Missives from Maravida

A Family's Caribbean Sailboat Adventure

By Sandy L. Davis

Copyright © 2013 by Sandy L. Davis

(Updated April 2016)

All rights reserved.

Published by Uncharted Ventures, Portland, Oregon.

ISBN: 978-0-9888432-0-2

CONTENTS

Prologue – Stepping off the Deep End 1

Preface – Details Preserved 9

Chapter 1 – A Boat in Trinidad 13

Chapter 2 – Decision Making in Connecticut 27

Chapter 3 – Marc in Trinidad 35

Chapter 4 – Apartment Life in Trinidad 49

Chapter 5 – Moving On to Venezuela 97

Chapter 6 – Puerto Rico, Friends, & Family 123

Chapter 7 – U.S. & British Virgin Islands 155

Chapter 8 – Six Weeks in Saint Martin 169

Chapter 9 – Island Hopping Down the Chain 191

Chapter 10 – Southern Caribbean Islands 241

Chapter 11 – Three Months in Colombia 287

Chapter 12 – Three Months in Panama 319

Chapter 13 – Colombia Again 347

Chapter 14 – Aruba and Curacao 387

Epilogue – Back to Terra Firma 399

Helpful Wikis 425

Acknowledgments 427

About the Author 429

A Favor 431

Two Months in Europe 432

Prologue

Stepping off the Deep End

Most people thought we were crazy. We sold our house and most of our belongings, keeping only the essentials that would fit into our suitcases. We were ready to venture out, but there was one hitch. We didn't know our destination. We scoured the Pacific Northwest; then we searched worldwide. We were shopping online for the boat that would be our home base for a new and different life.

In the early years of marriage, Marc and I fantasized about buying a sailboat and traveling the world. We decided to test out that fantasy during Marc's two-month sabbatical (after working for Intel for seven years). We arranged to charter a sailboat in Washington's San Juan Islands but changed our plans after receiving an overnight FedEx delivery that said we'd won $5,000 in American Airlines travel vouchers. I was sure it was a scam, but it turned out our names had been automatically entered in a drawing when we made a computer-related purchase.

We used the travel vouchers to fly to Europe, putting our sailing idea on hold—but not for long. We had another chance to try sailing while on sabbatical. Halfway through our two-month vacation in the fall of 1997, when the kids were ages three and five, and we were staying at a small harborside hotel in the French town of Villefranche-sur-Mer, Marc came back from a walk to the docks with an interesting plan: He had found a man who was willing to take us for a daylong outing on his sailboat. I agreed that this was an excellent opportunity, so we set sail the next morning under clear blue skies and calm seas for an exhilarating adventure on the Mediterranean Sea. Unfortunately, my enjoyment turned to misery after I went below to retrieve our lunch. This action took less than a minute but was enough to make me miserably seasick. Marc and the kids were fine, but we cut short the trip for my sake. Henceforth, I lost my enthusiasm for sailing, though at times we joked (or threatened) to take the kids and sail off into the wild blue yonder as an alternative to the potential agonies of middle school.

The subject of boating came up again in August 2003, after we attended a wedding in the coastal town of Port Townsend, Washington. We had rented an apartment for the weekend in the rear of a historic building on Water Street with a fantastic view of the bay. The kids and I settled in, leaving only for the wedding and a couple of outings for window-shopping and ice cream. Marc was restless, though, and repeatedly took off toward the docks at the end of Water Street. I didn't question his disappearances because he's often driven by his curiosity to seek out and learn about new things. On the drive back to Portland, I discovered that this time his interest went beyond mere curiosity. Here's the question he sprang on me: "How about we sell the airplane (one-half ownership of Piper Tri-Pacer plane) and buy a boat—something we could enjoy as a family on weekends and vacations?" This had to be a difficult compromise for Marc, but not for me. I answered "yes" without hesitation (a likely answer since the kids and I didn't enjoy flying in the small airplane).

I decided I'd better look into methods of dealing with seasickness. Through my research, I discovered that almost everyone gets seasick, but most people either acclimate with time or find reliable seasickness medications. My findings were good enough to convince me that I'd be okay on the water, so we proceeded to look at powerboats that would hold the four of us comfortably on weekend excursions. We were able to find several older boats that matched our budget, but before we got too invested in the idea, our boating plans changed course again.

We had started to brainstorm ideas for Marc's next two-month sabbatical, which was scheduled for the following year. Marc had borrowed several boating books from the library and was once again enthusiastic about chartering a sailboat in Washington's San Juan Islands; but I really wanted to go back to Europe. We had reached a stalemate.

One day Marc approached me with another idea: "Why don't we sell everything and travel the world in a sailboat just like we talked about years ago? We could even sail to Europe." This would take care of our disagreement about destinations, but he wanted to live on the water for the long term, not just during his sabbatical. This didn't surprise me, because over the past few years he had often proposed that we move to another state or even another country. My standard answer was, "No, all our family is here, and what about the kids? It would be too hard on them." But now I thought, yeah, what about the kids? They didn't fit into the typical molds at school. Alex, our 9-year-old son, was far ahead in math and reading, and he sometimes got in trouble for not listening in class. Madeline, our creative and dyslexic 11 year old, was exhausted by the end of each school day and had been having meltdowns over homework. Homeschooling was already a viable option, and what greater gift could we give our kids than the experience of traveling the world?

Over the next few days, I spent a lot of time contemplating Marc's proposition. At the time, we lived in a craftsman-style house we had designed and built ourselves. It was located on a half-acre of land on Bonny Slope in northwest Portland (Oregon), only 45 minutes away from most of our family. My priorities had always been my family and my house, though perhaps I needed more. I was happy to volunteer at the kids' school, but taking care of our big house and yard was a never-ending and thankless chore for me. Marc, however, loved his job as a prototype engineer at Intel. He also loved his airplane and his 1,300-square-foot shop in our basement garage. He had a full set of woodworking and metalworking equipment—to help him pursue any number of projects—but he never seemed to have enough time to use them. He went off to work each day in order to earn enough money to maintain our house, cars, and consumer lifestyle—and then he would ask, What if?

My biggest passion was travel, and I was most happy when I was planning an itinerary for a future trip. At this point, I wanted to go to Europe. What if I could go to Europe in a sailboat? What if I could travel the world? What if I could live on a sailboat and always be in traveling mode?

"Let's do it!" I exclaimed. Marc was dumbfounded by my answer but quickly pulled himself together and became fully engaged in preparing for this endeavor. His enthusiasm wasn't surprising because my husband is always gung ho about trying new things and rarely intimidated by them.

I must admit that one thing did surprise me: Marc had second thoughts many times over the course of the next year, but I didn't. I felt that we were destined to do this. Marc's experience of living in Turkey as a child had made him yearn to live in a foreign country as an adult. My well-honed knack for travel planning was about to be tested, and my constant desire for travel fulfilled. It was time to do something different with our lives, something that would add to our overall life experience.

> **How?**
>
> Did we have any experience? Nope. But Marc's impressive ability to learn anything and his strong mechanical and electrical skill sets gave us confidence. How did we learn to operate a sailboat? We took classes from the U.S. Power Squadrons to earn our Oregon Boater's Card, then we took a two-weekend beginner sailing class with the Willamette Sailing Club in Portland. That's it. Crazy? Perhaps, but we figured the best way to learn would be on our own boat. We had always been hands-on learners and often took on new projects without any experience.
>
> How could we afford to live without income? Sweat equity. Specifically, our home equity had increased as we bought, remodeled, sold; bought, remodeled, sold; and finally built and sold. We'd spent our marriage sweating equity out of our houses and building up our net worth. When we sold our last house, we netted enough money to buy a boat and provide a living allowance to last us a few years. We figured that we'd probably run out of money around the time the kids were ready to start college, which would make financial aid an option. In any case, they each had a small college fund and we were confident that we'd be able to find jobs when we needed them.

During the next year, we prepared to sell our house and our possessions. Have you ever considered what it would be like to get rid of everything you own? It's a long and difficult process, but the reward is a sense of freedom from a life complicated by "things." For us, paring down our belongings loosened the ties that bound us to our former life. Suddenly the world was open to us, and we were available for adventure.

Once the house sold, we had the money to buy a boat. After reading numerous books on cruising, we came up with three requirements: the boat should be made of steel (for peace of mind); it should have a minimum of three separate sleeping cabins; and total upfront costs shouldn't exceed $150k. We looked at one boat in Canada that would have been perfect—if it hadn't been designed for midgets. Another one on San Juan Island fit our requirements, but necessary updates and repairs would have raised our costs too far over the owner's firm $150k asking price. Yet another boat in

Olympia, Washington, was a stripped-down version of what we wanted and required too many modifications. It had two separate sitting areas with low coffee tables and no dining table. The large open spaces offered nothing to hold onto when walking through—not an issue when throwing a cocktail party in a marina, but definitely a problem when on passage. Finally, we had high hopes for a boat in Astoria, Oregon, but were disappointed when we went to view it and saw that its lone bathroom was located in the kitchen and could only be used if the door was open.

It was time to look at boats that were farther away than the convenient Pacific Northwest. Unfortunately, the three steel boats we found in Florida looked like they'd been built by amateurs and were fitted out roughly. This is a common problem; all steel boats are custom built, unlike fiberglass boats, most of which come off production lines.

At first, we discounted a boat that was up for sale in Trinidad. It looked beautiful in the pictures, but at $170k, it was priced higher than our budget allowed. We were afraid to insult the owners with a lowball offer because they'd already reduced the price considerably. It had been for sale for quite a while, though, so we suspected they might be getting desperate. After asking lots of questions and poring over the pictures and specs, we decided that we'd need about $25k to make necessary updates to the boat. I e-mailed the following message to the broker on August 7th:

> We're afraid that our top offer of $125k will not be acceptable to your sellers, but we're wondering if you could feel them out about it. $125k is the most we can pay, but it would be an easy sale because we have cash in hand and are ready to get into a boat ASAP.

On August 11th, the broker wrote back:

> We can make the deal work at $126.5k, shall I write it up for you?

We immediately filled out the Offer to Purchase and sent it off to the broker. On the 17th, we received an e-mail from the broker with the attached signed-off Offer to Purchase and instructions to execute the wire transfer. Though we immediately arranged for the transfer of the 10 percent deposit, the money didn't reach the Brazilian owner's bank until the 23rd. Meanwhile we made plans for the inspection, sea trial, and survey and then booked our air tickets to Trinidad.

Our adventure started when I was 42 years old, my husband Marc was 41, our daughter Madeline was 12, and our son Alex was 10. This story is about us and a Bruce Roberts steel boat built in 1984 in Brazil—a boat named MARAVIDA.

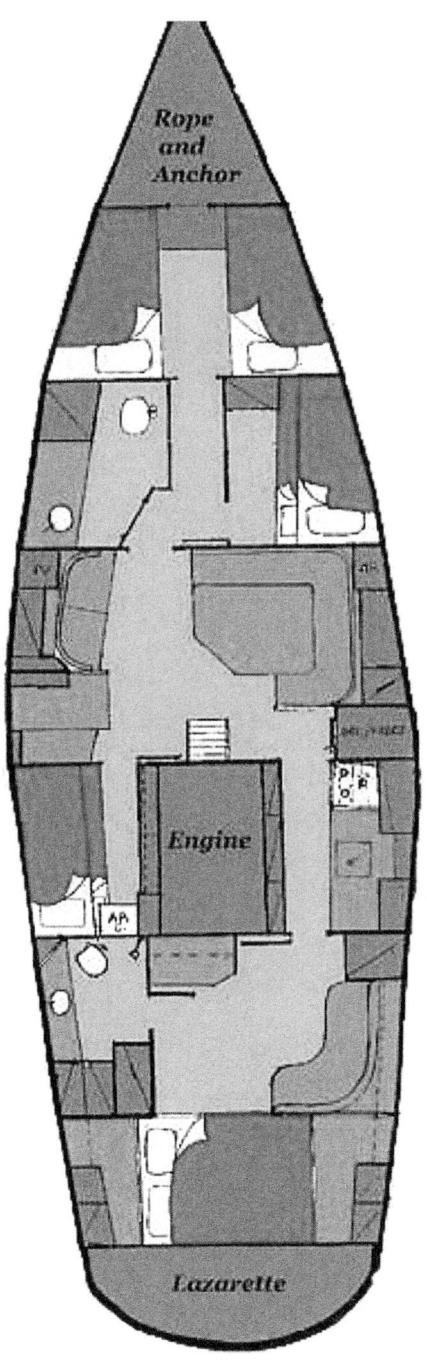

Specs—54' Steel Bruce Roberts Sloop

Name: MARAVIDA

Year: 1984

Location: Trinidad

Hull Material: Steel

Engine: Single diesel

Builder: Custom built in Brazil

Designer: Bruce Roberts design

Length: 53'designed length with 1'6" sugar-scoop extension

LOA: 54'4"

LWL: 46'9"

Beam: 16'4"

Displacement: 47,400 pounds

Draft: 7'5"

Balast: 16,000 pounds

Engine: Single diesel, 120 horsepower, Mercedes Benz OM352 (1984)

Cruise Speed: 7 knots

Max Speed: 8 knots

PREFACE

Details Preserved

This book is for my children, to help them remember. It is also for people out there yearning for the cruising life, or those about to embark on an adventure aboard their own boat. And for those looking for a way to live independently—"off the grid"—living on a sailboat is one option you may not have considered but probably should. Finally, but most important, this story is for people who want to read about a different kind of life. You don't have to be wealthy, brilliant, or crazy to try something different.

Most of this book is comprised of the e-mail messages I sent to friends and family after we met up with MARAVIDA in Trinidad. I have edited the missives slightly, just for readability, and supplemented the text with details and events that I had inadvertently omitted. Such additions appear in the running text in italicized type and in boldfaced boxes scattered throughout the book. I've also added facts about the places we visited, using Wikipedia as my source, which means the details might change over time.

Most of the names in this book (boats and people) are real, but a few have been changed. Typically, boat names are easy to remember, so cruisers tend to identify people by their boat's name—perhaps you'll run into some of these boats if you go out cruising.

As you follow this account of our travels, you'll see that I've done my best to preserve the small details of our life; they might prove useful for those who would like to follow in our footsteps or vicariously experience the day-to-day life of a family of cruisers. I've included lots of pictures. I regret that I didn't take more (isn't that always the case?), but I have enough to give you a peek at our cruising life.

If you're considering embarking on this kind of adventure, and you're anything like us, you'll want to read every how-to book out there. Like these:

Cantrell, Debra Ann. *Changing Course: A Woman's Guide to Choosing the Cruising Life*. Camden, ME: International Marine/Ragged Mountain Press, 2003.

Cornell, Jimmy. *World Cruising Destinations*. Camden, Me.: International Marine/Ragged Mountain Press, 2010.

Cornell, Jimmy. *World Cruising Routes: 1000 Sailing Routes in All Oceans of the World*. 7th edition. Cornell Sailing, 2014.

Goodlander, Cap'n Fatty. *How to Inexpensively & Safely Buy, Outfit, and Sail a Small Vessel around the World: Living Large, at Sea, on a Micro-budget*. Charleston, S.C.: CreateSpace, 2011.

Hill, Annie. *Voyaging on a Small Income*. Easton, MD: Tiller Publishing, 2001.

Jessie, Diana. *The Cruising Woman's Advisor: How to Prepare for the Voyaging Life*. Camden, ME: International Marine/Ragged Mountain Press, 2007.

Leonard, Beth A. *The Voyager's Handbook: The Essential Guide to Bluewater Cruising*. Camden, ME: International Marine/Ragged Mountain Press, 2006.

Neale, Tom. *All in the Same Boat: Living Aboard and Cruising*. Camden, ME: International Marine/Ragged Mountain Press, 2003.

Nicholas, Mark. *The Essentials of Living Aboard a Boat: The Definitive Guide for Liveaboards*. Updated and Revised. Arcata, CA: Paradise Cay Publications, 2013.

Pardey, Lin, and Larry Pardey. *Cost Conscious Cruiser: Champagne Cruising on a Beer Budget*. Arcata, CA: Paradise Cay Publications, 1998.

Rodriguez, Nicola. Sail Away: *How to Escape the Rat Race and Live the Dream*. 3rd ed. Hoboken, NJ: Wiley Nautical, 2012.

Slavinski, Nadine. *Cruising the Caribbean with Kids: Fun, Facts, and Educational Activities*. Kindle edition. Rolling Hitch Press. Amazon Digital Services, 2015.

Trefethen, Jim. *The Cruising Life: A Commonsense Guide for the Would-Be Voyager.* 2nd edition. Camden, ME: International Marine/Ragged Mountain Press, 2015.

Weatheritt, Les. *Caribbean Passagemaking: A Cruiser's Guide.* 3rd edition. Dobbs Ferry, NY: Sheridan House, 2015.

CHAPTER 1

A Boat in Trinidad

> **Trinidad**
>
> Trinidad is located in the southern Caribbean Sea, just off the northeast coast of South America. It is a part of the Republic of Trinidad and Tobago, which has a total population of about 1.3 million. Tobago is a much smaller island, covering only about 120 square miles of the archipelagic state's 2,000 total square miles.
>
> Trinidad's economy depends on oil, natural gas, manufacturing, and agriculture. The island contains both mountains and plains—the highest point is 3,000 feet above sea level.

New Digs?
August 26, 2004

The four of us exited Piarco International Airport into the hot and humid air of Trinidad. We each had two checked bags, a carry-on, and a personal backpack. Back in Oregon, we had pared down our belongings to what we thought we'd need to live on a boat for the next few years. Then we transported it with us across the United States to Miami and, from there, across the Caribbean Sea to Trinidad.

With relief, we found our prearranged taxi-van waiting as promised. Our destination was Chaguaramas *(pronounced something like: sha-ger-rah-mus)*.

> **Chaguaramas**
>
> Chaguaramas is located at the far northwest tip of Trinidad. In 1940, the United States leased the peninsula of Chaguaramas for use as a naval base. The U.S. government returned the leased lands in 1963, and now the region serves as Trinidad's center for yachting activity.

The 25-mile ride to Chaguaramas was enlightening, especially since this was our first visit to a developing nation. Along the route, we saw many unfinished buildings and even entire developments that had been abandoned mid-project. The average completed building was of simple construction, with concrete blocks stacked into a small square- or rectangular-shaped structure, sometimes painted, sometimes not. A small fraction of the island's dwellings were extravagant in comparison: mansions up on the hills and elegant high-rise apartments near the ocean. These offered a stark contrast to the shantytowns not far down the road.

Most structures had metal bars on the windows and doors, and the streetside shops served customers through barred openings in the wall. Many of the shops were fringed with people leaning against the buildings, looking as though they had nothing better to do.

The road was lined with broken sidewalks or dirt tracks and was generously sprinkled with litter. Our van bumped along the poorly maintained road, swaying from one side to the other as our driver swerved to miss the numerous potholes.

The drive took us through Port of Spain, Trinidad's capital and the most developed city on the island. Traffic was gridlocked—likely a common occurrence since the hawkers at every intersection displayed confidence as they offered their wares to the occupants of the stopped cars. Each vendor offered a different item: bottled water, snack foods, sunglasses, CD cases, and even windshield sunshades. I spied many drivers making purchases—mostly snacks or drinks—probably to help bide time while waiting in traffic.

We finally arrived at our destination, Coral Cove Marina, where the boat was stored. We were booked to stay in the marina's hotel.

> **Coral Cove**
>
> The Coral Cove compound houses a marina, a boatyard, a hotel, and a "mall" of several businesses. When we were there, these included a paint store, a hardware store, a mechanic's shop, a small chandlery, an Italian restaurant, and a mini-market.
>
> We booked two rooms at the hotel because each small room contained only two twin beds. The pink-walled rooms also had a television, bathroom, kitchenette, and tiny table with two chairs.
>
> http://www.coralcovemarina.com

The cool air in the rooms was welcoming, but we were anxious to view the boat we'd come so far to see. We quickly stuffed our luggage between and around the beds and then headed back out into the tropical heat to the boatyard.

Disappointment is the best word to describe how we felt when we first saw MARAVIDA. Our next reaction was "Oh no, we've made a huge mistake!" She looked terrible, nothing like the many pictures we had insisted on seeing before making our offer.

Now we could see that the exterior pictures had been taken from a distance, too far back for us to see the startling close-up details. What we saw now was rust, rust, and more rust; rust so bad in places you could poke a stick right through it and into the boat.

How could this be? We had received an ultrasound report showing the boat to be sound. However, it appeared that the person taking the ultrasound measurements had carefully avoided the problem areas, or the report had later been altered to remove the unfavorable measurements. Fraudulent? Maybe, but we weren't going to bother pointing fingers; it was too late now. Our only recourse was opting out of the deal.

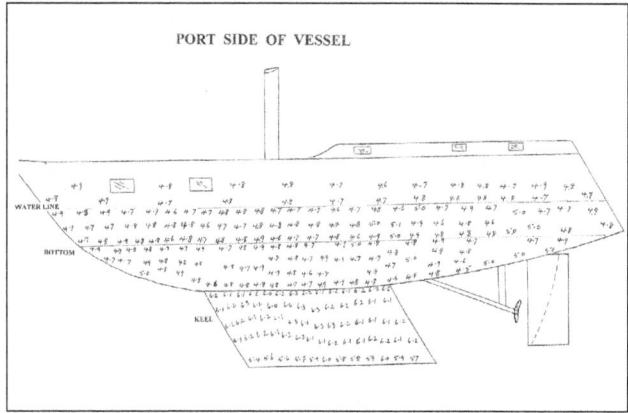

Davis News

I knew we had family and friends waiting to hear about our trip and the boat, so I decided to send one detailed e-mail to everyone. This was my first DAVIS NEWS missive, which became something our friends, family members, and their friends looked forward to receiving.

Notice I said "their friends"; this is because my mother would receive my newsletters and then forward them on to others. She used this as a way to keep the news coming: "Sandra, I haven't heard from you lately and my friends are asking about you." Thus, I became obligated to my "readers" to continue delivering these detailed and frequent e-mails. Here's the first one I wrote.

From: sandy_n_marc
To: Davis News Group
Subject: Davis News
Date: Sat, 28 Aug 2004

I'm writing this from an internet café located just around the corner from Coral Cove Marina, where we are staying. I'm playing reporter while Marc is at the pool with the kids.

It's hot and humid in Trinidad, but we're not complaining. The kids are spending the bulk of the day in the swimming pool, and I'm hanging out at a table in the shade provided by the poolside pavilion. The pool is tiny, but the kids don't mind.

Marc spent all day Friday examining the boat alongside the surveyor, the skipper, and the broker. (The skipper had been with the boat from when it was built until it was put into storage in Trinidad.) The good news is that the boat was built and owned by wealthy people who spared no expense. The interior is gorgeous. The bad news is that it's been here for four years, and the tropical weather has caused a lot of corrosion. We think it would take up to six months and at least $25k to restore the steel on the hull.

Marc wants to go ahead with the sailing survey on Monday. Even if we don't buy it, it will be a good sailing experience. He's become chummy with the Brazilian skipper and the French surveyor and feels he will learn a lot from them. Chances are the boat will take on some water because there are rust HOLES in the hull's steel exterior. *(Before the boat was splashed, the skipper epoxied tin can bottoms over the holes, though it still took on some water.)*

If we decide to take on this boat project, the owner will have to come way down in price. Meanwhile, we'll be looking into other boats. I met a man from Montreal who is going to sell his steel boat, but it has a retractable centerboard (which means no way, according to Marc—too many potential problems). I also just found a new listing for a steel boat in St. Vincent.

Food prices are very reasonable here, but we are spending too much on lodging because we had to take two rooms.

That's it for now, I have no idea what my internet time is going to cost.

Sandy

Slow Motion in Trinidad

From: sandy_n_marc
To: Davis News Group
Subject: Davis News
Date: Thu, 2 Sep 2004

We've been in Trinidad a week and haven't accomplished a lot by American standards. Things move slowly here, but it's understandable because of the heat.

The boat workers take their breaks in the shade under the boats, eating their sack lunches and then sleeping. Several of the regulars must have some kind of deal with Coral Cove: They're allowed to come into the marina and work on the boats, but Coral Cove isn't involved with their work or pay—the cruisers pay them directly. At the end of the workday, they hang around drinking beers, liming.

Liming

Trinis invented the term *liming*, and I bet that no one limes better than they do. It means hanging out with friends and can take place almost anywhere: at a bar, a party, the beach, at home, or even on the sidewalk.

Fetes

We met many Trinidadians whose sole motivation for working, it seemed, was to make enough money to party on the weekends. *Fete* posters are everywhere. Fetes are huge parties with hundreds, sometimes even thousands of attendees. There are fetes all year round, but they become more frequent around carnival time.

Soca Music

From our perspective, fetes are lively gatherings that involve lots of drinking, socializing, and dancing to very loud Soca music. Too rowdy for us.

Soca music originated in Trinidad and is named after the expression, "soul of calypso."

Everyone is friendly and helpful here. In fact, many people (both locals and cruisers) have approached Marc to tell him they are concerned that we are paying too much for the boat.

One of the boat workers approached me at the pool. He introduced himself as Junior. He is short, shaved bald, a little overweight, and has a nice smile. He said he helped clean MARAVIDA when the skipper first arrived, and he offered his services for any future work we might do on the boat if we buy it. The conversation was difficult because I had to ask Junior to repeat every phrase he uttered at least three times before I understood it.

> **Trinidadian English**
>
> Trinidadians speak English with a strong Caribbean accent that takes some time to get used to. They also use many English words and expressions in unique ways. To me, it was like listening to a foreign language.

We should have the boat survey results sometime tomorrow. Then we'll make a lower offer. Unfortunately, we've just heard that the owner has gone on vacation and will be unreachable until next Wednesday. So we've decided to give our new offer to the broker and check out of the hotel. Then we'll stow our excess luggage at the broker's office and go explore the island.

It rains every afternoon at 1:00 or 2:00; sometimes lightly, sometimes torrentially, and often accompanied by thunder and lightning. Since Portland rarely gets thunderstorms, these storms are exciting for us.

The hills around this harbor are thick with trees and vegetation and every speck of land down below is carpeted with grass. I've never seen jungle, but this must be it. I think it may be even greener here than in our Willamette Valley in Oregon. I'm looking forward to seeing more of Trinidad.

More later—
Sandy

Side Trip to Grande Riviere

> ### Grande Riviere
>
> Grande Riviere is an isolated village on the northeast coast of Trinidad, 72 miles from Port of Spain and 55 miles from the Piarco International Airport.
>
> It has a famous sea turtle nesting beach, though our stay did not coincide with the nesting season of March through August. We were told we had just missed the hatching season, which was proved by the empty shells we found on the beach.
>
> The village offers four small inns:
>
> Mt. Plaisir, Le Grande Almandier, Acajou, and Mc Eachnie's Haven.
>
> http://www.mtplaisir.com
>
> http://www.legrandealmandier.com
>
> http://www.acajoutrinidad.com

From: sandy_n_marc
To: Davis News Group
Subject: Davis News
Date: Thu, 9 Sep 2004

We were cut off from communication last weekend because we were at a remote beach community called Grande Riviere, about 80 miles from Chaguaramas. We rented a car for the excursion that turned into a hair-raising three-and-a-half-hour drive on twisty potholed roads. The car was from a reputable local rental company, but according to U.S. standards, it was worse than a "Rent-A-Wreck." It had no seatbelts, barely functioning brakes, and slow-motion acceleration.

We stayed at Mt. Plaisir Estate, a rustic ecolodge with rooms right on the beach. We had a wonderful time playing in the warm ocean, reading, and dining.

Unfortunately, the mosquitos were on a feeding frenzy in the evenings. We hadn't brought repellent and could not locate any to buy or borrow. So, we ended up leaving earlier than we'd planned because we couldn't endure any more bites.

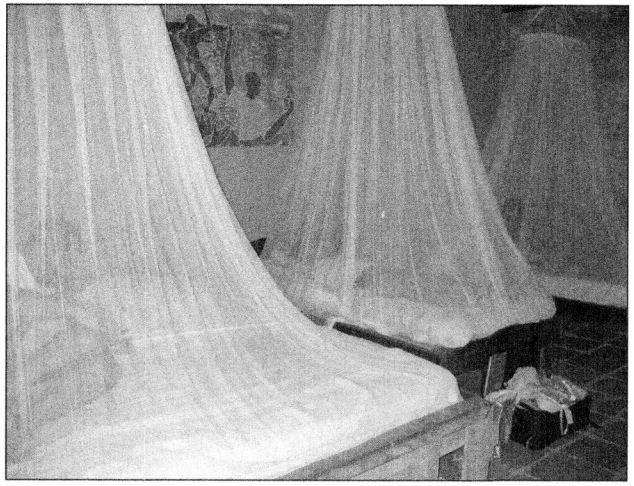

Back to Civilization and a Hurricane

Our departure from Grande Riviere was well timed: We soon discovered that Hurricane Ivan was expected to hit Trinidad the next day, and the beach areas would be most vulnerable. We decided to seek lodging in Port of Spain but had difficulty finding availability. Just when we started to get nervous that we would be homeless in a hurricane, we found a room available at The Normandie Hotel. We holed up in the hotel as everyone in Trinidad was instructed to brace for the storm.

> **The Normandie Hotel**
>
> Located in Port of Spain, The Normandie Hotel has 70 rooms that surround a courtyard with a pool. The furnishings were a bit dated, but the room was large and comfortable.
>
> http://www.normandiett.com

Ivan did not make it to Trinidad. *(Grenada, however, was not so lucky. On Tuesday, September 7th, Hurricane Ivan developed into a category 4 storm as it passed directly over Grenada, causing catastrophic damage.)*

On Wednesday afternoon, we received the call we'd been waiting for, but it wasn't good news. The boat owners had rejected our $70k offer and countered at $100k. That was too much, so we spent Thursday morning brainstorming for other options. There weren't any other boats in Trinidad we were interested in, we had to rule out visiting Florida because it was a wreck from hurricane Frances (which had swept through on September 5th), and now Hurricane Ivan was on its way to the Sunshine State. After much thought and discussion, we made a phone call to some dear friends (the Erreras) and then booked our tickets to go seek asylum with them in Connecticut.

After spending a couple of hours in downtown Port of Spain, we drove to Chaguaramas to stay overnight at CrewsInn.

CrewsInn

CrewsInn Hotel and Yachting Centre is near Coral Cove Marina, but it's more upscale and expensive and thus was a splurge for us. The room was large, the free internet access was helpful, and the large swimming pool was just steps away from our patio, nestled between palm trees and overlooking the marina and the distant jungled hills.

http://www.crewsinn.com

Soon after arriving, Marc drove to the broker's office to pick up our excess luggage. His intention was to drop off the luggage in our room and then return the car to the rental agency located here in CrewsInn Village. Unfortunately, Marc crashed into another car on his way back; he forgot that he was supposed to be driving on the left side of the road and went around a corner on the same side as the oncoming car. Luckily, the incident took place on the hotel road, and neither car was going fast. Nevertheless, it was a costly lesson because the insurance deductible was a whopping $750. Marc felt terrible about his mistake and gave the other driver enough cash to pay for three days' car rental to get him through the weekend.

Last-Minute Decisions

So there we were, giving up on Trinidad and MARAVIDA, with airline tickets in hand—and what happens? The broker calls us and says the owner has reconsidered and wants to accept our $70k offer. This new development generated additional hours of contemplation and discussion, but finally we called the broker to say that we were headed to Connecticut and would take some time to think about the offer. If we do decide to buy the boat, Marc will probably fly back to Trinidad to start work on it (with hired help), and the kids and I will join him later.

We're going to consider another option during our hiatus in Connecticut. Rather than pour time and money into a boat, we could travel around the world, renting apartments...

We will fly out of Trinidad tomorrow, September 10th, two weeks after our arrival.

We'll tell you more as we figure it out—
Sandy

CHAPTER 2

Decision Making in Connecticut

> **Connecticut**
>
> Although Connecticut is the third smallest of the 50 United States in terms of land area, it ranks number four in population density. The population wasn't noticeably dense to us, probably because we were staying in an area where the houses were comfortably spread apart and there were lots of green spaces. Connecticut's small size was more evident, though, because we were able to take easy day trips to Massachusetts, Rhode Island, and New York.

Skirting Ivan

From: sandy_n_marc
To: Davis News Group
Subject: Davis News
Date: Sat, 11 Sep 2004

Hurricane Ivan was battering Jamaica when we flew to Connecticut. The pilot made a point of assuring the passengers that he was steering around the disturbance. Nevertheless, we were nervous during the flight. Thankfully, we experienced no turbulence and no delays and arrived at the Hartford airport to find all eight suitcases on the baggage carousel.

We're enjoying the comfortable 65-degree weather and are happy to see our friends.

More later—
Sandy

Choices

From: sandy_n_marc
To: Davis News Group
Subject: Davis News
Date: Thu, 16 Sep 2004

We haven't made a decision yet. Marc has been studying steel boat repair and I've been researching ideal fiberglass offshore boats. We went to Long Island yesterday to check out three boats but weren't impressed with any of them. Tomorrow we're going to Newport, Rhode Island, to look at another boat and visit the Newport Boat Show, which is taking place September 16th through 19th. Good timing for us.

The Erreras are wonderful hosts; we feel right at home. Madeline and Alex have pronounced that they would be fine if we stayed here. I had to remind them that we are temporary guests, not a newfound family of nine.

Homeschooling is going well, though Becky says there's usually a honeymoon period (she's separately taken each of her kids out of public school for one year of homeschooling).

That's it for now—
Sandy

Ivan Again

From: sandy_n_marc
To: Davis News Group
Subject: Davis News
Date: Sun, 19 Sep 2004

Hurricane Ivan followed us here. Marc was in the garage when the house took a direct hit from lightning—we're still teasing him about his startled scream that echoed throughout the house. The well pump and most of the household electronics are dead.

Sandy

We're Doing It

From: sandy_n_marc
To: Davis News Group
Subject: Davis News
Date: Tue, 21 Sep 2004

After 10 days of agonizing deliberation, we decided to purchase MARAVIDA. Once the title is transferred, Marc will travel back to Trinidad to supervise the boat repairs. I'll follow with the kids once the boat is livable.

We finally recovered from the lightning hit. It fried every network card in the house, the T1 router, 10/100 switch, X-Box, cable TV, and the well pump. It took three days for Marc and Claude to get Claude's web host business running again.

The Newport Boat Show got us re-enthused for cruising.

More soon—
Sandy

From Marc

From: sandy_n_marc
To: Davis News Group
Subject: Davis News
Date: Fri, 24 Sep 2004

I will be in Oregon from the 25th to the 30th of September. I'm going to get a few things at my mother-in-law's house (mainly tools for working on the boat), do a little work at Intel, and see about getting a "leave of absence."

Marc

Alex Is 10 Years Old

From: sandy_n_marc
To: Davis News Group
Subject: Davis News
Date: Thu, 7 Oct 2004

Alex turned 10 on September 30th. We had a birthday party with eight kids, presents, pizza, and cake. Fortunately, Marc returned from Portland just in time for the party.

Marc was able to obtain a one-year leave of absence, which made him less anxious about his separation from mother Intel. While Marc was in Oregon, Becky and Claude took me and all five kids to a Renaissance Festival in Massachusetts. I'd never heard of such a thing—a make-believe world where people dress, talk, serve, perform, and sell their wares as Renaissance characters.

To Massachusetts

After school on October 1st, we headed north with the Errera family, minus Claude who stayed behind to host a Halo X-Box party. We spent Friday evening at Lake Compounce, which claims to be the oldest, continuously operating amusement park in North America. Our intent was to visit its famous Halloween Graveyard, but first we had time to try out some rides.

The next morning we drove into Boston to visit the Museum of Science. After spending the entire day exploring the museum, we drove to a motel in Lexington. On Sunday morning, we checked out the village green, where the first shot was fired in the Revolutionary War.

After lunch, Becky and her kids headed home so that they'd be back for school the next day. The four of us continued on to Concord to see the North Bridge. By midafternoon, the kids had reached their capacity for history lessons, so we headed to Cape Ann and the sea. We discovered a charming seaside town called Rockport. I'm sure it's bustling in tourist season, but it was peaceful at this time of year. We checked into a worn motel overlooking the water and ate dinner at the Fish Shack, where Madeline and I tried lobster for the first time. Madeline perked up in Rockport because the town has a plethora of tourist shops to explore.

We spent Monday night in the seaside town of Marblehead, which is crammed with three-story 16th-century houses on short winding streets. Our top-floor lodging had an excellent view of the boat-filled harbor.

We spent our last evening and morning in Plymouth, where we relearned the story of the pilgrims at the wax museum, checked out Plymouth Rock, and toured a full-sized replica of the Mayflower.

Our whirlwind five-day mini-vacation was blessed with clear blue skies, crisp air, and the hint of leaves turning red and gold—in other words, a perfect New England autumn.

Now we're back at the Errera house, and Marc has lots to do before leaving for Trinidad.

Go to http://www.maravida.org/photos/oldstuff.htm to view Madeline's slideshow of the trip. It's 8 MBs and you must have QuickTime installed to view it. Sorry some of the pictures are blurry. The same link leads you to "Fall colors" and "Our new friend." "Our new friend" is an amusing collection of photos on one subject that will make you laugh. It's an example of what homeschooled kids can come up with when they have the time to be creative.

We'll keep you posted—
Sandy

Progress Report from Marc

From: sandy_n_marc
To: Davis News Group
Subject: Davis News
Date: Fri, 22 Oct 2004

We're still waiting for the boat paperwork to go through. Some progress has been made, but it's taking longer than we expected due to international bureaucracy.

I passed my HAM radio test so we can have Winlink e-mail on the boat. I also acquired a license for Marine Single Side Band, which will allow us to call other ships, make expensive phone calls, and get weather reports. *(More info about Winlink and Marine SSB in Chapter 3.)*

We built a 1-square-meter crate to send to Trinidad by container ship. This will reduce the amount of luggage Sandy and the kids will have to take on the airplane. We'll pack it up with new equipment for the boat, including a radar set, radios, automatic inflating life jackets, and anything else we can think of.

We're still enjoying Becky and Claude's hospitality and feel comfortable being a part of this combined family.

Marc

Marc Is Leaving for Trinidad

From: sandy_n_marc
To: Davis News Group
Subject: Davis News
Date: Wed, 3 Nov 2004

MARAVIDA is now officially ours, the crate is packed, and the airline tickets are purchased. Marc and Claude are leaving today to take the crate to the shipping company in New Jersey, and then Claude will drop Marc at the Holiday Inn Express next to JFK International Airport in Queens. Marc leaves on a direct flight at 7:00 a.m. tomorrow, arriving in Port of Spain, Trinidad, at 12:45 p.m. Then the work begins....

The weather warmed up in Connecticut on Halloween day, and Becky finished installing her spooky outdoor display. The props, lighting, and music made an impressive set for trick-or-treaters that night. Madeline dressed as a prom queen and went to a party with Katie, who was dressed as water. The boys went trick-or-treating: Alex as the grim reaper, Tim as Robin Hood, and Ben as a ninja.

We plan to stay here another four to six weeks, which means Marc will have to spend his birthday and Thanksgiving without us. I hope that we'll be able to join him in Trinidad by Christmas.

All the best—
Sandy

Life in Connecticut

From: sandy_n_marc
To: Davis News Group
Subject: Davis News
Date: Thu, 18 Nov 2004

Our life in Connecticut is simple, and based largely around the Erreras' busy life. While the Errera kids are at school, Madeline and Alex do schoolwork, go for walks in the woods behind the house, watch television, play video games, and jump on the trampoline. After school, they hang out with the Errera kids as much as they can, but the Erreras are very busy: Katie has synchronized swimming practice, Tim has karate, and Ben has after-school sports. Doctor and dentist visits, school conferences, church activities, and the like also take up a lot of their time. Becky is in charge of the school book fair and has been working on it nonstop for the last week. Claude is involved with the Halo X-Box world, and with the recent release of Halo 2, he's been doing interviews, visits to New York, and specialty matches. There was an (almost full-page) article on him today in the *New Haven Register*.

We had snow last Friday night. Madeline and Alex are always thrilled with snow since we get so little of it in Oregon (except in the mountains), but the Errera kids were unimpressed since it's a commonplace event here.

Marc is delighted that his dad, Brian, is going to Trinidad to help work on the boat. He'll arrive just in time for Thanksgiving.

Sandy

Heading Out

From: sandy_n_marc
To: Davis News Group
Subject: Davis News
Date: Mon, 13 Dec 2004

This is it. We are leaving for Trinidad tomorrow morning. We've been comfortably situated here for three months, but now it's time to start another chapter of our life. Unfortunately, we won't be living on the boat, which is still being dismantled. Instead, we'll be staying in a two-bedroom apartment that Marc and Brian found for us.

Our apartment is one of two rentals in the lower level of a house. Its owners are of East-Indian ancestry and live on the upper level. The house is situated on a major roadway about 5 miles from the boatyard. The biggest benefit of this location? Convenience. It's a major thoroughfare for maxi-taxis, and there's a large grocery store and shopping mall within walking distance. (Madeline is thrilled about this.) The downside is the traffic noise.

Life has been enjoyably easy with the Erreras. I think things will get more challenging from here on out.

Take Care—
Sandy

CHAPTER 3

Marc in Trinidad

Marc sent me frequent e-mails detailing his days in Trinidad, and I forwarded them to my growing base of "readers" as I received them. I've put them together here in one long daily journal.

Marc's Diary of Boat Work

November 4, 2004

I arrived in Trinidad at 12:30 p.m., and one of Jessie James's drivers met me at the airport and took me to Coral Cove Marina.

> **"Members Only" Maxi-Taxi Service**
>
> Jesse James's Maxi-Taxi Service caters to cruisers in Chaguaramas. He provides weekly shopping trips and 24-hour airport shuttle service, along with sightseeing, cultural, and seasonal adventures. His office is run by his wife, Sharon Rose, and is located at Crews Inn Marina (inside YSATT office), Pointe Gourde Road, Chaguaramas. Phone numbers and more info are available at http://www.membersonlymaxitaxi.com.

Despite making arrangements ahead of time, nothing was ready for me at the marina. No power, no water, no key to the boat. After two hours of cajoling, I finally gained access to the boat and got power.

For dinner, I went to Joe's Italian Restaurant, which is located here in the Coral Cove compound. While I sat eating a pizza and drinking a couple of beers, there was a huge downpour. I returned to the boat to find pools of water on the floor below the hatches I'd left open. After cleaning up, I went to bed. When I woke up, it was dark and I was completed disoriented; I had no clue what time it was. I walked over to the marina office and peeked in a window. It was only 9:30 p.m. Back at the boat, I found a clock and put a battery in it—my first repair. I figured out how to get a television channel on the small built-in TV and watched it until 11:00 p.m.

November 5, 2004

Got water to the boat, fixed the sink pump, figured out the water system, and filled the tanks.

Bastien, the French boat surveyor, came by about 5:00 p.m. and took me to a local bar where all the local contractors meet at the end of the week. Drank lots of beer and talked politics.

> **AMD**
>
> Bastien Pouthier is cofounder and managing director of AMD (A. Marine Design), which is based in Chaguaramas, Trinidad. AMD offers surveys, design, and refit management for yacht and powercraft.
>
> http://www.pouthier.eu

November 6, 2004

Examined the boat bottom and used a hammer to find weak spots. When I removed the anchor chain box to gain access to the first hole on the hull, I discovered that it had formed because a limber hole had plugged up, allowing water to pool against the hull. It should be an easy fix. Limber holes are small drainage holes drilled into the ribs and stringers that allow water, which gets inside the hull, to flow into the bilge.

November 7, 2004

Did grinding and cutting on the hull.

November 8, 2004

Went to the tool store in the yard and bought a compressor, hearing protection, and dust masks. Started working in the hull using a needle gun.

MISSIVES FROM MARAVIDA

Bastien took me out for beer for my B-day.

November 9, 2004

Refrigeration guy came and fixed the air-cooled fridge. Went shopping for food. Worked on the hull.

November 10, 2004

Listened to the morning VHF radio cruisers' net. It meets daily at 8:00 a.m. on Channel 68 and is a great way for cruisers in the area to communicate with each other. One person is in charge *(the net controller)* and starts out by asking for safety and security issues, then for general questions, and then for who has things to sell, etc. I asked about—and located—a manual for the boat's HF radio. I then joined a Jesse James outing to PriceSmart. It's a spinoff of Costco and has most of the same stuff. Got some basics then came back and got the radio e-mail working.

VHF Radio

All seagoing vessels should have marine VHF (very high frequency) radio installed. The frequency range for marine VHF radios is between 156.000 and 162.025 megahertz (MHz). A marine VHF radio transmits and receives on standard channels. Channel 16 is the international distress channel and is used for "hailing" (calling another vessel), as well. Boaters should monitor this channel continuously while on passage and even at anchor. Once contact is made between parties, both are expected to switch to an agreed-upon noncommercial channel.

HF Radio

While VHF radio operation is short range with a limit of around 5 to 25 miles, HF radio is capable of longer ranges. Worldwide communications are possible with an HF radio, but marine antennas tend to limit the range to approximately 500 miles. Cruisers often refer to HF radios as SSB (single sideband) radios.

> **Radio E-mail**
>
> There are several systems available that allow users to send and receive e-mail while at sea or in remote areas. Most are prohibitively expensive. Two of the most affordable are Winlink and Sailmail. They are very similar systems that use Marine SSB or Amateur Radio SSB to transmit mail from your boat to a radio on shore. The shore-based radio station then relays your mail, over the internet, to the intended recipient. Sailmail is a nonprofit association using Marine SSB (or satellite). Winlink is a volunteer organization using Amateur radio frequencies. On MARAVIDA, we had Winlink and used Marc's General class call sign KE7BZI. (Marc has since upgraded his call sign to AE7UV because he now has an Extra Class License.)

November 11, 2004

Got up at 6:30 a.m. and started work at 7:30. I've been working on the section under the master bath and master berth in the aft of the boat. The damage is considerable, but so far it's the only real area of concern. I need to remove the entire bath and part of the bedroom area, which means I'll have to find a place to put all the stuff and I'll need to sleep in another part of the boat.

The fridge is working well. It's been great to have cold drinks handy while working.

This afternoon I started to remove the interior port side of the aft cabin. It went pretty well. It looks like most of the rust here was caused by the shower. I think I'll try to find a regular shower base to install. The current setup was a small pan under the floor to catch the water, but I can't see how more than 30 percent went in—the rest went in the bilge.

November 12, 2004

It rained all night, so I had to keep the hatches closed. This made the boat too hot and stuffy to sleep well.

Met a guy with a 46-foot steel Bruce Roberts. He built it himself. He and his wife have almost finished their first circumnavigation. I went to his boat and asked a bunch of questions. When he came over to check out

MARAVIDA, I told him how much we paid for her and he said it was a good deal. He had some suggestions about the repairs and told me it shouldn't be too much of a problem. This was a big boost because I was feeling overwhelmed. Another guy had come by the boat earlier and told me we'd made a big mistake. He turned out to be a dork, but it bummed me out anyway.

I removed more of the bathroom, but didn't get as much done as I should have. Too much BS-ing, though it was useful.

November 13, 2004

I got an e-mail from my friend Kelly asking me to continue sending out this work log because the "old-man lunch" is following with interest. They are a group of guys back home who get together for lunch to talk airplanes; many are old-timers.

Here's today's installment:

I signed up for a Thanksgiving dinner. About 130 people are expected. As soon as I signed up, I was called and invited to sit at someone's table. I guess I had talked with them at the pool.

Looks like it's gonna rain all day. It started to pour at 6:30 this morning. I have a hatch over my bed, so I woke up when I started to get wet. I had to rush around the boat closing up things. Guess I'm working inside today.

I removed most of the master bath. Just the wall against the hull remains in place. Tomorrow I'll get a good look at the damage in that area. I hope I can remember how to put the joinery back together. It's a real jigsaw puzzle.

I got some info on how to treat the interior steel after removing the rust. You wash it with a strong acid—like phosphoric or muriatic—and then use a product called tar epoxy.

I did my first load of laundry, then went to the store so I would have something to eat tomorrow when stores are closed for a Hindu holiday.

I met a nice cruising family from Brazil. I gave them the Portuguese books from the boat. They were grateful. They have a wooden boat and are clearly living on a shoestring. The two teenagers are very enthusiastic about cruising.

The days are rushing by.

November 14, 2004

Today I finished removing the bathroom wall and started in on the aft center cabin. This is where the saltwater pump, watermaker, pressure water pump, seawater strainer, and starting batteries are located. It's a maze of hoses and wires. This is the area with the worst damage, probably because the saltwater pump leaked and the shower water came through this section. It's hard to get to, so it wasn't maintained as well as it should have been. We'll probably have to replace about 4 square feet of hull plating here. So far I've found only one place where a structural member needs to be patched.

I met another steel boat owner today. They have a nice round-bilge boat. They bought the bare hull and finished it out themselves. They had some good ideas about proper ham radio installation in a steel boat.

A flock of about 30 bright green parrots hang out in the bamboo across the road. They make quite a racket, though they're not as annoying as the local disco. Last night it was wound up to a fever pitch until 4:00 a.m. Even though the club is almost a mile away, it's still loud on the boat. Earlier in the evening I was at the little restaurant in Tropical Marine Marina, next door to Coral Cove. I was listening to a local jazz musician playing classics on the sax. Very nice, but I felt bad that he had to compete with the strange reggae/rap the disco was playing with the amp turned to 11.

Tonight is the weekly BBQ at Coral Cove. Surprisingly, I managed to plan ahead and buy some meat for the grill. I think I'll try to get a bit more work done before heading over to the pool/grill area.

Just for Sandy:

I'm working hard but it's difficult to keep up my motivation. I get lonely and overwhelmed. My main incentive is to get the boat ready enough for you guys to come join me. I guess I'm not a good loner. I was bummed when my dad said he might take a driving vacation across the U.S. before coming here. I tried to talk him out of it but don't know if I was successful.

Please don't send out the last paragraph. It's too depressing.

Love you and miss you—
Marc

November 15, 2004

I have most of the aft center cabin removed. I still have to remove a bit more of the aft cabin before I can start repairing the steel. Just in case I haven't been clear about what I'm doing: I'm getting access to all of the port side of the boat that is aft of the navigation station. This is where 90 percent of the welding will be done. I finished removing the watermaker, battery, and saltwater pump. I also removed most of the woodwork in the aft center cabin.

Went for a dip in the pool and got invited to get a burger at Tropical Marine. She was 24 and … just kidding. It was the couple from the boat PASTIME, the same couple that invited me to sit at their table for Thanksgiving dinner. They are very nice people with lots of down-to-earth advice for cruising.

Just for Sandy:

Please keep this to yourself. I've just had a bit of a shock. I removed some paneling in the salon and realized that I'd set the boat on fire. The insulation had burned in a 3-square-foot section. I'm sure it was my doing because it was near where I had been grinding. I never smelled anything, even though it must have been burning for 15 or 20 minutes. Luckily, only the insulation was damaged. Don't worry; I'll be more careful.

November 16, 2004

Not a lot of visible progress today. I went to several stores to get paint supplies. I also talked at length to the local paint supplier who sells a brand called Jotun. He claims it's the largest marine paint supplier in the world. He was quite convincing in his confidence in the product. I think I'll use it. The total cost for the paint will be $2,400. I also took the watermaker in to be tuned up. That'll cost $380, but includes a new membrane.

With a project of this size, and being so foreign to me, it's hard to keep positive all the time. Many "expert" boaters around here prognosticate anything from complete doom to instant success. While they have lots of information to share, I have to be careful not to take what they say to heart. Most of the time I feel pretty good about my progress, and I don't see any immediate land mines ahead, but I still don't know what I'm doing well enough to hire a helper.

The head guard at Coral Cove recommended a refrigeration guy who turned out to be a real craftsman. He's also found a welder for me to use when I'm ready. I'm still looking for a reputable painter who's experienced with steel boats. I think I found a good sandblaster, but I don't have a quote from him yet.

The yard workers are experts of the worst kind. Many are amateur con men trying to fleece the "rich American boaters." One guy started hanging out and making nice. When he asked for work, I asked him to quote the job of replacing one of the Plexiglas windows. In the U.S., the job would cost about $200. This guy wanted $800, claiming that the plastic was expensive here because it's imported. When I asked around, the cost was no more than U.S. list prices.

I haven't been taking photos like I should. However, I've been making notes on the pieces I remove, and since the construction methods used are the same throughout the boat, I've got good examples. I'll take some photos and put them on the web page soon.

So far, the sailing people I've met have been great. You just have to filter the "expert factor" a bit.

November 17, 2004

I went to PriceSmart in the morning. In the afternoon I worked in the aft center cabin with the needle gun. Rust is EVIL!

November 18, 2004

To Sandy and Dad:

I decided to come up with a complete repair list. I thought this might help you think about the job before you come.

From this I realized that every cabin will have to have woodwork removed and welding done before the paint job starts. This means I won't be able to use any part of the boat for storage. It also means it will be impossible to live aboard the boat. We'll have to rent some storage and an apartment for at least two months.

Sandy:

In looking at this list, it seems that we have several months of work to do here. This means leaving here mid-February, perhaps after Carnival. You might want to think about what this means to our route and other plans.

TO-DO LIST

Before Sandblasting:

- **Through-hulls (defined later):**
  Plan number and locations.
  Buy pipe and have it threaded.
  Cut holes for through-hull locations.
  Have pipe welded in.

- **Portholes:**
  Remove woodwork.
  Cut patch pieces for old openings.
  Weld in patches.
  Cut new openings.

- **Repair rust problems:**
  Remove woodwork as needed.
  Use grinder/needle gun to clean and remove rusted areas.
  Cut out bad spots.
  Weld in replacement pieces.
  Clean and paint inside hull where repairs are made.

In Sandblast Yard:

- Drop rudder/skeg.
- Remove prop shaft.
- Mask.
- Sandblast and apply primer in 4-hour cycles.
- Repair any new problems revealed by sandblasting.
- Re-blast and re-prime as needed.
- Apply second primer coat.
- Add filler to hull as needed.
- Prime filled areas.
- Paint topsides.
- Paint antifouling on bottom.

Before Splashing Boat:

- Install all port lights and fixed lights (windows).
- Install prop shaft.

- *Repack shaft log.*
- *Install rudder/skeg.*
- *Repack rudder log.*
- *Install ball valves on through-hulls.*

Before Sailing Off:

- *Reinstall woodwork.*
- *Replace batteries.*
- *Treat rust on deck.*
- *Install stereo.*
- *Life raft?*
- *Flares?*
- *Check EPIRB (emergency position-indicating radio beacon) battery.*
- *Install new voltage regulator for main alternator.*
- *Change all filters/belts/oil for main engine and generator.*
- *Pump out main fuel tank sump.*
- *Check fire extinguishers.*
- *Rebuild engine raw water pump.*
- *Grease prop.*
- *Clean and grease winches.*
- *Check manual bilge pump.*
- *Check ropes to tie to dock.*
- *Check halyards for mainsail and genoa, mainsheet and reefs.*
- *Replace cowl vents.*
- *Cockpit vents.*
- *Buy dinghy.*
- *Check outboard.*
- *Service toilets.*
- *Lube main mast track.*
- *Fix saltwater pump in kitchen.*
- *Backstay insulators for radio antenna.*
- *Oil pressure alarm main engine.*
- *Fix kitchen macerator pump.*
- *Fix freezer door hinge.*
- *Lube anchor windlass.*
- *Check electrical contacts for anchor windlass.*

Buy Spares:

- *Foot-pump*
- *Mercedes saltwater pump*
- *Macerator*
- *Pressure freshwater pump*
- *Belts*
- *Toilets*
- *Bulbs*

November 19, 2004

Peakes Yacht Services looks good for the sandblasting and painting. It will cost $300 to move the boat, which includes splashing the boat when it's done. Yard time will cost $650 a month, and the blasting and painting will cost about $5,000, not including costs to fair the hull *(smooth with filler)*. They don't use a tent. They just wait for good weather then blast/paint in short cycles. It takes two days to blast and apply the first coat of primer.

I think I've worked out a good scheme for storage on deck using the spinnaker pole and tarps. I'll put it up and see. If it works out, then I think we'll keep MARAVIDA in Coral Cove until the welding is done.

November 20, 2004

Now that hurricane season is almost over, the yard's starting to thin out. People are finishing up their boat repairs and getting ready to leave. Many of the boats were from Grenada, getting repaired from hurricane damage.

You get to know people from hearing them on the morning net, and then when you meet them in person you sort of know each other already. I meet people at the pool as well. I've talked to everyone with a metal boat to ask what works and what doesn't. People also stop to ask about MARAVIDA.

I had dinner last night with the people from PASTIME and CAVA *(pronounced sava)*. PASTIME and CAVA first met when they were both talking on the radio with the Canadian weather guy who helps cruisers plan their trips according to weather conditions (see http://www3.sympatico.ca/hehilgen/vax498.htm). Both boats left New England at the same time, late in the season, and met off and on as they cruised down the island chain.

The more people I meet here, the more I'm sure we made the right choice. I haven't met anyone I didn't like.

I spent the last two days building on-deck storage and moving woodwork to it. I also cleared out a cabin for my dad, who is coming soon.

November 22, 2004

I cut more holes in the hull and squared up some of the odd-shaped ones I'd already cut. I took some measurements of the corrosion depth and found very little that was deeper than 2 mm. The plating of the hull is 5 mm. I've set a limit of 2.5 mm for isolated pits. Any deeper and I will fix them. Less than 2.5 and they will get sandblasted and epoxy painted along with the rest of the hull.

My dad sent me a note that he's in Caracas and will be taking a 12-hour overnight bus ride tomorrow to Guiria, Venezuela. He'll take a ferry from Guiria and arrive here about 6:30 p.m. on Wednesday. He just got back from a month in Vietnam—he's quite the adventurer.

To get ready for my dad's arrival, I did laundry, washed dishes, and worked at overall cleaning and organizing.

November 25, 2004

My father arrived the night before Thanksgiving. The Thanksgiving dinner was held at the TTHTI (Trinidad and Tobago Hospitality and Tourism Institute) in a former military hospital about a 10-minute ride from Coral Cove. The students did a great job with the dinner, and our server was a beautiful and articulate young woman. It was great to see the students working so hard to better their circumstances. We had six at the table, which included the couple from PASTIME and two sisters from another boat. The meal included all the classics plus a few new items.

My dad and I went on a three-hour guided excursion to see the Gasparee limestone caves on nearby Gaspar Grande Island. At the bottom of the cave is a large pool of salt water that rises and falls with the tides. We swam in the pool for about 20 minutes, feeling the warmer ocean water coming in and watching the bats flying overhead.

November 28, 2004

A fellow cruiser invited a group for a day sail on his catamaran. We went to the west side of an island called Chacachacare *(pronounced something like: sha-ka-sha-ka-ree)*, where we swam, snorkeled, and had a BBQ. We then sailed to the east side of the island, where there are buildings still standing from an old leper colony that was established there in the 1920s. I read that the patients were moved to the Port of Spain Hospital in 1984. It looks like they left in a hurry because of the many items left behind: filing cabinets, furniture, even patient records. There's also a generator and many overhead power lines still going between the buildings, but the jungle is starting to encroach. The return sail was nice with lots of wind.

December 1, 2004

Renewing my visa turned out to be a challenge. I went to the Chaguaramas immigration/customs station located at the CrewsInn Yachting Centre. They told me they couldn't help me because I had arrived on a vacation visa, not as a boat captain. They sent me to the main office in Port of Spain (locals call it POS). At the POS immigration office, I was told that only the Chaguaramas office could do the necessary paperwork. When I told them I'd just come from there, I was told to wait to talk to the supervisor. After 45 minutes, I was called in to a small office. The supervisor turned out to be in charge of the Chaguaramas office as well and read them the riot act over the phone. He apologized to me and sent me back to Chaguaramas. It was a bit chilly in the Chaguaramas office, but I was given my three-month extension.

Four of the windows on the boat are flat Plexiglas. They are old and cracked, so we ordered replacements made. We hired a day laborer, named Junior, to work at grinding around the window openings to remove rust. He worked hard and got quite a bit done, so I think we'll use him again. At the end of the day the importer called me on the radio and told me to come over because he had a reasonable deal on the new port lights we need. I placed the order ($3,100). He says they will arrive in two weeks, but he doesn't have a good reputation for being on time.

Two of my new cruiser friends leave tomorrow. I can already tell my least favorite part of this life will be saying goodbye to friends.

CHAPTER 4

Apartment Life in Trinidad

Settling In

From: sandy_n_marc
To: Davis News Group
Subject: Davis News
Date: Fri, 24 Dec 2004

The kids and I arrived in Trinidad 10 days ago. We're experiencing culture shock, but it's different this time because we're living as locals, not tourists. Our apartment is situated in a neighborhood, away from the yachting world. We ride with the locals in maxi-taxis. We shop with them downtown, in malls, and at neighborhood grocery stores. We are completely immersed in a new and different culture.

Our apartment is in a concrete house surrounded by a concrete fence. Like all houses here, it has bars on the windows and doors. The concrete walls have open lattice along the top for ventilation, but we covered them with foam to decrease street noise and let the bedrooms' air conditioners cool the entire apartment. The foam also blocks out the grime that comes from living next to the highway.

We have use of a washing machine located in a padlocked outbuilding behind the house. The first time I did laundry and hung the clothes out on the lines, the rain soaked the clothes so that they wouldn't dry before the next day's rain. Hmmm ... Marc's solution was to rig up lines inside the house. They add to the already cluttered appearance that comes with storing the contents of MARAVIDA in the apartment. I'm still wading through the boxes of books and boat items; most will be useful, but some are a mystery.

Marc has hired Junior to work with him on MARAVIDA. He's the guy who approached me about work when we first came to Trinidad. To ensure that he'll continue to work for us until the boat is finished, Marc's decided to up his salary to TT$300 per day (US$50). He's cheerful, works hard, looks out for us, and so much more. He also has a car!

We took our first public maxi-taxi ride to PriceSmart the day after our arrival. We had to limit our purchases to what we could carry back. That's okay, though, because yesterday Junior took us for a return trip in his car so we could stock up on essentials.

The second day after our arrival, Grandpa Brian (Marc's dad) stayed home with Alex while Madeline and I walked to the Hi-Lo Supermarket with our handy rolling cooler, purchased in Connecticut before we left. The long, hot walk along the highway wore us out, so we decided to drag ourselves to the shopping mall, located on the far side of the supermarket, where we could rest our legs and cool down before we tackled the grocery shopping.

Madeline is excited to have a shopping mall within walking distance, even if it's a tortuous walk in the glaring sun. From the outside, West Mall looks like a demolition site, but the inside appears to be undergoing a cosmetic renovation judging by all the glass and marble that's being installed. I guess the facelift is designed to indulge the inhabitants of the high-rise condos lined up behind it along the ocean and to entice the residents of the mansions up in the hills.

Madeline and Brian went on an adventure to Tobago over the weekend. They had the choice of a short plane hop *(approximately 50 miles)* or a longer, uncomfortable ferry ride *(approximately 86 miles)*. They chose the plane.

> **Tobago**
>
> Though Tobago is part of the Republic of Trinidad and Tobago, it is very different from Trinidad. Lying northeast of Trinidad, Tobago is a much smaller island, covering only 116 square miles compared to Trinidad's 1,833 square miles. Trinidad's million and a quarter population dwarfs Tobago's 60,000 or so inhabitants, but Tobago is more tourist-friendly with better diving, nicer beaches, and a more laid-back atmosphere.

On Saturday night, Marc, Alex, and I went to Coral Cove's annual holiday party at Joe's Pizza. They served local food and provided steel drum music as entertainment. *(Both the steel pan drum and calypso music originated in Trinidad.)* We chatted with Coral Cove business owners, employees, and fellow tenants while Alex and a six-year-old local boy played Gameboy games.

On Sunday, the three of us went sailing with some cruisers on a catamaran. We sailed to another island, went snorkeling, and barbecued on the boat.

On Tuesday, Brian and Alex took a maxi to the zoo while Madeline and I took one into Port of Spain. We purchased a miniature artificial Christmas tree, wrapping paper, and some kitchen items.

Brian left Wednesday morning. We will miss him.

An American cruising couple (docked at Coral Cove) asked us to join them and their visiting grandchildren on Wednesday for a day tour with Jesse James. The first stop was a roadside stand for breakfast *doubles* (curried chickpeas in a homemade pita). From there we headed out on a scenic drive through the rainforest. Along the way, Jesse pointed out various plants and trees and told us about the Asa Wright Nature Centre as we passed by the entrance (famous for bird watching http://asawright.org). Our final destination was Maracas Bay beach, where we swam and ate "Shark and Bake."

Everyone in Trinidad knows about and craves "Shark and Bake" from Maracas. The breaded shark is tucked into a flatbread sandwich, which is then loaded up with veggies and condiments such as tomatoes, lettuce, mayo, and chutneys.

A Dinghy for Christmas

On Thursday *(December 23rd)*, Madeline and I went grocery shopping while Alex and Marc went to pick up the new dinghy that Marc ordered a month ago. The 25-horsepower dinghy engine that came with MARAVIDA was already tuned-up and ready to go. And that it did—the guys came home that night with big smiles on their faces, excited about our fast dinghy.

Most sailboat tenders use 5- to 10-horsepower motors, but they're mounted on smaller craft than our new 11.5-foot, six-person dinghy. It's large enough to handle the bigger engine, and MARAVIDA has a large deck to hold it. We chose AB Inflatable's aluminum bottom model, which makes it lightweight for its size (see http://www.abinflatables.com).

We'll spend Christmas Eve at our apartment and open presents the next morning. Fortunately, I brought lots of presents with me from the States. It'll be the first time the kids and I will experience Christmas in warm weather and with an artificial Christmas tree.

Anjuli has invited us to her boat for Christmas dinner. She's from New Zealand and is both crew and nanny on a sailboat owned by a family of five. They are gone until February, so she's watching their boat and making repairs.

MERRY CHRISTMAS!

Love—
Sandy, Marc, Madeline, and Alex

Transportation Issues at Christmas

From: sandy_n_marc
To: Davis News Group
Subject: Davis News
Date: Tue, 28 Dec 2004

We had a difficult time getting to Coral Cove on Christmas Eve day because all the maxi-taxis were full. Our mission was to get to the internet café to send an e-mail out to everyone. We finally walked to West Mall, where the maxis were unloading shoppers in droves, and easily hopped aboard.

The stores were closed on Christmas Day, and the roads were quiet. We didn't realize how hard it would be to find a maxi-taxi. Since Anjuli expected us for Christmas dinner, we stayed out on the road until we finally managed to hail a personal taxi. When we asked the driver why he was working when no one else was, he answered that he's a Jehovah's Witness.

The stores were also closed on Boxing Day, but we had an easier time getting transportation into Chaguaramas. Once there, we hopped into our dinghy—which is tied up at Coral Cove's dinghy dock—picked up Anjuli at her boat in the anchorage, and headed to Scotland Bay, about 15 miles away. We tethered the dinghy to a tree, ate our picnic lunch, and then went snorkeling. I can't wait until we can snorkel where the water is clearer.

Today is our first school day since we left Connecticut. Both kids were in tears at different times this morning, but they're doing okay this afternoon.

We fired the first welder. His welds cracked after they cooled, and Junior didn't like him. We weren't surprised by Junior's animosity toward the welder since the man was disrespectful to the Trini workers. Marc had a second welder lined up, but Junior asked if he could hire someone he knew—a guy named Michael. So we're trying Junior's guy. Marc is giving Junior and Michael lots of space. So far they've worked every afternoon and evening, even on Christmas.

The Culture of Trinidad

Since Trinidad is our home for now, I'm glad it's an English-speaking country. People are helpful, friendly, and welcoming despite our white skin and perceived affluence. Trinis are poor by American standards, but they don't look it. Trinidadian women put more effort into their hair, makeup, and clothing than I ever have. I spend a minimum amount of time on my hair, and I wear no makeup in this humid climate. Most of my summer wardrobe is fine to wear in Chaguaramas, but it is unacceptable for the rest of Trinidad. The women in Trinidad dress conservatively, but there's a definite sexiness to their style. They wear high-heeled shoes, tight pants or jeans or knee-length skirts, and fitted tops—nothing sloppy and nothing too short. The men wear pants or jeans or long shorts and, more often than not, gold jewelry.

Trinis seem to be paranoid about theft and robbery, but perhaps that's for good reason. Was it paranoia or firsthand experience that led to the installation of bars on the windows and doors of the houses and businesses here? We are constantly warned: Don't go in such and such areas at night, watch your purse and wallet in Port of Spain, don't trust this person or that person. Both friends and strangers are concerned for our safety.

We finally figured out the language for using maxi-taxis. The driver honks to ask if we want a ride, and we tell him our desired destination by pointing our finger. If we stand near our apartment (on the side of the highway heading north), we point toward the ocean to indicate we want to go toward Chaguaramas. Pointing inland would indicate Diego Martin as our intended destination, and pointing to the ground means we want to do a short hop, like to the mall.

We've learned a lot about young Trini women by watching them get maxi-taxis. They don't use the hand signals; in fact, they appear uninterested in obtaining a maxi at all. But the maxi driver stops for them and they slowly walk up to the vehicle and climb aboard, making sure to ignore the driver and the other men in the van. Trinidadian women are aloof and disdainful of men, but the men are patient and accept it as normal. It's a game that we don't totally understand. The guidebooks describe this country as a male chauvinist society, but I think the women stay in command by using their sex appeal to manage the men.

Interesting Info:

- In our apartment, we get lukewarm water from the cold water tap and nothing from the hot water side. Nevertheless, we can have a warm water shower because of a nifty device that's attached to the showerhead. I guess you'd call it a tankless hot water showerhead. It warms the water right before it comes out, and you can adjust the temperature by increasing or decreasing the flow rate. Sounds great, but we have to use a small stream to get it warm enough to be comfortable. I don't mind, but Marc and Madeline both love a hot shower with lots of water pressure.

- We drink milk and juice out of liter boxes (just like in Europe). They take up less space than the plastic jugs at home.

- Imported food is expensive, but the local fare is reasonably priced and food stands offer tasty items at bargain prices.

- We don't drink the tap water because it's overchlorinated; you can smell the chlorine.

- Trinis put ketchup on everything, even pizza.

- Importing used "tyres" is big business here; no sense buying new tires when the roads are in such bad condition.

- When a landslide removes part of a road, the road is "repaired" by simply drawing a white line around the edge of the hole. Sometimes a flimsy bamboo guardrail is added for effect. We're amazed at the poor condition of the roads considering that Trinidad possesses the largest natural tar lake in the world.

- "New Year's Eve" is called "Old Year's Night" here.

Happy New Year!

Love—
Sandy, Marc, Madeline, and Alex

Hurricane Season Has Ended

From: sandy_n_marc
To: Davis News Group
Subject: Davis News
Date: Thu, 13 Jan 2005

Marc worries about how much time and money we're spending here. I assure him that it's all part of the adventure. We are learning about the culture of Trinidad as well as the subculture of cruising and cruisers.

Regrettably, many cruisers are departing now that hurricane season has ended. That leaves people like us, stuck in huge projects; people like Bill and Benita, our Canadian friends on ALCHERINGA II, who are waiting for a new mast to come from the U.K. (they were dismasted in the hurricane in Grenada); and our New Zealand friend, Anjuli, who's looking after her host family's sailboat while they are away. We've been told, however, that more boats will come for Carnival (Feb. 7th–8th this year).

> **Carnival**
>
> Carnival takes place on the Monday and Tuesday immediately before Ash Wednesday. Trinidadians start preparations months in advance—each "band" must choose a theme, music, costumes, and dance moves. Participants, "mas players," choose the band they want to join and then attend many practices and costume fittings. They are preparing for the huge parade where they will dance down the streets of Port of Spain wearing their elaborate costumes. This festival is the premier event of each year for Trinidadians and is more about being a participant than a spectator.
>
> We went to the Children's Carnival on Saturday, February 5th. It was loud, crowded, and exciting enough that we decided to watch Carnival Monday and Tuesday on TV rather than in person.

We now possess library cards from the National Library of Trinidad and Tobago. The Port of Spain branch was built in 2003 and stands in proud contrast to the worn buildings of downtown. Whenever we step inside, we are excited to be in the company of books: Libraries have always been an important part of our life, and we definitely welcome the cool air as we take shelter from the uncomfortable heat outside. But the library itself does not feel welcoming—the big spaces, high ceilings, empty shelves, and strict rules are disappointing. Each of us has a library card, but because the book checkout limit is so small, we must put the kids' books on all four cards. I guess I shouldn't complain, because having a library we can use is better than not having one at all.

Junior

The Sunday before last, Junior showed up at our apartment at 9:00 a.m. with fresh doubles, coconut water, and sugarcane from his yard. He proceeded to expertly cut up the sugarcane and showed us how to chew on it for the sugar juice. He also brought *The Garfield Movie*—pirated, of course.

We often rent pirated DVD movies from the internet café for TT$7. (There are 6 Trinidad and Tobago dollars to the U.S. dollar.) It seems to be a big business here. Many of the available titles have not yet been released to video. The movies vary in quality, but most hold extra entertainment value due to the additional action that occurred in the theater while filming: flies buzzing by, people coming and going, laughing, coughing, etc.

Last Saturday, Junior brought us another movie and also barbecued chicken and salad made by his girlfriend, Michelle. We first met Michelle last Sunday, when we all went to the zoo. She was shy at first, but over time she became more comfortable, and her seemingly negative disposition turned out to be just a dour sense of humor. Like many Trinidadian women, she has a justifiably jaded outlook on Trinidadian men because, we're told, they are often unfaithful and many seem to be stuck in teenage-boy mode.

Junior is definitely a teenager at heart, but he's thoughtful and kind, and we're quite fond of him. Nevertheless, we have to watch him carefully. Many Trinidadian workers will take advantage of cruisers if given the opportunity, and Junior is no exception. Thus, Marc has a weekly talk with him about writing down the actual hours that he works and being fair when he asks for reimbursement for his black market purchases. He explains to Junior that we are not rich and can't afford to be cheated. Nevertheless, the only way to keep a handle on this is for Marc to work at the boat alongside the workers and to accompany Junior on boat purchase errands.

Since we arrived in Trinidad, we've had to develop a new mindset about trusting others. It seems that the majority of Trinidadians look out for themselves first; they don't feel bad about taking advantage of the "system" and of people more fortunate. To outsiders, they appear to be greedy, but there's no mean-spiritedness to the act of cheating the system or other people. It's a fact of life and even a matter of pride. They feel it's their duty to give it a good try. So, we must also play the game by not being gullible Americans. We should be cautious, but we can do this cheerfully and without hard feelings once we come to accept this as the norm in Trinidad.

Transportation

We didn't have a car in Trinidad; instead, we rode with the locals in maxi-taxis. The drivers of the 12-passenger vans pick up passengers anywhere along their route if they have a vacant seat. They work hard to keep occupancy full, so we often had difficulty hailing one in front of our apartment, especially during heavy traffic times. We had the best luck at the pedestrian overpass down the street. The wait was shorter there because it's a busy spot, and we could usually take the seats from someone alighting.

As we waited, we took turns announcing each passing van's egocentric name branded across the top of the windshield: "Righteous," "Ultimate," "Number-One Lover," etc. The typical driver was always in a hurry: He screeched to a stop, music blaring, and the copilot would throw open the side door. Squatting next to the door so he wouldn't take up a valuable seat, this "conductor" of sorts speeded up the process.

We winced as we climbed aboard and regretted that once again we'd forgotten to bring earplugs. Our goal was to sit down quickly so we weren't slammed down at take-off, but we always made sure to greet our fellow passengers as is customary. Then we turned our attention to the interior décor to speculate about the driver/owner's personality from the signs, photos, and artwork plastered around the vehicle.

The driver would accelerate quickly: He doesn't have a set time schedule, so the more ground he covers, the more money he'll collect. The ride is definitely not for the faint of heart. There are many hazards to slow the driver's progress, but he speeds around them, often switching lanes into the oncoming traffic to avoid potholes and double-parked cars. We'd attempt to stay in our seats as we bumped and swayed through the white-knuckle ride, wondering why we trusted these crazy drivers with our lives.

When our destination was close, we'd tell the copilot where we wanted to get off so he could relay it to the driver. The van would screech to a stop. As we exited, the copilot took our money and gave change from the wad of cash he proudly clutched in one hand. As we stepped down from the roller-coaster ride—weak in the knees and ears ringing—we'd chuckle about how the taxi business was probably the only service industry in Trinidad that doesn't move at a snail's pace.

The kids and I take the maxi-taxis downtown to shop and to go to the library. Marc rode them daily to the marina in the late mornings until he realized that the workers accomplished little before his arrival. So he started to ride with Junior, but they would get to the yard late because neither Junior nor Marc is punctual. Fortunately, since we've hired Junior's friend Richard, who is more mindful of schedules, the three of them now arrive at Coral Cove at a reasonable time each morning.

Junior is proud of his car. But where he sees a thing of beauty, I see a junker. I'd compare his pride to that of a teenager thrilled with owning his first ride.

Junior's car is typical for Trinidad. Most are Japanese imports from the roll-on/roll-off foreign used-vehicle industry that got going here in the 1990s. His car has probably been through a few owners since its roll-off and has withstood several "improvements." The hood and fenders are various colors, though I'd guess the original color was blue. The interior is missing everything except the seats and dashboard. There are no seatbelts, and the back seat is not even bolted down.

It's scary, but entertaining, to ride in the back and watch the driver and his assistant drive the car. Junior starts the car like a car thief, reaching under the dash to touch two wires together. Richard operates the windshield washers, when necessary, with a screwdriver. When the horn is needed, which is often in Trinidad, Junior uses the high beam switch, which he somehow repurposed to blow the horn.

More Later—
Sandy

Health Care

Our only experience with health care in Trinidad was when I had a persistent earache in January, not long after our arrival. Marc and I decided to walk to the nearby community of St. James to look for a doctor. We walked into the first doctor's office we encountered. It had a small waiting room with a couple of people waiting and no receptionist. We took a seat. Eventually the doctor poked his head out, and we asked if we could make an appointment. He said to wait. A few minutes later he waved us into his office. As we sat down in front of his desk, I told him that I had an earache and was worried I might have an ear infection. His response was, "Okay, I'll write you a prescription." But Marc asked, "Don't you want to look into her ears?" He said, "Sure," picked up his otoscope, and walked around the desk. After taking a perfunctory peek into my ear, he wrote the prescription. The appointment lasted only a couple of minutes, and though I wasn't assured that I actually had an ear infection, I decided to take the antibiotics prescribed anyway.

The Trinis we met don't trust the healthcare system because they've heard too many horror stories about hospital visits gone wrong. They tell us about friends and family members who are admitted to the hospital with minor problems and come out with new or worse problems, or don't come out at all. Many feel that going to the hospital is a death sentence. I honestly don't know if this is warranted or unwarranted paranoia.

Living "With" Our Boat

From: sandy_n_marc
To: Davis News Group
Subject: Davis News
Date: Thu, 3 Feb 2005

We brought more of the boat to our apartment. Last time we brought the contents of the cupboards and storage areas; this time we brought the cupboards themselves, along with most of the other wooden interior pieces, walls and bed frames among them. We crammed as much as possible into the apartment, making sure to leave narrow pathways to the beds, chairs, and dining table. The remaining pieces went to Junior's father's house. (Junior and Michelle live with Junior's father.) We may not be living on our boat, but we are certainly living "with" it.

Our experience with welders has not been good, and we had to do more welder shuffling this past month. We let welder #4 go last Wednesday (he only lasted a week) and rehired welder #2 this week (Michael, Junior's friend). Hopefully we're settled on him now.

The workers are going over the boat thoroughly and are still finding places to cut and weld. Yesterday, they found rust holes in the fuel tanks!

Marc is designing a new through-hull plan for the boat.

Through-Hull

A through-hull (or thru-hull) is a hole in the hull of the boat with a plastic or metal lining. It has a fitting that accepts hoses, pipes, or valves and allows water to pass in or out of the vessel. A seacock attaches to the inside tail of the through-hull fitting and is opened and closed with a valve. The through-hull must be easily accessible so that if a hose breaks, the seacock can be closed and the boat won't sink.

MARAVIDA's original through-hull fittings were plastic flange valves. The hull rusted badly at the points where the fittings were bolted, so Marc plans to weld the holes closed. He also plans to reduce the number of holes and move some to locations above the waterline. Speaking of holes, Marc ordered two new Lavac toilets, which he says are supposed to be the most reliable.

January was cloudy and rainy. The upside was that we didn't have to use sunscreen all month. Nevertheless, I'm happy the rainy season is over; now I can hang clothes on the outside lines.

We've found a reliable taxi driver to use for bulk shopping trips. We take a maxi-taxi to the store, and then midway through our shopping expedition we call the taxi driver from the store phone. So far he's been available or he's sent someone else in his place. We usually call him from PriceSmart or Tru Valu Supermarket at Long Circular Mall. It's only TT$20 (US$3.25) for the trip home.

The four of us quarrel often, but we're becoming closer because we spend so much time together. I see the benefit of our life to come.

Talk to you later—
Sandy

The Drums

From: sandy_n_marc
To: Davis News Group
Subject: Davis News
Date: Fri, 25 Feb 2005

This week the guys removed the teak toerail. We've decided to choose practical over pretty by replacing it with a steel tube rail. The new rail will be mounted farther off the deck than the wooden rail so that rust won't form underneath as easily.

Marc now spends ten hours a day at Coral Cove. We're worried that we'll run out of "boat money" before we're finished, so we want to hurry up the process as much as possible.

Alex is cheerful as usual, though he talks often about his friends in Oregon. Madeline is feeling stir-crazy, but that's normal for her. I'm doing fine; still fascinated with the culture of Trinidad.

At 11:00 p.m. last Wednesday, we awoke to the sound of drums getting louder as they came close to our apartment. We woke again at 3:00 a.m. when they came past again. The next night, we hadn't gone to bed when we heard the drums, so we ran outside and watched as a large group of drummers, flag bearers, and spectators inched along Western Main Road in front of our apartment, blocking two of the three lanes of traffic. We were fascinated and intrigued by the spectacle. When we heard the drums and went outside again on Friday night, we found our landlords already outside watching. They explained that it's an annual Islamic event. The Hosay procession comes from various neighborhoods and meets in nearby St. James before parading down the streets.

> **Hosay**
>
> The dates of Hosay vary each year based on the Islamic lunar calendar's observance of Ashura (the 10th day of Muharram). On the 7th and 8th nights of Muharram, the procession carries drums and flags; on the 9th and 10th nights, the participants roll an ornate handmade temple behind the drummers; and on the final day, the temples are taken to touch the sea.

Anjuli stayed overnight at our apartment last Friday; it was our last chance to see her before she left the country. She's been in Trinidad for more than three months (about the same as Marc) and has had an interesting life experience over the past year or so, but she's broke and ready to go home now. (She's only 24.) Anjuli sailed from New Zealand to the United States and from there to Trinidad with her host family. Although she intended to sail back to New Zealand with them, many concerned friends (including Marc) have said that the boat isn't in acceptable condition to sail across the South Pacific. So, she told the family that if the necessary repairs weren't made to the boat, she'd have to leave them. Alas, they don't want to spend the money to make the boat safer, so Anjuli's leaving for England to visit two of her brothers, and then she'll fly home to New Zealand, where she wants to take courses to be an "Outward Bound" instructor. We'll miss her.

Take Care—
Sandy

Schedule

From: sandy_n_marc
To: Davis News Group
Subject: Davis News
Date: Tue, 15 Mar 2005

We now have phone and internet at the apartment thanks to Junior's use of personal connections to shorten the wait.

Michelle's sister braided Madeline's hair.

Current Boat Schedule:

- Reinforce rudder skeg (today)
- Install new through-hulls (1 day)
- Weld on studs for zinc anodes (2 hours)
- Install new toerail (3 days)
- Move boat to new yard; sandblast and paint outside of hull (?)
- Install interior and systems (3 months or longer)

More Later—
Sandy

Demographics

While we were living in Trinidad, I went downtown often, sometimes with one or both kids, other times by myself. I rarely saw another person with white skin. Clearly, I stood out as a foreigner, yet nobody treated me differently.

Trinidad has three primary ethnic groups: (1) The Indo-Trinidadians (approximately 40 percent of the population) originally emigrated from India as indentured servants. (2) The Afro-Trinidadians (approximately 38 percent of the population) came from Africa as slaves. (3) People of mixed racial background make up another 19 percent of the island's population.

When I did see fair-skinned people, they were usually foreign nationals.

Finishing Up at Coral Cove

From: sandy_n_marc
To: Davis News Group
Subject: Davis News
Date: Tue, 5 Apr 2005

Alex made a friend at Coral Cove's swimming pool. His name is Tyler, and his German father, Karl, has just purchased a "fixer upper" catamaran that resides in the yard. The boat needs a lot of fiberglass work, but that's Karl's specialty: He runs a fiberglass repair business here in Chaguaramas. Tyler's mother is Trinidadian, and she and Karl are a couple anymore, but we've met her a couple of times.

Tyler was born here and lives on Gaspar Grande Island with Karl and Karl's Trinidadian girlfriend, Lily. The island is accessible from Chaguaramas by a small ferry. Last week, the four of us drove our dinghy to the island to pick up Tyler, who has a two-week break from school for Easter. We hiked up one of the concrete "roads" (there are no cars on the island) to his house, which overlooks the ocean, as all houses do on the hilly island. It's quiet and peaceful, though a bit eerie with every third house or so abandoned and taken over by jungle.

ALCHERINGA II went into the water last Thursday. Bill and Benita (our friends from Canada) will be leaving soon because their new mast is installed and the rigging is finished. On Sunday, they invited us to go with them to test sail the new setup. The kids became nervous when the boat started to heel, but they adjusted fast. Marc, Madeline, and I took turns at the helm. When we returned to the marina, Benita expertly backed their 44-foot boat into its narrow slip. This gave Marc the idea to ask her to steer and captain MARAVIDA to Peakes Boatyard, where the sandblasting and painting will be done.

Marc and crew have worked eight days straight to prepare MARAVIDA to go to Peakes. Once they finished installing the new toerail, they thought they were ready to go, but another problem arose: After a day of heavy rain, the bilge mysteriously filled with diesel fuel. Upon thorough investigation, the crew discovered an additional fuel tank under the engine in the keel. It had filled with rainwater from two small holes on deck and then overflowed into the connecting saddle fuel tanks, which in turn overflowed into the bilge (all because of the way the hoses were set up). The guys cut three holes into each baffle of the keel tank, emptied out the fuel and water, then pressure-washed the insides. They found an area that needed welding, so they opened up a larger hole and did the necessary repairs. We're grateful for the heavy rainstorm that helped us discover the fuel tank and holes.

Yesterday morning, Coral Cove's travel lift picked up MARAVIDA and set her into the water. Because MARAVIDA's motor and steering aren't hooked up yet, Marc and Bill pushed her with dinghies while Benita steered with the emergency tiller. Peakes' travel lift hauled MARAVIDA out, and she's now sitting in the sandblasting yard. Today the workers will prep and mask, and tomorrow the sandblasting will begin. Marc, Junior, and Richard have gone over to pull the prop shaft and do a few other things. Marc plans to go every day to supervise the sandblasting and painting.

Sandy

Work Continues at Peakes

From: sandy_n_marc
To: Davis News Group
Subject: Davis News
Date: Fri, 15 Apr 2005

The sandblasting was postponed for three days because the propeller shaft wouldn't cooperate. Marc and the guys spent hours fabricating special tools to help remove it from the boat.

The sandblasting, which is now complete, uncovered pinholes that need welding. However, it didn't clean out the rust in the shaft log, so Marc will have to figure out another method. Meanwhile, Marc, Michael, and Junior spent Sunday welding up the pinholes.

We intend to stay at Peakes long enough to do minimal fairing (smooth out the roughest areas of the hull using epoxy mixed with fumed silica) and then have the painters spray on the final coats of paint (we'll live with white for now). In addition, Marc has to hook up the engine and its required plumbing, reassemble the propeller system, and install the port lights. He won't be able to get help from Junior and Richard, though. We just found out that Peakes doesn't allow outside contractors.

After Peakes, Marc wants to reassemble MARAVIDA's interior out at anchor to save on marina costs. Junior and Madeline want to return to Coral Cove. I'm arguing for the latter for two reasons: (1) It takes longer to do the work at anchor because of transport time—all that shuttling back and forth of people and materials—and (2) the anchorage is rough, and it's difficult to work on a boat that's constantly moving. We'll see.

The kids started a beginner sailing class last Saturday with the Trinidad and Tobago Sailing Association (TTSA). Alex liked it, Madeline didn't. Partway through the first lesson, she refused to continue because the class was comprised entirely of boys Alex's age and younger. (It also didn't help that she had to wake up three hours earlier than usual.) I told her she would have to ask for a refund. The lady in the office said no refunds, but she gave Madeline the option of trying out a larger boat with one of the teenage male instructors on Saturday.

Alex returned from his Wednesday lesson with a big smile on his face. The students took the boats out—tied together—and practiced using their rudders and daggerboards. They fell in the water multiple times, which he says made the class more fun (see http://www.ttsailing.org).

On Saturday, a fire gutted a couple of blocks in Port of Spain. Marc and I saw the charred remains of the buildings on Monday when we went downtown to do errands. Many people were standing behind the barricades, gaping in awe. The major damage covered at least two square blocks (between Frederick and Chacon Streets on the north side of Queen Street). In addition to the 300 vendor "People's Mall," the flames destroyed six stores, one restaurant, and a government office. Fortunately, the fire started in the early morning, when the businesses were empty. The public is understandably angry that it took so long to extinguish due to complications with fire hydrants and firefighting equipment.

Later—
Sandy

> **In the News**
>
> Morris, Gizelle. "Fire Downtown." *The Trinidad Guardian*. 10 Apr. 2005. Web. 23 Feb. 2012.
>
> http://legacy.guardian.co.tt/archives/2005-04-10/news1.html.

From Marc

From: sandy_n_marc
To: Davis News Group
Subject: Davis News
Date: Sun, 17 Apr 2005

MARAVIDA is sitting in the sandblast yard with a small fleet of large Vietnamese fishing boats. For the first few days, I just sat and watched the work being done on our boat. Despite my best efforts, the Vietnamese fishermen ignored me. Not a smile or a nod—nothing. I was surprised because my father had recently traveled to Vietnam and reported the people to be happy and friendly. But when I started to physically work on MARAVIDA, something changed. Small groups of men would come over to MARAVIDA and watch me work. Using sign language and a few words of English, they would ask questions about the boat, America, and my family. I had a hard time getting work done with so many men showing up for introductions! Today, Sandy came to the boat to work. Not only did this do nothing to stem the tide, but all work on the fishing boats suddenly needed to be done where a view of Sandy was possible.

Chronicles

From: sandy_n_marc
To: Davis News Group
Subject: Davis News
Date: Fri, 22 Apr 2005

Marc is lonely working on the boat by himself. He wants to finish filling and sanding by Sunday and then have it painted on Monday. After that, we'll move the boat to a more pleasant spot in the yard where we'll prepare it for the water. I told Marc I'd work with him every other day once MARAVIDA's moved away from the sandblasting yard (where too many eyes watch my every move). I'll get the kids out and about on the days I don't work on the boat.

On Monday, the kids and I walked to the mall and grocery store. Madeline insists we visit the mall at least once a week. On Tuesday we went to CrewsInn Marina. We've made friends with a Dutch couple on a large powerboat named SOUTHERN CROSS. We first met them when their boat was on the hard in Coral Cove, but now it's docked in the water at CrewsInn. They lent us one of their keys to use the facilities at CrewsInn. The pool is at least six times larger than the pool at Coral Cove, and Alex loves the computerized treadmills in the exercise room.

> **On The Hard**
>
> On the hard: Description of a boat that has been hauled and is now sitting on dry land.

I took Alex to his sailing class on Wednesday afternoon. (Madeline refuses to continue, even with the private lessons.) I sit in the shade while he's in class, intending to read my book, but I usually spend the time talking with other parents. They are interested in the concept of homeschooling, which is unheard of in Trinidad.

Yesterday I went into Port of Spain by myself. I borrowed school books for Alex at the library and did a few other errands. I had to detour around a commotion on the Promenade, but I couldn't see over the heads of the bystanders to identify the cause. I heard later that a shooting had taken place on the Promenade—the 102nd murder of the year.

> **In the News**
>
> "Man Shot Dead on Lara Promenade." *Trinidad and Tobago's Newsday*. 22 Apr. 2005. Web.
> http://www.newsday.co.tt/news/0,27176.html

The kids and I will go back to CrewsInn today, and tomorrow I'll take Alex to sailing class again. My life probably sounds easier than Marc's, but dealing with Madeline's severe hormonal mood swings has been difficult for me. I hope for improvement as she matures; meanwhile, I need lots of patience.

Take Care—
Sandy

Davis News

From: sandy_n_marc
To: Davis News Group
Subject: Davis News
Date: Mon, 2 May 2005

Marc didn't finish the filling and sanding by last Sunday as he'd hoped, but Junior asked around and discovered that the sandblasting yard—with its own separate security guard—isn't monitored by Peakes. So Junior and Richard joined Marc, and the three of them finished by the end of this weekend. Today the boat will be power washed, tomorrow it will be masked, and then the painting will begin. I'm not sure how many days it'll take because the process requires multiple coats of paint, and it's been raining in the afternoons.

We spent last Sunday afternoon and evening on SOUTHERN CROSS. The beautiful, restored steel yacht was built in the 1970s. We went along for the boat's first run in five months. After the outing, we had dinner on board. Marc taught the couple how to make corn tortillas, and I showed them how to make refried beans. (We picked up these culinary skills out of necessity. Tortillas and refried beans aren't available in the stores here, and they're a staple in our family—especially for Alex.)

Our pleasant day ended with a bad experience. On the way home in the maxi-taxi, one of three teenage boys grabbed our cooler as they exited the maxi. Marc ran after them, and they dropped it. I'm not sure if they dropped it because they were being pursued or because it was so heavy. The other passengers in the van were surprised by Marc's audacity to chase the culprits down, and the kids and I were angry with Marc for endangering himself, since the miscreants outnumbered him and could have turned on him. Marc's own outrage increased when we got home and discovered that his Leatherman must have fallen out of the front pocket of the cooler. We were all disturbed by the incident, but it reminded us to be more cautious.

This Sunday we went to Tyler's house on Gaspar Grande Island again. I spent the afternoon with the boys and Lily while Marc and Karl went diving and spearfishing, with Madeline along to man the dinghy. They speared five fish and had a great time diving on a new shipwreck, a coastal freighter only 20 feet down and near to shore. We returned to Coral Cove late, so we decided to call our private taxi driver since last Sunday's incident was still fresh in our minds.

From Marc

I had a fantastic time diving on the freighter. Karl had a rough idea of the location, so we went out with the dinghy and towed the anchor around on 50 feet of rope, hoping to hook the wreck. After a while, we gave up on the search. I jumped in the water to scrub the barnacles off the dinghy so we could make better time to our next spot. When I put on my mask and looked down, there it was: The bridge of the freighter was only about 20 feet below me. It was spooky. We spent the next two hours scuba diving and free diving the wreck. The freighter sank about nine months ago and is still in good shape. Its cargo (spools of cable) has spilled out on the ocean floor. Karl is an excellent free diver and can stay down several minutes at a time. He speared his first fish before I had finished putting on all my gear! We speared four more fish, explored the wreck, and then headed home. I can't wait to go back for more exploring.

Paint!

From: sandy_n_marc
To: Davis News Group
Subject: Davis News
Date: Fri, 6 May 2005

MARAVIDA with fresh paint.

Sea Trial

From: sandy_n_marc
To: Davis News Group
Subject: Davis News
Date: Tue, 17 May 2005

Richard got a worker's pass for Peakes and worked on MARAVIDA from Tuesday through Friday. Because of his help, we were able to launch today. The four of us, along with Junior and Richard, took MARAVIDA out on a sea trial, and everything worked! We stayed out an additional half hour to practice docking maneuvers before taking her to her new slip at Coral Cove. We expect to stay here for a month or more.

More Later—
Sandy

On the Water

From: sandy_n_marc
To: Davis News Group
Subject: Davis News
Date: Sun, 22 May 2005

I'm thrilled that we're on the dock in Coral Cove. We finally convinced Marc that it was more practical to have MARAVIDA on the dock than out at anchor. So now the only difference between us and other cruisers is that at the end of the day, we go to our apartment. We've found one downside to doing boat work on the water, though—the tendency to drop tools off the side. Junior dropped two wrenches the first day, but he got someone to dive for them.

There are two types of cruisers: full-time and part-time. Because Trinidad is considered to be outside of the hurricane belt, many part-time cruisers store their boats here during the summer hurricane season and return for winter cruising. Most are older and retired, but we know a few younger couples who organize their cruising life around seasonal jobs.

The yards are filling up as boats come in after winter cruising. Every day we see more of the familiar faces of cruisers we met at the beginning of winter. No one seems surprised to see us still here. The year-round cruisers we meet in Trinidad are often working on extensive projects. Eventually they finish their projects and leave, and ultimately we will, too. Trinidad is a cruiser's destination primarily for storing one's boat or working on it.

Marc is working on the window installation by himself. Before he installs the Lexan windows on the doghouse, he has to grind, sand, and fill around the openings.

> **Doghouse**
>
> Doghouse: A slang term (in the U.S., mostly) for a raised portion of a ship's deck. A doghouse is usually added to improve headroom below or to shelter a hatch.

Marc will also cut new holes for the port lights on the topsides. Earlier in the renovation process, most of those openings had to be welded over because of excessive rust. Junior and Richard are working on the interior. They sprayed the boat thoroughly to make sure water flows straight to the bilge. Where necessary, they drilled additional holes in the frames and bulkheads. Next they'll grind and epoxy paint any interior rust and apply a final coat on all interior steel. My job is to juggle the kids, clean up the tools and garbage that all three guys shed everywhere, and assist Marc.

Friday afternoon we went swimming off Bill and Benita's boat in the anchorage. They're back from Guyana to tie up loose ends before they head back into the Caribbean. Marc went diving again today with Karl and brought home four fish.

That's it for now—
Sandy

Birds, and Stingrays, and Lobsters! Oh My!

From: sandy_n_marc
To: Davis News Group
Subject: Davis News
Date: Mon, 30 May 2005

Alex has been going to the marina every day to see a new friend from the boat BLUE RABBIT. Espion is Dutch and doesn't speak English, but his parents—Christian and Trine—speak English well and encourage Alex to speak English to Espion. At first, Alex didn't do much talking. The boys just swam or played Gameboys together. But now Alex speaks directly to Espion, and Espion can say a few English words in return. Most important, though, they are both fluent in Pokémon. *(I found out the correct spelling of his name much later: Asbjørn.)*

On the daily ride to and from the marina, Junior has been detouring into Chaguaramas Park. He drives on the grass to the middle of the field to check on a bird that's been sitting on her eggs for weeks. He wants to see if the babies have hatched yet. The father bird keeps watch nearby and tries to scare us away.

On Wednesday, Junior pointed to a mango tree in the park. Richard and I declared our love of mangoes, which prompted Junior to drive up to the tree, jump out of the car, climb the tree, and shake the branches, forcing the tree to surrender its fruit. Once Richard and I realized what Junior was up to, we climbed out of the car and gathered up the mangoes.

Yesterday was a designated (and much-needed) day off from the boat. In the morning we sorted, measured, and counted hundreds of screws collected from the boat's interior disassembly. The purpose? To see how many and what sizes of stainless steel screws we need to order from the States. They are too expensive here. In the afternoon, we met Karl, Lily, and Tyler downtown at the Globe Theater to watch a double feature of *Star Wars* and *Monster-in-Law*. After the movies, all seven of us crammed into Karl's tiny car and headed to our apartment for a spaghetti dinner. Junior and Michelle showed up and it became a small party until everyone left at 11:00. It was a busy but very enjoyable day off.

This morning we stopped again to see the birds and discovered that two of the three eggs had hatched. Junior says the fourth egg disappeared after he asked the park employee to avoid the nest when mowing. He thinks the guy took the egg home for his pigeons to lie on.

Late this afternoon Marc and Karl went spearfishing. Alex, Tyler, and Junior went along in the dinghy and swam around while the guys were diving. Marc speared a huge lobster and Karl speared a stingray. We ate the lobster for dinner tonight—a gourmet feast.

Cheers—
Sandy

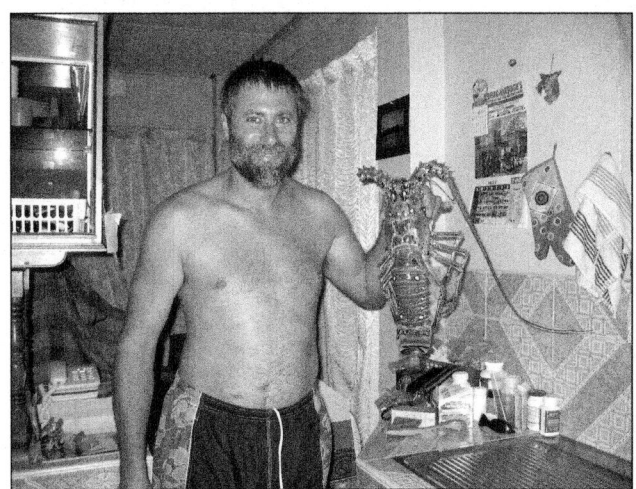

Maracas Beach

From: sandy_n_marc
To: Davis News Group
Subject: Davis News
Date: Thu, 9 Jun 2005

On Sunday, we went to Maracas Beach with Junior, Richard, and Richard's girlfriend, Natalie. We played in the waves, went boogie boarding, and ate "Shark and Bake." It's 45 minutes away, but Maracas is the closest swimming beach to Chaguaramas and Port of Spain. The water in Chaguaramas Bay is dirty, though we do see people swimming there. Maracas Beach is not the idyllic deserted Caribbean beach with pure white sand and brilliant turquoise waters that you'd envision, but it's nice enough, and the Trinis think highly of it.

Food

My favorite food in Trinidad was *roti*, purchased from street vendors or roti shops. The flatbread roti skin is made from flour and ground yellow split peas. The filling is a stew of curried chicken, beef, goat, duck, shrimp, or potato. Additional ingredients may include green beans, channa, pumpkin, mango kuchela, and greens. Our favorite place to buy roti was the Roti Hut in Power Boats Marina. Hidden in a corner of the large boatyard, the small blue building has lots of window openings and houses the cooks and cashier. On one side of the building is an open-air eating area with a thatched roof and long wooden tables with benches. There's always a line of customers patiently standing behind the order window; most are yard workers and cruisers.

Other popular Trinidadian foods are cowheel soup; callaloo made from dasheen leaves, okra, and coconut milk; and macaroni pie—baked pasta, eggs, and cheese.

I didn't care for the popular Malta drinks (non-alcoholic, made from malt and hops), but peanut punch (a creamy peanut butter drink) became a comfort drink for me. Marc drank the locally brewed beers, Carib and Stag, which are nothing like Oregon's craft beers but refreshing enough when you're hot and thirsty.

Junior took us to Queen's Park Savannah, a large park in Port of Spain, for coconut water. The vendor stands in the back of a truck filled with green coconuts, slices off the top with a machete, and hands it to you with a straw. You can find these vendors many places, but Junior liked to go to Queen's Park for the spicy raw oysters.

From time to time throughout our stay, we visited the numerous cafeterias, Chinese restaurants, and KFCs on the island. We also patronized the restaurants in Chaguaramas: The Bight Restaurant (now Zanzibar) at Peakes, The Roti Hut and Sails Restaurant at Power Boats, The Wheelhouse Pub at Tropical Marine, The Lighthouse Restaurant at CrewsInn, and Joe's Pizza at Coral Cove. (Now there's also The Lure Restaurant at Sweetwater Marine.)

Marc and I finished installing the Lexan windows last week, which made the boat more rainproof. Now we're working on port lights and the anchoring system.

Junior and Richard have removed rust and applied three layers of epoxy paint on about two-thirds of the inside of the hull. It looks good and should protect the hull well. Now they're tackling the hard to reach area under the engine.

On Wednesday afternoon, Marc stopped a man walking through Coral Cove with his two daughters—our first teenage girl sighting. He succeeded in acquiring their stats without coming across as creepy: The girls are ages 12 and 15 and from Canada; their mother is Egyptian, their step-father is Dutch, and their 43-foot Catana catamaran is docked at CrewsInn Marina. Unfortunately, they're leaving Friday afternoon for Venezuela. Nevertheless, Marc was able to arrange for Madeline to spend Thursday with the girls. They must have had a good time together, because now Madeline is eager to finish up the boat and go to Venezuela, which was not a priority for her before now. I'm trying to evaluate what projects need to be done to get MARAVIDA minimally functional for passage to Venezuela. We can continue to work on her there, where things are supposed to be cheaper.

Talk to you later—
Sandy

Sweating and Sorting

From: sandy_n_marc
To: Davis News Group
Subject: Davis News
Date: Sun, 19 Jun 2005

It's been six months, and I still haven't adjusted to the heat in Trinidad. The high humidity and high temperatures make working—and even walking—quite difficult. I truly understand why the locals move in slow motion. Fortunately, veteran cruisers assure us that the rest of the Caribbean is more comfortable. I hope so.

We're working even harder with Venezuela as our goal. I'm exhausted and ready for bed by 9:00 every night.

Junior borrowed his father's pickup truck to bring the boat furniture stored at his house to our apartment. Since the other downstairs tenant has moved out and the landlords plan to remodel the bathroom before they re-rent the unit, they've allowed us to use that unit's storage area and bedrooms to hold the furniture. We've sorted the pieces by type so we can locate what we need more easily. Our first project is to assemble a side cabin that doesn't require wiring or plumbing in the walls. Once it's done, Marc can sleep on the boat when he wants to do electrical work in the evenings. That way he won't get in the way of Junior and Richard's work during the day.

Our Danish friends from BLUE RABBIT plan to leave tomorrow. The boys (Espion and his younger brother, Siggy) are spending the day at our apartment while their parents button up their boat for long-term storage. Alex will be lonely after they go. For the past few weeks, he has spent almost every day with Espion.

Sandy

From Marc

From: sandy_n_marc
To: Davis News Group
Subject: Davis News
Date: Wed, 22 Jun 2005

This afternoon I heard a loud noise and crawled out from the bilge to investigate. I spied a ship on fire in the harbor. I later found out that four people died in the blast on the oil tanker: Three were found floating some distance away, and one was never located. The fire burned for several hours before it was put out by the service boats from the nearby offshore wells. The local fireboat came the next day. The cause is thought to be a welding accident, since welding work was being done in the area where the explosion blew a large hole in the deck.

Marc

In the News
Thomas, Norman "Gus." "Four Dead in Oil Tanker Explosion in Trinidad." *Caribbean News Now!* 23 June 2005. Web.
http://www.caribbeannewsnow.com/caribnet/2005/06/24/explosion.shtml.

Speeding Up

From: sandy_n_marc
To: Davis News Group
Subject: Davis News
Date: Thu, 30 Jun 2005

We installed the last port light and the v-berth yesterday. Now we have three bunks for sleeping. There would be four, but we haven't located two little, but necessary, pieces that support the upper bunk. Now we're working on the forward bathroom.

We received an e-mail from the family on the Catana catamaran. They are now at Bahia Redonda Marina in Puerto la Cruz, Venezuela. They say the marinas are booked up and suggest we get on a waiting list.

This afternoon we went to an informal meeting of cruisers interested in going to Venezuela. We learned about cruising in Venezuela from a few cruisers who had already been there and added our names to an e-mail contact list. All four of us are getting revved up for this upcoming change of venue.

Sandy

Waiting Out the Storm

From: sandy_n_marc
To: Davis News Group
Subject: Davis News
Date: Wed, 13 Jul 2005

We continue to read, hear about, and see crime here. Another incident in Port of Spain came a little too close again. A bomb exploded in a trash can yesterday, injuring 14 people. It happened on the corner of Frederick and Queen Streets, in the very district where I had shopped the previous day.

> **In the News**
>
> "Explosion in Port of Spain." *Trinidad and Tobago News*. 11 July 2005. Web.
>
> http://www.trinidadandtobagonews.com/special/1107 05.html.

We've installed the kitchen walls and cabinets, the battery box and its 10 batteries, and the forward toilet—no running water to any sinks yet, but the bathroom toilet works. Now Marc's working to identify all the electrical wires.

Yesterday we gave our 30-day notice at the apartment. The deadline means we'll have to move into MARAVIDA by August 11th, regardless of her state of completion.

We are waiting for Tropical Storm Emily to hit Trinidad this evening. Marc has been tracking tropical storm formations on the internet and predicted that Emily would come our way. He has stuck with his prediction even though the experts expected the storm to hit north of us in the Leeward Islands. The forecast has changed now though, and at 12:30 p.m. today, the prime minister of Trinidad told people to go home and brace for the storm. This is the first the Trinis have heard about it. The cruisers, however, have been preparing since yesterday. Now that the announcement has been made, the streets are jammed with cars, and there are lots of people standing along the road waiting for maxis. I think many maxi drivers went home already, so I felt fortunate to get a ride with Junior.

Junior has been doing as little as possible the past two days because he's hurt his back, though not from working on MARAVIDA, thank goodness. Marc and I spent yesterday and this morning preparing the boat for the storm while the kids stayed back at the apartment. Getting the deck cleared off was our biggest challenge. First, we had to organize the contents of the boat to make room for everything stored on deck—a frustrating and time-consuming task. Then we had to string lines to the docks across from MARAVIDA. Other boat owners had already done this; there are lines spider-webbing in all directions between the boats and docks. Before we hauled the dinghy onto the deck, I drove it over to the grocery store at CrewsInn and stocked up on food for the apartment and the boat. Upon my return, we lifted the dinghy onto the deck by using the boom. Marc was tying down the dinghy when Junior and I left Chaguaramas around 1:30 in the afternoon. Marc had decided to stay with the boat and ride out the storm. Most of the other cruisers in the marina were doing the same, so I wasn't worried about him being alone.

A couple of months ago, a feral cat had kittens in our neighbor's storage unit. We heard persistent meows coming from the outbuilding a few days ago and discovered one remaining kitten, probably calling for her mother. Since she was still meowing the next day, we surmised that she'd been abandoned and was starving. So Madeline started to put out tuna fish on the back patio—each time she kept her distance while she watched the wary gray tabby eat, hoping the kitten would get used to her presence. Yesterday we asked—and received permission from—the landlord to bring the kitten inside the apartment. Junior brought us a litter box this morning, and today I purchased cat litter. Madeline has just now managed to entice the kitten into the apartment by laying a tuna fish trail. The kitten is frightened and hiding; I hope we can tame her. In any case, I'm glad we got her inside before the storm. If we domesticate her successfully, she'll soon be a boat cat.

I'll let you know how the storm goes. We hope it will change course and be a nonevent.

Sandy

Lucky Break

From: sandy_n_marc
To: Davis News Group
Subject: Davis News
Date: Thu, 14 Jul 2005

Hurricane Emily bypassed Trinidad. The only effects were a little wind and a lot of rain. Grenada was not so lucky ... again.

I'm still at the apartment but got an update from Marc. He says he ate a delicious dinner on a neighbor's boat and had a wonderful night's sleep. It might be challenging to work on the boat today because it's bouncing around a lot from residual wave action from the storm. I'm going to stay here and catch up on laundry.

Kitty update: She's still afraid. We were thrilled when she used the litter box last night—now we don't have to worry about that anymore. She spends a lot of time thrashing around in the box; she likes it, I guess. She also likes to eat—food is VERY important to her. We've decided to name her Emily, after Hurricane Emily—our motivation for bringing her inside the apartment.

Talk to you later—
Sandy

Getting to Be That Time...

From: sandy_n_marc
To: Davis News Group
Subject: Davis News
Date: Sat, 23 Jul 2005

I'm amazed at how many cruisers we've met in the past seven months. We've met people from Canada, Australia, New Zealand, South Africa, Turkey, Egypt, Italy, Denmark, France, Britain, Holland, Germany, all over the United States, and probably more. We're getting to know the world before we even begin to travel. This is the advantage of being in Trinidad for our retrofit. Most people who sail the Caribbean end up here eventually, either to dodge hurricanes or to do boat repairs.

Nevertheless, we're more than ready to move on and continue to work as fast as possible to accomplish this. The kitchen sink is fully operational now, and Marc and I have been working on the walls in the salon, but we can't continue until the floor support boards are reinstalled. Unfortunately, many of these boards were damaged during removal, and others had been hacked up from former retrofits. (We've found evidence of many changes done to the salon over the course of MARAVIDA's 20-year life.) So, Marc has decided he must buy a jigsaw and a circular saw to construct new support boards. (Almost nothing makes Marc happier than buying tools.) Junior is still off with an injured back and also had a fever this week. Michelle says she's tired of taking care of him.

Last Saturday, Madeline insisted that we go to the mall to buy the just released *Harry Potter and the Half-Blood Prince*. Once home, she proceeded to read the entire book within 24 hours. Alex finished reading it this morning, and Marc plans to start reading it tonight.

Alex slept on the boat with Marc last Friday night, and Madeline slept on it last night. Neither kid slept well, but neither is worried about it. They realize that it'll take time to get accustomed to sleeping on a moving boat.

Emily is still skittish but is more comfortable with us. Madeline can hold her and get her to purr, and she'll hop on anyone's lap for food. She eats dry cat food from her bowl but gets tuna as a treat to tempt her to come close. We can now pet her, though only while she eats. She spends a lot of time playing and loves to attack things: her back feet, Madeline's rabbit's foot (now an official cat toy), a string we hung from the table, and all our toes.

We're getting ready for our move in 18 days. It's overwhelming to think about how we're going to get ourselves and all our belongings onto the unfinished boat.

We'll keep you posted—
Sandy

Davis News

From: sandy_n_marc
To: Davis News Group
Subject: Davis News
Date: Mon, 8 Aug 2005

Marc, Junior, and I continue to work seven days a week on the boat. Richard left a few weeks ago to start a "regular" job in the city.

The kitten is thriving. Madeline holds her often so that she gets used to human contact. Her favorite toys are two yellow foam ear plugs. They are baby mice to her. She pounces on them, bats them around, and then carries them in her mouth to another destination where she starts the game again. Her curiosity gets her into everything. She follows us around and attempts to get into the cupboards and the refrigerator whenever they're opened. Our biggest challenge is to keep her off the table when we eat. When we move onto the boat we'll concentrate on training her to stay off counters and tables. We hope her curiosity will keep her from being too traumatized by the move.

My mango supply is nearly exhausted. After my stockpile from Junior's raid of the park's tree ran out, Lily started to bring me mangoes from her trees on Gaspar Grande Island. I had no idea how many different varieties exist; my favorite is one that's bigger than a grapefruit. Today Lily gave me a fruit called a sugar apple. It's the strangest looking fruit I've ever eaten: It's round, green, and has a pinecone-like outer skin; inside, there's a sweet, white flesh with black seeds. There are many other fruits in the stores that I've never seen before, along with some familiar fruits that are easy to miss because they look different than they do back home. The oranges are ugly with mottled brown, orange, and green skin, but their visual imperfection is merely a disguise: They taste great. Avocados are in season now. They are two or three times larger than the avocados sold in the States.

Madeline and Alex came with us to Coral Cove the last two Saturdays. Alex played in the weekly Chaguaramas dominoes game with the "old people."

The game lasted three hours, which would be too long for most kids Alex's age, but Alex loves serious game play.

Last Saturday night, MARAVIDA was broken into ... or so we thought. The wimpy hasp lock was broken, but the hatch and slats were still in place, as if someone had been scared away before entering. The contents of the interior appeared undisturbed, which was a relief since we had lots of new electronics inside waiting for installation. Marc decided he'd better spend the next night on the boat until we could get to a store to buy new hardware. We later heard that two other boats had been boarded the same night—one about 9:30 p.m. by a swimmer (who was chased away), the other by someone who got away with a charge card. The thief must have known about a concert that many cruisers were attending that evening. We later discovered a flashlight and rubber hammer missing, which might have been taken to use on other boats. I guess they were looking for money and not large and obvious items like our electronics.

We've never worried about our personal safety at the marina, and this incident doesn't change that. Coral Cove management is allegedly working on a new system to keep the night guards awake. We've become fond of the day guards: Lal mans the security booth at the yard entrance, while Winston patrols the marina area.

Thursday is move-in day. We're looking forward to it, even though we'll be "roughing it." All our beds will be installed, but the refrigerator and stove won't be working. We won't be able to check e-mail as often but will get to it periodically at the internet café next door.

Marc has been in Trinidad for nine months, the kids and I for eight.

Talk to you again after we're moved in—
Sandy

Cramming In

From: sandy_n_marc
To: Davis News Group
Subject: Davis News
Date: Fri, 19 Aug 2005

So much stuff and so little space to cram it. MARAVIDA is larger than the average cruising boat, and I think we might eventually find places to put all this stuff; for now, though, storage is a challenge.

Our first night here, the kitchen counters were piled high with tools, and there was no place to sit. At least we had places to sleep.

We cleaned up the kitchen and put in the banquet seats the next day. Junior installed the table yesterday.

It's hard to move around without bumping into a toolbox or tripping on an extension cord; I have the bruises to prove it. Nevertheless, we are excited to be on the boat. We're using a cooler for our fridge and the microwave for cooking.

Emily settled in right away. She loves to explore the messy boat. She has no interest in going up on deck, which is a relief for Madeline since she worries that Emily will fall into the water.

We just heard there's a slip available to sublet at Bahia Redonda Marina starting August 22nd. We will pay to keep the spot open for MARAVIDA, and hopefully we can leave sometime next week. If you're interested, the website is http://www.bahiaredonda.com. Marc's biggest concern is not the passage but maneuvering the boat into the slip upon arrival.

Sandy

Leaving Trinidad

From: sandy_n_marc
To: Davis News Group
Subject: Davis News
Date: Fri, 25 Aug 2005

We plan to leave Trinidad at 4:00 p.m. tomorrow with three other boats. Our first destination is Los Testigos, supposedly a tropical island paradise. Then we'll head to the island of Margarita, which is touted as a duty-free shopping haven.

You may not hear from us for a few days, but as soon as we get to the marina, we'll sign up for wireless internet.

To clear the decks for passage, we had to pile things onto the master bed. Marc and I will have to bunk with the kids.

We are dead tired from pushing ourselves so hard, but we're excited for the change.

Talk to you from Venezuela—
Sandy

On the afternoon of August 27th, we left Chaguaramas for a short passage to the island of Chacachacare, where we met up with our three companion boats: LA COLOMBE, JJ, *and* AMORGOS. *We worked on our passage preparations while we waited for the evening departure. However, before our scheduled departure time, one of the boats started to leave. Once the other boats noticed, they hauled their anchors. We weren't ready but started to rush through our remaining tasks. It turned out to be a false alarm; the boat wasn't moving on purpose, they were just tweaking the engine down below and didn't realize that the engine was in gear and dragging the anchor. A newbie mistake—one we could have made ourselves. Once everyone heard what had happened, we decided to leave anyway, especially since two of the boats had already hauled their anchors. They went ahead, and we followed soon after, at about 5:00 p.m.*

Some Observations on Trinidad

We found Trinidadians friendly and caring people. Many felt compelled to warn us about dangers on the island. They are frightened of the serious crimes occurring in their country, which they blame on drugs and political corruption.

By the time we left, we realized that the dangers were real and it was time to be on our way.

> **In the News**
> "Thousands March on Trinidad Crime." *BBC News.* 23 Oct. 2005. Web.
> http://news.bbc.co.uk/2/hi/americas/4368582.stm.

Cruising Guides

We bought every cruising guide we could find and wore out most of them in the course of our travels. They were indispensable for choosing the best anchorages, as well as for navigating through reefy areas, locating ports of entry, and understanding the procedures for clearing in and out of each country. I can't imagine cruising without these guides. Another important feature for me was a description of what's onshore at each stop and how you can get around once you've arrived (by walking, biking, taking buses, and/or renting cars). We found that some guides were more helpful than others on certain topics, but each one seemed to have its own area of expertise. Many of the popular guides update every few years, others haven't ... yet.

Trinidad doesn't have many anchorages, but you can glean some other tidbits from these guides:

Doyle, Chris. *The Cruising Guide to Trinidad and Tobago, Plus Barbados and Guyana.* Dunedin, FL: Cruising Guide Publications, 2013.

Pavlidis, Stephen J. *A Cruising Guide to the Windward Islands: Martinique, St. Lucia, St. Vincent & the Grenadines, The Tobago Cays, Carriacou, Grenada, Barbados, Trinidad and Tobago.* 2nd edition. Port Washington, WI: Seaworthy Publications, 2013.

Street, Donald M. *Martinique to Trinidad: Including Martinique, St. Lucia, St. Vincent, Barbados, Northern Grenadines, Southern Grenadines, Grenada, and Trinidad & Tobago.* Bloomington, IN: iUniverse, 2001.

Virgintino, Frank. *The Yachtsman's Guide to Trinidad with Directory.* Kindle edition. Amazon Digital Services, 2012. **I haven't read this cruising guide.**

CHAPTER 5

Moving On to Venezuela

Venezuela

Venezuela is located on the north coast of South America and covers 353,841 square miles. The country's biodiverse habitats include the Andes Mountains, the Amazon Basin Rainforest, the llanos (plains), the Caribbean coast, and the Orinoco River Delta. The climate varies accordingly.

About two-thirds of Venezuela's 30 million inhabitants are *mestizo* (mixed Amerindian and European), a little more than 20 percent are white, approximately 10 percent are African, and just 1 percent of the people are indigenous. Most Venezuelans are Roman Catholic and literate.

Venezuela has a mixed economy, but the dominant sector is petroleum.

Islas Los Testigos

Los Testigos

Los Testigos Islands are comprised of six islands and several rock islets. Their total area adds up to only 2.5 square miles. The island group is under the jurisdiction of the Federal Dependencies of Venezuela, which encompasses most of the offshore islands of Venezuela.

From: sandy_n_marc
To: Davis News Group
Subject: Davis News
Date: Mon, 29 Aug 2005

We made it to Islas Los Testigos at 7:00 a.m., escorted in by a troop of dolphins—a much appreciated welcome after a challenging 14-hour passage. This passage in MARAVIDA was our first in any boat, and it was made at night and without electronics.

Making the trip at night was a calculated decision: We wanted to evade pirates. The plan was to travel without running lights and head straight north from Trinidad for 50 miles before turning west to Los Testigos. This would put us farther from the Venezuelan Peninsula of Paria, a coastal area notorious for pirates.

We didn't have enough time to finish the electrical wiring before our departure. Consequently, our autopilot was not hooked up, so we had to self-steer; our compass light was not hooked up, so we had to use a flashlight to monitor our direction; and our radar was not hooked up, so we couldn't locate other boats in the dark. Concerned that we might run into our companion boats, we decided to turn west earlier than planned. This cut off some time and put us in front—hopefully far enough ahead to decrease the risk of collision. Up to this point, we had experienced rolling seas and were all feeling seasick; but once we turned, the ride became more comfortable. Because it was dark and this was our first time out, we motored the whole way using only the staysail, not the bigger jib and/or mainsail.

We're settled into the anchorage with a dozen other boats. We now have proof that the quintessential tropical paradise exists and all the typical descriptions apply: crystal clear aquamarine water, bright white sandy beaches, and palm trees swaying in the breeze. It's all here.

From where we're anchored, it's hard to believe that there are 200 inhabitants in this small group of islands. From what I understand, the population is composed of fishing families and a few coast guard officials. We won't check in unless we're asked to.

We may stay until Wednesday morning, even though our ice will probably be melted, our bread moldy, and our cup-a-soup supply depleted. But then we'll have an easy day-sail to the civilized island of Margarita where we can do some shopping ... because that's what you do in Margarita. From there, we'll head to our new home base in Puerto La Cruz.

Isla de Margarita

> **Margarita**
>
> Isla de Margarita is not a Federal Dependency of Venezuela like Venezuela's other offshore islands; instead, it's the largest island of the state of Nueva Esparta (which also includes Coche and Cubagua Islands). Margarita is oddly shaped, covers almost 400 square miles, and is home to more than 400,000 residents.
>
> With its duty-free shopping and 106 miles of coastline, Margarita is a popular vacation spot for Venezuelan mainlanders.
>
> Cruisers' net: Monday through Saturday, 8:00 a.m., on VHF channel 72.

From: sandy_n_marc
To: Davis News Group
Subject: Davis News
Date: Wed, 31 Aug 2005

We've moved on to Margarita. We had an uneventful passage, except that our microwave took a header. Our average speed motorsailing with the jib sail was 8 knots. When we turned off the engine for a while, we made only 5 knots. We'll stay here a day or two and then move on to Puerto La Cruz.

Catching Up

From: sandy_n_marc
To: Davis News Group
Subject: Davis News
Date: Fri, 9 Sep 2005

Sorry it's been so long. The laptop crashed after the last e-mail and I wasn't able to send another until after we settled into Bahia Redonda Marina in Puerto La Cruz. I've got lots to catch you up on, starting with our time spent at Isla de Margarita.

There were maybe a hundred boats anchored in Margarita's Porlamar Bay; quite overwhelming. To get to town, we dinghied to Juan's Marina and tied up at the guarded dock. Juan's Marina is a ramshackle wooden building in the middle of a dirt patch. Juan speaks many different languages and arranges for clearing-in paperwork and free bus trips each day to one of two large grocery stores.

On Thursday, September 1st, we went on the 10:00 a.m. to 1:00 p.m. grocery excursion. We were given special passes for discounts and entry to the VIP room, so Alex was happy to park himself there with the comfy couches, free internet, big screen TV, and free beverages.

An escort shepherded us to a basement office to make our money exchange. We'd been warned not to use our debit and credit cards in Venezuela because the banks might double charge our cards, the stores might double swipe, and the exchange rates would be bad. To avoid any of these unpleasant scenarios, we opted for the black market money exchange—U.S. checks for bolivars.

We returned upstairs with cash in hand, ready to tackle the store that was more amusement park than grocery store—overwhelming in size and sparkle. One major theme was liquor. "Duty free" means big business in liquor, and this store capitalized on it by offering aisle after aisle of booze and scantily clad sample-girls representing various labels. We spent more time buying food than booze, though, and left thoroughly satisfied with our experience.

We joined our friends from Trinidad for dinner at Jak's, which is just down the beach from Juan's Marina.

A sense of uneasiness hung over us while we were anchored in Porlamar Bay. Other cruisers had warned us to raise and lock our dinghy when not using it and to be wary of thieves who might board the boat. Our plan was to get in and out as fast as possible.

Complications

We left Margarita at 7:00 a.m., September 2nd. We expected an easy passage to Puerto La Cruz, but complications arose. A couple of hours into our passage, Marc thought he heard a strange noise coming from the engine compartment. I didn't hear it, but thank goodness he did, because he discovered the raw water pump had spit out its bearings and was pumping seawater into the bilge rather than through the engine. The bilge was full of water. We immediately turned off the engine and turned on the electric bilge pump. Unfortunately, the small pump immediately became clogged and seized up. We were left with one option—the manual bilge pump—but it didn't seem to be working either. Fortunately, Marc soon realized that it was pumping air into the bilge instead of water out of it, which meant it had been assembled backward. In order to access the bilge pump, we had to empty the contents of a kitchen cabinet and remove the back wall. We hit another obstacle when Marc realized that Junior had installed the cabinet permanently, not for easy entry as was necessary for an access panel. At this point, Marc was cursing the pumps, Junior, and himself. But he was able to disassemble the pump, reverse the valves, and reinstall it with no further complications. We then took turns hand pumping and emptied the bilge.

Our new circumstances meant that we'd have to sail without an engine and that we might have to be towed into the marina. It was a scary prospect for rookie cruisers. Our first challenge came when we unexpectedly found ourselves in the midst of dozens of fishing boats. We had no choice but to maneuver through them—without an engine. Once we got past them without any casualties, we relaxed and enjoyed sailing without the noise of the engine.

We made 5 knots for most of the morning and into the afternoon. Eventually the wind started to die off, and we decided to put up the mainsail (for the first time). This increased our speed to 6.9 knots, despite the decrease in wind. We should have done this before, but we were still learning.

A little after dusk, we took down the sails because we were approaching an island chain and didn't feel comfortable navigating through the islands at night without reliable power. We turned on the anchor light, set a waypoint on the GPS, and went to bed (on deck so we could keep watch). The wind blew hard most of the night. Marc got up frequently to check our distance from the waypoint. By morning, we had drifted 2.5 miles.

By the time we put the sails up in the morning, the wind had died completely. We were stuck. Not for long, though, thanks to Marc's ingenuity. He jury-rigged an old "water puppy" electric bilge pump to replace the defunct raw water pump. It worked, but because this pump was smaller, we had to run the engine at a slow speed. We kept our speed at 3.5 knots, grateful to be moving at all. How nice to be married to a human Swiss Army knife!

We finally reached our destination, Bahia Redonda Marina, at 4:00 p.m. on September 3rd. The stern-to mooring was a challenge, but we managed to dock without inflicting damage on our neighboring boats.

Settling in at Bahia Redonda

> **Puerto La Cruz**
>
> The city of Puerto La Cruz is located in northeast Venezuela on the Caribbean Sea. It is both a resort town and an important hub of the oil industry. The population is around 400,000.
>
> Bahia Redonda Marina is located in Puerto La Cruz. (See http://bahiaredonda.com.)
>
> Cruisers' net: Monday through Saturday, 7:45 a.m., on VHF channel 72.

Our slip at the marina is far from the pool and services, but the water out here is less stale and the walk is good for us. The marina's landscaping is beautiful and more polished than our former home at Coral Cove.

Alex has already become good friends with an eight-year-old boy named Patrick who lives with his parents and older brother on their current project boat, TARA. It's a former Texas shrimp trawler that they are converting into a luxury yacht. They've been here a year.

Madeline is happy hanging out with three girls her age. One of them is from the family we met in Trinidad right before they left for Venezuela. They've been very helpful since our arrival.

We got yellow fever shots yesterday.

Good/Bad—Up/Down

From: sandy_n_marc
To: Davis News Group
Subject: Davis News
Date: Mon, 19 Sep 2005

Marina life has its good and bad points. I think it's much like RVing in the U.S. Most people are older than we are and many are heavy drinkers. Some stay in marinas for months (hurricane season makes that understandable) or even years (laziness, perhaps?), and they tend to form large social groups. About one-quarter of the boats here are "blue-water" (offshore) sailboats, another quarter are coastal sailboats (Hunter, Beneteau, etc.), yet another quarter are catamarans, and the rest are large powerboats owned by locals.

Chaguaramas, Trinidad, is a place for cruisers to work on their boats; Puerto La Cruz is a place where cruisers "hang out." The social network makes us feel a bit isolated, but we're not in a hurry to join the club. I've enjoyed the friends we've made since journeying to the West Indies, but I'm overwhelmed by the large groups here. I guess I prefer one-on-one interaction.

Madeline has been having a lot of ups and downs. Since my last e-mail about the other girls, she has been excluded by them for an entire week. But then, two days ago, they asked her to hang out with them for the evening. This boosted her mood, but I have a feeling the problem might persist. I can only tell her that middle-school-aged girls can be a pain when it comes to friendships. I think Patrick's 14-year-old brother, Sean, is also lonely, but Madeline won't take his hints because she has missed being around girls her own age.

Alex is happy with his routine: electronic games, breakfast, schoolwork, lunch, Patrick at our boat, Alex at Patrick's boat, swimming with Patrick and Sean, dinner, and maybe back to Patrick's boat after dinner. Sometimes Sean comes over and hangs out at our boat. His long blonde hair gives him that California surfer dude look. He loves to surf, wind surf, and play electronic games. Both are attractive kids. Their mother, Virginia, is French. She has long blonde hair and a vivacious personality, wears short shorts and midriff tops, and is two years older than I am. Their father, Sam, is originally from the East Coast but spent many years in Port Townsend, Washington, where he built hundreds of wooden boats and helped establish the Wooden Boat Foundation. They do what we did with houses, but with boats: buy one, fix it up, sell it, and start over again.

Venezuela seems more developed than Trinidad, but there are also many poor people. Like Trinidad, it's not safe to go out at night. It appears cleaner, the roads are in better shape, and the drivers are less reckless. Because labor rates and gas prices are low, taxi trips are cheap. So far I've been to three different grocery stores, one mall, the public vegetable market, and downtown (sometimes all four of us go, or I go with Madeline or other cruisers). There's one downside to getting out and about here: We don't speak Spanish and few people speak English. We use a few Spanish words and do a lot of gesturing and smiling.

We purchased a 1st through 12th grade schooling program on CD. It's called the Robinson Self-Teaching Homeschool Curriculum. It's a bit radical, but not unreasonable. I like that it's based on learning by reading—but not from dry textbooks. English is learned by example, mainly through the reading of great works of literature. History is learned by reading autobiographies and historical novels. The program recommends Saxon Math, which we hear is a well-liked math program for homeschoolers.

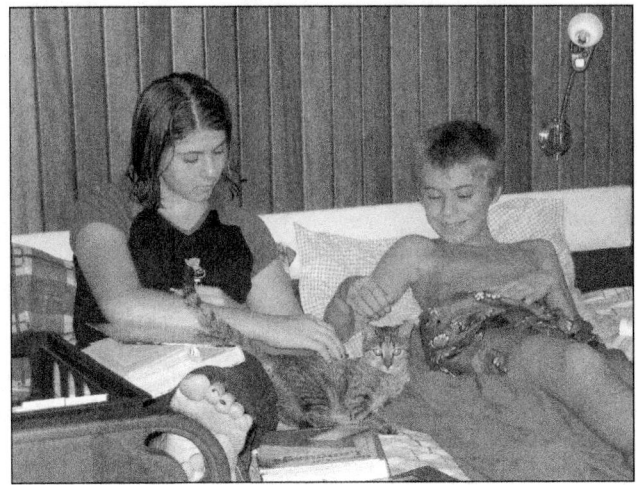

It's Hot

From: sandy_n_marc
To: Davis News Group
Subject: Davis News
Date: Thu, 29 Sep 2005

We found a computer store in town and purchased a new hard drive for our laptop. Now we can use the internet at our boat via the marina's wireless service.

It's hot, in the 90s. The temperature is similar to that of Trinidad, but it's less humid here. Unfortunately, it doesn't cool off at night as much as it does in Trinidad.

The facilities at our marina are handy, though the walk in the heat is exhausting. Every day we visit the marina's mini-market to purchase two or three bags of ice for our cooler. Our rolling cooler is indispensable for getting the ice all the way to the boat without melting. We often stop at the marina restaurant for a coffee or an iced fruit drink on our way to or from doing errands. Marc and I don't use the pool because the water is hot—not refreshing at all.

We're also using the personal service facilities in the marina compound. Last week Marc and I went to the dentist, and Madeline and I got manicures (US$2.50 each). This week Marc and I got haircuts (total US$10 for the both of us). They don't have a self-service Laundromat, but the wash/dry/fold service is the same price as Coral Cove's self-service (US$2 per load). It's a better deal, without the work; but it's also a long walk and a few days' wait.

Madeline and Alex are in the same routine now. They do schoolwork in the morning and then go to TARA for electronics time until 3 p.m. (Sean and Madeline have finally hit it off). Next they go to the pool until 6:00 p.m. After dinner, they head back over to TARA for one hour of evening electronics time. Madeline often stays later to watch a movie with their family. Our cats have hit it off also. Their extremely large male cat, Skipper, jumps onto our boat and little Emily comes out to greet him. They usually hop off the boat and play on land for a while until Emily gets scared and runs back. Later, Skipper comes back for her and off they go again.

We spent our first week here setting up the boat for basic living. Marc was sick the next week. Now we are devoting more time to the kids' schoolwork. If we don't have errands to run, we try to get a little boat work done in the afternoons. Not enough, though. I hope we can speed up our progress because we plan to leave here the first of November.

From Marc

Boat parts are hard to get here. There are about eight boat stores in town. Each has the same hundred or so items in stock. Shipping parts from the States is expensive (about US$100 for a small package). Non-boat-specific parts are available, but you have to search all over town to find them.

Most of the cruisers are older than we are and many are here to stay. Cruisers here seem more paranoid to go outside the marina complex than they were in Trinidad. Most only go out in a taxi to a specific destination. I think this may say more about the cruisers than the safety situation.

Property crimes are common here, and there's a lot of police corruption. The upside is that police officers are paid well and there are a lot of them around.

Venezuelans are friendly and some speak a little English if pressed. Between taxis, buses, and cab sharing, transportation is easy. But I'll never get accustomed to giving a cab driver 5,000 bolivars (though it's only about two bucks).

Since we've been advised not to use credit or debit cards here because the exchange rate is bad (2,150 bolivars to the dollar) and there is a fear of credit card fraud, we must find other ways to get bolivars. The local travel agents will cash a personal check or take U.S. cash at 2,400 bolivars to the dollar (USD). Some local reputable money changers will give 2,500 bolivars to the USD, but you have to wait on a list until they have the money to sell. Rumor has it that you can get 3,000 bolivars to the dollar in Caracas if you have cash and can avoid being cheated or robbed.

I started working on the fridge this week but haven't found a source for the foam I need for the job. In the meantime, I'm looking for the parts to rebuild the water pump, and Sandy and I are cleaning up the v-berth and installing more interior ceiling pieces. Next, I think we'll empty out the back storage room (lazarette) and build in storage shelves for the scuba tanks, scuba compressor, washing machine (to be purchased), watermaker, tools, beach stuff, etc.

Sandy and I went downtown this afternoon to shop and eat dinner. We purchased a few things for Alex's 11th birthday (coming up this Friday). Sandy also showed me a fabric store she had discovered—it's the largest fabric shop I've ever seen. It has three floors and is packed with material. It even has an escalator. The prices run around $2 to $5 (US) per meter of fabric. We topped off our outing by eating two large gyros (called *schwaramas* here) for dinner, and then headed home.

I like it here and can imagine taking the time to get to know it better. However, after visiting Los Testigos, I'm yearning to explore more islands.

MISSIVES FROM MARAVIDA

October in Venezuela

From: sandy_n_marc
To: Davis News Group
Subject: Davis News
Date: Wed, 19 Oct 2005

October 7, 2005

Gas costs about 15 cents (US) per gallon here—no kidding!

On Alex's birthday, we dinghied to an island about 4 miles away—it took 30 minutes to get there. We went with Virginia, Sean, and Patrick of TARA. We found a sandy beach and hung out for the morning. On Wednesday, we sailed to the same island with Bill and Benita on ALCHERINGA II (yes, they're here too). We snorkeled and saw our first live coral.

The kids have been spending a lot of time over by the bathroom facilities where three stray kittens (about four weeks old) are being fed and medicated by one of the cruisers. It's fun to watch the cats play with each other, and all three like to be held. Madeline wants to adopt one.

October 10, 2005

We're out of money again and will have to get more today. I can't believe that we're getting money on the "black market." What's even crazier is that they take a U.S. check for $1,000—no I.D. needed.

We did get one of the kittens; yes, we're weak. Since Emily is named after a hurricane, we thought we'd pick a name from this year's hurricane list for the new cat. We chose Maria because it's a popular name in Spanish cultures and thus links her to her Venezuelan heritage. Madeline used two arguments for adopting another cat: Emily needs a playmate, and we need a lap cat. We've had Maria for three days, but Emily—who is three times the size of five-week-old Maria—is still scared of her. Madeline originally wanted the beautiful blue-eyed gray kitten, but after I said that the scrawny black one might not get adopted as easily, she chose it instead. Maria is black with a white nose, white legs, white tummy, and a flat face. She looks like a rat when she lies on her back (which she does often).

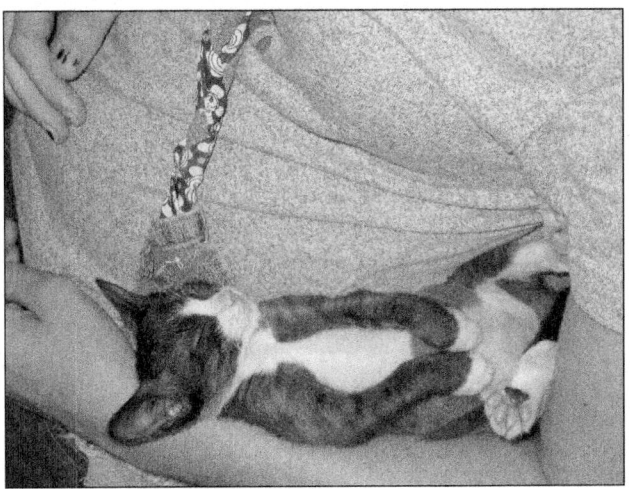

October 14, 2005

Yesterday afternoon Marc and I went on errands with Leo. He's one of three taxi drivers used by the cruisers here. All three speak English and charge around 10,000 bolivars per hour (US$4). They've become familiar with cruisers' needs and know where to go; they save us time, money, and the great frustration of trying to do find everything we need on our own. They also translate and negotiate prices.

Leo has a VHF radio in his taxi that a cruiser gave him. He often gets on the morning radio net to advertise his services, always starting with, "This is Leo...." He's well loved by the cruisers for his enthusiasm, though some don't care for his nonstop chatter.

Leo took us to the Yamaha parts dealer, a fuel injection shop, a photocopy place to copy marine charts, a print shop to make laminated cards, an auto parts store, a pet store, a bakery, and McDonalds (to surprise the kids for dinner). We did it all in less than four hours. We have an appointment with him again next Thursday morning and have already started on a to-do list.

The marina is sponsoring a sailing regatta this weekend. Marc will crew for Bill and Benita. They're checking out the course right now. Tomorrow night the marina restaurant will host an after-race party at the pool.

October 19, 2005

Bill, Benita, and Marc raced ALCHERINGA II Saturday and Sunday alongside 14 other boats in the Cruising class. They placed second and received a plaque and a certificate for a free haul-out. Marc had a great time.

We're in the middle of many projects but won't finish them all before we leave: refrigeration, generator repair, water pump repair, propeller shaft alignment, electrical wiring, rigging adjustments, navigation station setup, lazarette shelving, etc.

The cats are starting to get along now. Thank goodness.

Still in Venezuela

From: sandy_n_marc
To: Davis News Group
Subject: Davis News
Date: Thu, 3 Nov 2005

November 1, 2005

President Hugo Chavez asked the Venezuelans not to celebrate Halloween because it's part of the U.S. culture that's "putting fear into other nations, putting fear into their own people." I'm not sure if his announcement made a difference or not, but it certainly didn't here at the marina. There was a big Halloween party at the restaurant that included costume contests, pumpkin carving, a special dinner, a DJ, and dancing. Madeline went with the family from TARA. Marc and I went to a BBQ that was for the quieter set, and Alex chose to stay home.

In the News

"Chavez Calls for Ban on Halloween." *BBC News*. 30 Oct. 2005. Web.

http://news.bbc.co.uk/2/hi/americas/4391166.stm.

There's still much to do, but we plan to go to Puerto Rico before December, when the Christmas winds arrive. Our friends (the Opp family—Ron and Kathryn and their sons Brian and David, the former a classmate of Alex's) will be joining us there from December 16th through January 7th. Later in January, my mother and my aunt and uncle will meet up with us. We haven't picked the place yet.

By making these commitments in the future, we realize that Marc isn't going back to Intel. His one-year sabbatical—put in place as an emergency backup plan—ends November 8th. It would be severely disappointing if we had to give this up now, before we'd done any real cruising. Our funds have depleted faster than we had hoped, so we may have to skip Europe and the Eastern U.S. in order to save money. It's possible we'll head for Mexico and the Sea of Cortez instead. We've heard that it's beautiful, friendly, and inexpensive.

November 2, 2005

We woke this morning to the stench of diesel fuel. News travels fast among cruisers, so it didn't take long to get the scoop. Employees at the fuel dock got caught selling fuel to smugglers. To hide the evidence, the smugglers dumped the fuel from their boat into the water. It must have been a lot of fuel because the entire marina has a layer of diesel coating the water. Now we're worried about how long the fuel dock will be closed, since we've been planning to fill our 450-gallon tanks with cheap fuel before our departure. Current gossip says that the nearest port—Cumana—has stopped selling diesel fuel to foreign-flagged vessels.

The boat is a mess. MARAVIDA's deck is strewn with the contents of the lazarette so we can build its shelving. To add to the chaos, the huge Westerbeke generator is sitting in the middle of the kitchen. Two neighbors helped Marc pull it out of the engine compartment today, but it was too heavy to take any farther. Needless to say, we ate dinner out.

There's no way we're going to get out of here by early November.

November 3, 2005

The filthy generator is now off the boat and up against the rock jetty behind us. The same two men helped Marc get it out and off the boat (after he had removed a few external parts to lighten the load). One of the men is Wayne from DAYDREAM. He and his wife, Susan, arrived a couple of weeks ago. They are about our age and lots of fun. Marc has a lot in common with Wayne, and the two of them can talk for hours. The couple bought an unfinished aluminum sailboat in St. Martin and stayed there working on it about the same length of time we spent in Trinidad. They were building interior pieces and installing systems while we were dismantling and welding. They did a fantastic job. The other man and his wife have a steel fishing trawler that he built himself. It's called CHESHIRE TOO. It's like TARA but on a much smaller scale.

The generator has a piston seized in the bore. Even if the problem is limited to severe carbon deposits, the disassembly, cleaning, reassembly, and reinstallation gives us another time-consuming project.

Haven't Left Yet

From: sandy_n_marc
To: Davis News Group
Subject: Davis News
Date: Wed, 16 Nov 2005

November 8, 2005

Last week we bought a used dinghy and motor from a couple who had purchased a new one. A second dinghy will be handy for the kids or for when we have visitors. We paid US$250 for the 20-year-old inflatable Avon dinghy with a 10-year-old Suzuki 4.5-horsepower outboard motor.

We've decided to scrap the old stove in the boat and purchase a new one in Puerto Rico. We're also going to scrap the generator. It has a bad cylinder bore, and the cost to overhaul is more than we want to spend on a 20-year-old generator. Marc is shopping the internet for a replacement; so far, the leading contender is made by NextGen and uses a Kubota one-cylinder diesel engine.

Today is Marc's 43rd birthday. The event was overshadowed by our push to leave, but at least he gets to shop for a new generator; he loves shopping online.

November 12, 2005

Our new friends, Wayne and Susan from DAYDREAM, had planned to leave for Tortuga by now but are stuck waiting for diesel. We also hope to stop in Tortuga on our way to Puerto Rico. We won't stop at any of the close-in islands, though, because there was a robbery a couple of days ago on a boat anchored at Boracha Island. Armed men boarded the boat and tied up the crew, robbing them of $7,000 cash and $12,000 in electronics (US).

The cats eat together, drink together, play together, and then nap together. Emily has a water fetish. She plays with the water in the bowl until it's empty or overturned.

We realized this morning that Emily is in heat. We've kept both cats inside since we got Maria, but now we have to be extra diligent about closing the hatch. The plan is to wait until Maria is old enough, and then have them fixed at the same time.

Marc had some parts made at a machine shop that will enable him to adjust the engine motor mounts to better align the propeller shaft.

November 16, 2005

The propeller shaft is aligned.

On Monday, Wayne and Susan took their boat over to the Puerto La Cruz fuel dock (about a mile away). They arrived at 8:00 a.m. and waited until 4:00 p.m., when the diesel was finally delivered. After learning the diesel usually lasts only about a day and a half, they offered to help us go over the next day. By the time we arrived, however, it was already sold out; word is the dock probably won't have more fuel until Friday. We did benefit from the trip, though: We calibrated the autopilot, learned helpful driving tips from Susan, and felt the fresh ocean breeze for the first time in a long while.

Wayne and Susan are ready to leave but have to wait another day or two because of a tropical depression heading west. It's unusual to have these storms brewing this late in the season. When there's finally quiet on the storm front and diesel becomes available, there will likely be a rush of boats leaving their hurricane season hideaways.

Fuel Dock Finally Open

From: sandy_n_marc
To: Davis News Group
Subject: Davis News
Date: Sat, 26 Nov 2005

DAYDREAM left November 17th and TARA left November 20th.

The fuel dock finally opened on Monday. We had no problem getting the boat over to it, but there was a snag in the actual fueling process. A hole in the keel tank caused the bilge to fill up with diesel. Marc ended up pumping about 50 gallons of fuel through a filter and into one of the saddle tanks. We'll have to avoid filling the keel tank more than half full until we haul out next time. Then we'll need to open up the keel, find the hole, and repair it.

We hope this will be our last day at Bahia Redonda Marina. It's been a fine place to hang out, though time went too fast and we didn't get as much marked off our to-do list as we'd hoped. By far our most important achievement, though, was being able to retrieve the new water pump from customs on Thursday. Now it's installed.

Laundry Held Hostage

From: sandy_n_marc
To: Davis News Group
Subject: Davis News
Date: Tue, 29 Nov 2005

We didn't leave on Sunday after all. Our laundry was supposed to be done on Saturday, but when we went to pick it up, the Laundromat was closed. It was probably because the water supply had been on and off all week. Our laundry was held hostage until Monday, but since other cruisers were also complaining, the laundry manager was called in on Sunday. To speed things up, we retrieved our unfinished laundry, and I spent the afternoon hand washing as much of it as I could. Marc continued to get ready to leave. Realistically, we wouldn't have been ready to leave Sunday morning anyway, since the water supply was sporadic throughout the weekend, making it difficult to get our water tanks filled.

Isla La Tortuga

> **Tortuga**
>
> When researching Tortuga, I found some conflicting information. Was it named Turtle Island because of its shape or because of the presence of turtles on the island hundreds of years ago? Can it be considered uninhabited because there are no permanent residents—even though there is a small sandy airstrip, a temporary fishing village, and a "hotel type place"? I don't know, but from our vantage point, it looked like an uninhabited paradise.

We got up at 5:30 Monday morning, left Bahia Redonda at 7:15, and arrived at the Tortuga anchorage about 8:30 p.m. It was well after sunset, which comes promptly at 6:00 p.m. We wouldn't have attempted to enter the reefed area at night, but Wayne and Susan of DAYDREAM had mapped GPS readings of the entrance to the anchorage. Wayne and another friend, Art of CASA DEL MAR, used the readings to meet us in a dinghy and lead us into the anchorage. We anchored in a rolly area, but it was preferable to staying out at sea all night. (Rolly is a word used by cruisers to describe anchorages that are uncomfortable due to rough water conditions that keep the boat in constant movement.) The next morning we moved to a calmer spot next to DAYDREAM.

The autopilot is a joy. It's like a crew member who never tires or complains. I can see why cruisers often give it a name.

Isla La Tortuga is uninhabited and pristine, another paradise of white sand and turquoise clear waters. We walked the beaches, snorkeled, and Marc scuba dived. He speared a fish, but it was small. I've attached a photo of the local fishing boats. Wayne calls them "African Queens" because their outline is similar to the boat in the Bogart movie.

Rationing Food

From: sandy_n_marc
To: Davis News Group
Subject: Davis News
Date: Tue, 6 Dec 2005

Time flies in paradise; it's been a week already. We had to say goodbye yesterday to our close friends Wayne and Susan of DAYDREAM and Bill and Benita of ALCHERINGA II. They are off to Los Roques Islands. They didn't leave us alone, though; we still have the friendly company of the couples on CENTIME, PSYCHE, HEART OF TEXAS, ANYTHING GOES, FRANCESCA, and CAYENNE III.

We planned to be in Puerto Rico by now, but the weather has delayed our departure. Our goal was to get there and purchase a new stove and generator before our friends arrive on the 16th. However, a storm is on its way and we prefer to face it here rather than out at sea.

We hate listening to the engine racket when we want to cook or use anything electronic. We can't wait to get a new generator ... and a new stove. We're still cooking on the single electric burner hotplate.

The cats also hate when the engine is running, but they seem to love boat life otherwise. They have no fear of being on deck.

The ice in our cooler melted after our fourth day here, but it doesn't matter since we're out of meat and soft drinks. We have plenty of cheap Venezuelan beer, which Marc is willing to drink warm. Ugh!

To make sure we have enough water in MARAVIDA's tanks to get us to Puerto Rico, we're taking saltwater baths. It's easy: put on your swimsuit and jump off the back of the boat.

The only other concern is our food supply. We didn't plan to be here this long, so we're rationing food items that we'll need for the long passage. But no worries—we won't starve because we have lots of canned beans.

Madeline is not happy about the power and food situation. Alex is okay about it, but he's not thrilled with our distance from civilization.

Marc has caught three fish and two lobsters while snorkeling. He loves it here. I think his male hunting instinct has emerged. Unfortunately, the fishing possibilities at our new anchorage (Cayo Herradura, where we think we'll be better off in the approaching storm) are not on a par with those of the last one (Los Tortuguillos).

High Winds

From: sandy_n_marc
To: Davis News Group
Subject: Davis News
Date: Sat, 10 Dec 2005

We hope to leave Tortuga for Puerto Rico early tomorrow morning. We've been making preparations all day.

It's been a blustery week. The wind has been blowing 20 knots on average, and sometimes as high as 35 knots. Marc has set up the wind generator; we're getting a steady trickle of power from it. The high winds make the anchorage rolly, but I figure this will help us get our sea legs for the ocean passage.

We've had new neighbors for the last two nights and all day yesterday. All—or most—of the local fishermen of these islands came to stay in our anchorage for protection from the storm. At one point, we were surrounded by 16 "African Queens." Our only concern was that if we dragged anchor, we might wipe out a few of them (they are made of wood).

Lack of refrigeration started to hinder the quality and variety of our diet, but our friends generously donated to our cause. DAYDREAM gave us ground beef before their departure; PSYCHE gave us pork chops, fish, and hotdogs; CENTIME had us over for dinner; and HEART OF TEXAS gave us a fresh loaf of homemade bread. Thanks guys!

On Our Way to Puerto Rico

From: sandy_n_marc
To: Davis News Group
Subject: Davis News
Date: Mon, 12 Dec 2005

We left Tortuga yesterday at 6:00 a.m. It would have been easier to wait another day until the conditions calmed down a bit more, but we needed to get going. The first day was rough. The wind blew at 20 knots, the waves were as high as 15 feet, and the seas were confused. We were relieved when late last night the seas settled to 5 feet high and the winds slowed to 15 knots. We're making 4 to 7 knots an hour, depending on wind and seas. Our current location is N 13.57 W 065.19 at 1:00 p.m. AST.

Some Observations on Venezuela

As in Trinidad, most Venezuelans we met were unhappy with their country. Many of the taxi drivers told us they had university degrees and used to have good jobs and nice homes, but they'd lost it all and were now forced to drive a taxi. They did not blame their country's problems on drugs, though. They blamed President Chavez.

United States and Venezuelan relations deteriorated considerably after our stay. You should do a lot of research before considering a visit to the area.

Stay Current on Safety Issues

http://www.safetyandsecuritynet.com

http://www.noonsite.com/General/Piracy

http://www.noonsite.com/Countries/Venezuela

http://www.noonsite.com/Countries/Venezuela/Countries/Venezuela/venezuela-pirate-attack-first-person-report-from-sy-explorer

http://www.noonsite.com/Countries/Venezuela/Countries/Venezuela/venezuela-isla-margarita-dutch-sailor-killed-whilst-resisting-robbery-on-board-september-2013

Cruising Guides

Doyle, Chris. *Cruising Guide to Venezuela and Bonaire.* 3rd ed. Dunedin, FL: Chris Doyle Pub. in association with Cruising Guide Publications, 2007.

Van Sant, Bruce. *The Gentleman's Guide to Passages South: The Thornless Path to Windward.* 10th ed. Charleston, S.C.: CreateSpace, 2012. **I haven't read this cruising guide; the cover says it has sailing directions from Florida to South America.**

CHAPTER 6

Puerto Rico, Friends, & Family

Puerto Rico

The island of Puerto Rico lies about 1,000 miles east-southeast of Miami, Florida, between the Dominican Republic and the U.S. Virgin Islands.

Puerto Rico is a volunteer commonwealth of the United States. Its status as an unincorporated U.S. territory has sparked an ongoing debate: Will Puerto Rico remain a territory, become a U.S. state, or declare itself an independent country? The people of Puerto Rico are U.S. citizens, but only the fundamental rights under the U.S. Constitution apply to them, and they are not allowed to vote in presidential elections.

Puerto Rico is the smallest island (3,515 square miles) of the Greater Antilles (a group of islands that also includes Cuba, Jamaica, and Hispaniola). Its terrain is mountainous, and its highest elevation is Cerro de Punta at 4,393 feet. The island has a tropical marine climate with temperatures ranging between 70 and 90 degrees Fahrenheit.

The population of Puerto Rico is roughly 3.7 million (2010 census) and is predominantly Roman Catholic, Spanish speaking, and of Spanish origin.

Ahh, Luxury!

From: sandy_n_marc
To: Davis News Group
Subject: Davis News
Date: Wed, 14 Dec 2005

We arrived at Puerto Del Rey Marina at 5:00 p.m. today, after crossing the Caribbean Sea between Tortuga and Puerto Rico. As newbie sailors, we're proud to say that we sailed without the engine for 69 of the 82 hours. The distance between the islands is 500 miles, but we took a slightly longer route to take advantage of the wind direction.

We decided to go to a marina to recuperate and get organized; however, the high-priced slip rental confirms that we're not in South America anymore and can't afford to remain here for long. We'll stay just long enough to reprovision and collect our visiting friends. Then we'll anchor out, like diehard budget cruisers do.

> **Puerto Del Rey Marina**
>
> We chose Puerto Del Rey Marina because it was the only marina in the Fajardo area that could accommodate our depth and length. Since then, another large marina has opened closer in to the town of Fajardo. It's called Sunbay Marina.
>
> http://www.puertodelrey.com
>
> http://www.sunbaymarina.com

Tomorrow we have to go grocery shopping. We're out of most foods, even cat food. We managed to get pizza delivered for dinner, which was a treat after the limited diet we ate on the crossing.

We're already enjoying the luxuries of shore power: The kids are watching movies; Marc has turned all the lights on; and we can use the microwave, hotplate, and computer without having to run the engine at the same time. The most important tasks to accomplish at dock are to fully charge the batteries, hose down the salt-covered boat, and do laundry.

Right now, I'm off for my first freshwater shower in 16 days. Yay!

The Passage

Here's a day-by-day summary of our trip from Venezuela to Puerto Rico.

Day One: The roughest ride we've had yet, with waves as high as 15 feet. Despite strong winds, we could only make 4.5 knots. All of us felt queasy, even though we took seasickness meds. After dark, the seas calmed down. The kids slept in their bunks, and Marc and I slept in the cockpit. We're both light sleepers, and there are so many noises on the boat that one or the other of us would wake up on average every half hour to look out for other boats. We weren't worried about it, since we appeared to be out there alone for the entire trip. *(In hindsight, this was not a good idea. It only takes 10 minutes for a freighter to get from the horizon to you. Even though we were outside the shipping lanes and the chance of hitting another boat was small, the consequences are too horrible to contemplate. From this point on, we made sure someone was on watch at all times. We didn't run formal shifts, though. One of us stayed up as long as possible and then woke the other. This worked out fine for us, because we never slept well on passage and often the person sleeping would awaken early.)*

Day Two: We were in good spirits and spent a lot of time talking about the foods we wanted to eat when we reached civilization. The seas were more comfortable and the wind was variable. We welcomed the small squalls that came through occasionally, giving us bursts of speed. After dark, we had more wind and higher seas, which sprayed my side of the cockpit and kept me perpetually damp.

When MARAVIDA got up to 7 knots of speed in 20 knots of wind, it felt as though we were speeding up and down hills in a '69 Cadillac with bad shocks. We were delighted to discover that when MARAVIDA reaches 7 knots, she hums like a whale. Marc says the hull is resonating.

Day Three: We made slower progress because of low winds. Cats boldly went on deck. We feared that we'd lose Maria over the side, but we didn't—thank goodness. The kids were grumpy and bickered with each other.

Day Four: We were in a great mood because we could see Puerto Rico in the distance. Seas were calm with light winds. We motorsailed the last few hours in order to reach land in daylight.

Walmart = Civilization

From: sandy_n_marc
To: Davis News Group
Subject: Davis News
Date: Mon, 19 Dec 2005

On Thursday morning, we rented a car at the marina and went into town. We spent most of the day at West Marine and Walmart, thrilled with the variety of shopping choices and reasonable prices.

The next morning, a cruiser in the marina hailed us on the radio to tell us that we'd been reported missing on the Caribbean Safety and Security Net (see http://www.safetyandsecuritynet.com). That meant the Winlink e-mail announcing our arrival in Puerto Rico hadn't gone through, and our friends in Venezuela must have reported us missing. We decided we'd better send out another e-mail through the internet this time, but since the internet was down at the marina, we had to wait until noon when a local internet café opened.

After we sent the e-mail, we realized that the Opp family's plane would be landing soon and they wouldn't have received the e-mail disclosing our location. Marc and I quickly rented a minivan and arrived at the San Juan airport just in time to greet Ron, Kathryn, David, and Brian as they exited the arrival gate.

On Saturday, all eight of us hopped in the minivan and went to West Marine, Kmart, and Sears (all local—in Fajardo). We went shopping again on Sunday, this time to Home Depot and Costco (about 45 minutes away). Today we plan to take MARAVIDA to Isla Palominos, which is only a few miles from the Puerto Rican mainland. We'll anchor overnight and then go back to Fajardo to pick up our new stove before heading off to the Spanish Virgin Islands of Culebra and Vieques.

Talk to you later—
Sandy

Isla Palominos

> **Palominos**
> Isla Palominos is a three-quarter-mile-long private island off the eastern coast of Puerto Rico.

From: sandy_n_marc
To: Davis News Group
Subject: Davis News
Date: Sat, 24 Dec 2005

We motored to Isla Palominos on Monday and took one of the free mooring buoys set up by the Department of Natural Resources. We were the only boat there. Most of the 100-acre private island is rented to El Conquistador Resort. They have a private beach on the island and use a ferry to shuttle their guests back and forth between the resort and the island.

On Tuesday afternoon, we dinghied to nearby Palominitos Island and spent hours playing on and around the tiny island.

The next day, we anchored off the mainland near Fajardo and dinghied to a public dock, where we met a West Marine employee who had brought our new stove. Later on, we realized that we needed additional parts to hook up the stove—and that we could use more food supplies as well. So we went back to Puerto Del Rey Marina on Thursday and rented a car. While there, we caught up on laundry and fully charged the batteries. We finally left for Culebra on Saturday at about noon.

Spanish Virgin Islands

> **Spanish Virgin Islands**
>
> The Spanish Virgin Islands lie between Puerto Rico and the U.S. Virgin Islands. They belong to Puerto Rico but are geographically part of the Virgin Island chain. In addition to the larger islands of Culebra and Vieques, there are many smaller islands and islets.

Cayo de Luis Pena

> **Cayo de Luis Pena**
>
> The uninhabited island called Cayo de Luis Pena is a U.S. Fish and Wildlife Refuge off the coast of Culebra.

We had a brisk sail to Cayo de Luis Pena, arriving around 5:00 p.m. We hooked up to the single mooring buoy in the tiny bay and are now settled in for the night.

Merry Christmas Eve!
Sandy

Christmas Day

From: sandy_n_marc
To: Davis News Group
Subject: Davis News
Date: Sun, 25 Dec 2005

This morning we opened Christmas presents, ate a pancake breakfast, and then went snorkeling in the clear water. We immediately spied a sunken sailboat (about 20 feet long) directly under us. Since these islands had been navy occupied for years, Marc guessed that the sailboat could be a U.S. Navy drone used for bombing practice.

Because our moorage was uncomfortably rolly, we decided to move. We left at 3:00 p.m. for Ensenada Honda, a large bay on Culebra Island. Two hours later, we anchored off the town of Dewey.

Culebra

> **Culebra**
>
> Culebra is about 17 miles east of Puerto Rico and 12 miles west of St. Thomas. It has a population close to 2,000 on 11 square miles of land.
>
> Ensenada Honda is a deep sheltered bay, about a mile and a half by a half mile in size. The bay was once used as a refuge by pirates but was not ideal because the island has no natural freshwater source. Nowadays Culebra gets its water through an underwater pipe from Puerto Rico.

We used the new stove to make Christmas dinner. Unfortunately, it has two problems: (1) it won't gimbal (balance) properly—it wants to dump pots off the top; and (2) the oven clearance is tiny—it'll only hold items up to two inches tall. What a disappointment. Marc called the manager of the West Marine store on Saturday morning to say we wanted to return it. Thankfully, the manager said it was okay to use it over the Christmas holiday since we couldn't get back to the store before then.

Tomorrow we'll explore the town of Dewey.

Merry Christmas!
Sandy

St. Thomas

St. Thomas

The island of St. Thomas is a district of the U.S. Virgin Islands (USVI), which have been an unincorporated organized territory of the United States since 1917. St. Thomas covers 31 square miles and has a population of about 50,000. The town of Charlotte Amalie is the territorial capital of the USVI and is the busiest cruise ship destination in the Caribbean.

From: sandy_n_marc
To: Davis News Group
Subject: Davis News
Date: Sun, 1 Jan 2006

We made an unplanned trip to St. Thomas on December 27th. The Opps had hoped to get their scuba open water certifications while on vacation, but the dive shop on Culebra didn't have any openings. However, a dive shop on St. Thomas had spots available for the next two days. It took about four hours to get to the island; we averaged only 5 knots of speed because we had to motor directly into the wind.

We docked at Crown Bay Marina for four nights.

> **Crown Bay Marina**
>
> This marina has 99 slips, a pub and restaurant, a fuel dock, a grocery store, a Laundromat, and a chandlery. (See http://www.crownbay.com.)

While the Opps worked on their certification, we checked out the town of Charlotte Amalie. We rode the dollar safari bus (a truck with open-air bench seating) into town. Once there, we had to stick to window-shopping because the stores sell luxury goods that are beyond our means. The town is obviously dependent on cruise ship passengers who have plenty of money to burn.

Vieques

> **Vieques**
>
> Isla de Vieques lies approximately 10 miles south of Culebra and 8 miles east of Puerto Rico. It covers 52 square miles of land and has almost 10,000 inhabitants.
>
> From 1941 to 2003, the U.S. Navy occupied about two-thirds of the island and used it for training and weapons testing until a series of protests led to the military's departure. The area is now a national wildlife refuge under the protection of the U.S. Fish and Wildlife Service.

We left St. Thomas on New Year's Eve to return to the Spanish Virgin Islands; this time, we were bound for Vieques Island. We sailed, running the engine just two of the seven hours, then anchored in Bahia Salinas del Sur on the undeveloped side of the island. Bahia Salinas del Sur was formerly under U.S. military possession, and from the anchorage we could see burned-out military tanks on the hillside and many signs telling visitors not to go inland because of unexploded bombs. While snorkeling, we saw two landing craft and a lot of bomb casings and artillery shells.

Today we decided to head farther west along the south coast. It took about two hours to get to Sun Bay near the town of Esperanza. We may stay here for a while.

Alex and Brian (both 11 years old) play together nonstop. If it isn't electronics, it's Yu-Gi-Oh! cards, Harry Potter cards, or just pretend stuff; and, of course, they swim. They usually sleep in the cockpit rather than in the cabins down below with their siblings. Madeline and David (ages 13 and 15) are also getting along well. They play cards, snorkel, and tease each other.

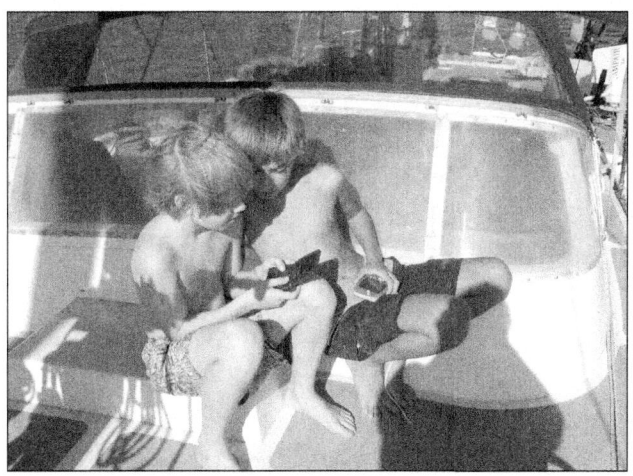

More later—
Sandy

Sun Bay

From: sandy_n_marc
To: Davis News Group
Subject: Davis News
Date: Fri, 6 Jan 2006

While anchored in Sun Bay, the Opps treated us to a bio-bay tour at nearby Mosquito Bay, which is purported to be one of the brightest bioluminescent bays in the world. After dark, we put on life jackets and paddled kayaks into the bay. The tour operator gave us a short lesson before we slipped into the water to swim with the dinoflagellate microorganisms that lit up magically when disturbed by our movements.

We left Sun Bay at 9:30 a.m. on January 5th, stopped to snorkel at the corner of the island, and then continued on to the western tip to anchor at Green Beach for the night. Total travel time was about three hours.

The next afternoon, we motored three hours to Puerto Del Rey Marina.

That's all for now—
Sandy

Crazy Cats in Rich Marinas

From: sandy_n_marc
To: Davis News Group
Subject: Davis News
Date: Tue, 10 Jan 2006

On January 7th, we rented a car to take the Opps to the airport. Before we returned the car, we took the stove back to West Marine and ran some other errands.

We decided to stay at the marina an extra night to do laundry and general cleanup. In the meantime, we met a Brazilian family—two boats down—

with three boys a little younger than Alex. They are getting ready to embark on a two-year cruise to the Pacific Islands on their 62-foot Deerfoot monohull, but have been struggling to fix their electronics after a lightning strike in Florida (where they purchased the boat). Marc worked on their boat Saturday evening and Sunday morning but informed them we were leaving the marina on Sunday because our budget doesn't cover marina fees. They offered to pay our slip fee for another night so that he could continue to help them. This worked out well, and we might even stay a couple more nights.

Madeline was unhappy to see our new stove removed and returned. We need to do some research to figure out the best replacement, but since the internet is still down at the marina, we'll have to wait until we can use it at my family's rented condo. My mom, aunt, and uncle arrive on the 11th for a four-week stay. We're excited to see family after a year and a half. They plan to rent a minivan so we can go on excursions together.

Puerto Del Rey Marina is amazing. It's the largest marina in the Caribbean, capable of holding a thousand boats. I've never seen so many shiny white motor yachts in one place. The average size is probably 50 feet, but there are also several mega yachts. We're docked in the mega yacht section, which means we have to step down from the dock to our boat. It also means we're a long way from land where the office, laundry, store, restaurant, and parking lot are located. Fortunately, they have valet cart service (VHF 71), which we use when we have laundry or groceries to haul. The drivers of these six-seat golf carts, with trailers attached, maneuver them as though they are skilled race car drivers. Whenever I use them, especially at night, I feel like I'm on a Disneyland ride.

The cats are jumping off MARAVIDA and exploring the million-dollar boats docked around us. Luckily, the boats are unoccupied. When I see the employees washing the boats—which is an ongoing process here, even though they look sparkling white already—I imagine they must be finding paw prints. Oh well, now they have something tangible to clean.

Maria lost one of her nine lives while we were in the islands. Marc woke up to a "plop, plop, plop" sound early one morning. He thought it might be a dolphin or other sea creature, but instead he discovered Maria swimming around the boat. Unfortunately, she was unfazed by the incident and continues to race around the decks in all conditions.

Later—
Sandy

From (Aunt) Carolyn—Dear Family and Friends

From: cj.laughlin
To: Family & Friends
Subject: Puerto Rico
Date: Wed, 25 Jan 2006

I can't believe our trip is halfway over. We've been in Puerto Rico for two weeks and are getting somewhat adjusted to the climate and slow lifestyle that's expected with this heat and humidity. It's been cooler this past week since we've been having windstorms.

Spanish is the primary language spoken here, but most people know some English and many speak it well.

The grocery stores are similar to those in the U.S. They have their produce, meat, and fish flown in, which is surprising since Puerto Rico is a large island.

We made a trip to El Yunque rainforest. It's very lush with huge plants and lots of waterfalls. It even rained a little when we were there. We plan to go back to do more exploring since it's close.

El Yunque National Forest

El Yunque is the only rainforest that belongs to the U.S. Forest Service. It was established in 1903 and covers 28,000 acres.

Yesterday we all went to San Juan, Puerto Rico's capital. The girls went to the mall while the guys went to customs—they had to take care of the paperwork necessary to get the new boat generator onto the island and to buy marine Plexiglas for a new windshield. When the guys were finished, we all went to Old San Juan to tour the town and walk along the beach. It was a nice day.

Today Marc and Sandra are at the boat, getting it ready to leave the marina once the generator is delivered (either today or tomorrow). They plan to anchor in the bay and will access the boat by dinghy. On Thursday or Friday, we hope to sail over to a small island that's known for its beautiful beach.

The kids bought a sewing machine, and Janice has been teaching Madeline to sew. They are both enjoying it. So far, Madeline has made a scarf and an apron—she's doing well. Both Madeline and Alex have a hard time sticking to their homework, much to their father's aggravation. Bribery helps a little.

We have a nice place to stay, and Sandra and the kids have spent the night off and on (Madeline the most). Marc's staying on the boat every night because he's afraid it might drag anchor due to the high winds we've been having.

We are really enjoying spending time with Sandra, Marc, and the kids. We eat most evening meals at the condo and are often out at lunchtime.

All for now—
Carolyn, John, and Janice

From (Aunt) Carolyn—Dear Family and Friends

From: cj.laughlin
To: Family & Friends
Subject: Puerto Rico
Date: Sat, 4 Feb 2006

We are enjoying the warm weather and moving lazily along. When not sightseeing, we enjoy the view, take walks, read, fix meals, and sometimes go out to eat. The kids play on the computer, watch television, or read books. Marc and John have been working on improvements and maintenance on the boat. We go shopping at the few stores around here.

On Sunday, we went on a two-hour trolley ride through Las Cabezas de San Juan Nature Reserve. We saw mangrove forests, a bioluminescent bay, a rainforest, a rocky beach, and a historic lighthouse. Very interesting, and much different from what we're used to in Oregon.

Las Cabezas de San Juan Nature Reserve

The Conservation Trust of Puerto Rico owns this nature reserve which has seven different ecological systems within its 316 acres.

On Wednesday, the wind finally calmed down enough to take the boat out, so we headed to Palominos Island and tied up to a mooring ball. After barbecuing hot dogs on the boat, we took the dinghy to Palominitos Island.

The island is tiny—at best a quarter of a mile long and half that in width. We put up an umbrella for shade and spread towels on the small sandy beach. The weather was perfect, the water was warm—it was nice. After about three hours on the island, we went back to the boat, had snacks, sat for a while, talked to cruisers on another boat that was also moored there, and then sailed back. It was a great day.

On Thursday, we dropped the cats at the vet to get fixed. Then Sandra, Janice, Madeline and I took the ferry to the northern coast of Vieques Island. The guys stayed to work on the boat and pick up the cats. The ferry was supposed to leave at 9:30 a.m., but didn't leave until 10:30. We aren't sure why it was delayed, but no one seemed too worried about it. The ferry ride took about an hour and dropped us off at the town of Isabel Segunda, an interesting place—much like a small town in Mexico (though not a border town). It's picturesque, but right now the streets are torn up for construction. We wandered around and had sandwiches at a bakery. The national sandwich seems to be ham, cheese, and egg toasted on French bread. It's tasty, hearty, and cheap—usually $3.00. We bought a few little things in the town and then wandered back down to the ferry dock area and up a little hill to an artist's gallery. Both the view and art were beautiful. The artist sold paintings, watercolors, and painted china (see www.siddhiahutchinsongallery.com). The afternoon ferry came on time.

We've been reading a lot of books. It's nice to get to really relax, but it'll probably be hard to readjust to the cold and the faster pace when we're back in the States.

We expect to be home on Thursday, February 9th.

Love to all—
Carolyn, John, and Janice

From Sandy

From: sandy_n_marc
To: Davis News Group
Subject: Davis News
Date: Sat, 11 Feb 2006

February 9, 2006

Our visitors have extended their stay another five days. John wants to help us get further along on our projects. It's been great having them here!

The boat is settled into the anchorage at Cayo Obispo, formerly known as Isleta Marina. Most of the boats there seem to be empty and anchored permanently, which makes the area feel a bit spooky. We're on the outskirts near the ferry route, so the waters get rolly; but that doesn't matter too much since we are all sleeping at the condo now that the wind has finally settled down.

Marc and John have the lazarette and master bedroom taken apart to lay wire and plumbing for the new generator while simultaneously prepping for the watermaker and future washing machine. The new stove is waiting at the condo for its turn at installation, and the refrigerator is on hold for now.

The guys take the dinghy back and forth between Villa Marina and MARAVIDA in the anchorage. The marina is handy because it is close to the condo, and they are kindly letting us tie up our dinghy in a covered boat slip for no charge (see http://www.villamarinapr.com). Before the guys go to the boat in the mornings, they often stop to purchase more parts at the hardware store, Pep Boys, and West Marine. It's been great for Marc to have John to work with and to have a vehicle for running errands.

We went to Costco on Monday and loaded two shopping carts with food. We held out on items that will cost less at the grocery store. Even so—and with the highest ticket item just $30—we spent $900. I continue to buy additional food items each time we go to the grocery store and Walmart. (I bought all the refried beans at Walmart!)

Maria has been unhappy with our absence at night, but she gets lots of attention from John during the day. (He doesn't normally like cats, but because she's both demanding and charming, she's now on his good side.) Both cats got spayed last week. Their first visit to the vet was for shots, the second was to get "fixed," and the third was to get the stitches removed. They hated the noisy dinghy trips.

Puerto Ricans are warm and friendly. Though Spanish is their native language, most can switch to English without a problem and without much of an accent. Most houses are modest, one-story concrete buildings with flat roofs, which seems practical for hurricanes. Despite having simple houses, most people drive fairly new cars and public transportation seems almost nonexistent: This makes it feel almost too Americanized here. Outside the towns, are lush mountainous landscapes.

The Fajardo area is not very cruiser friendly. Grocery stores, chandleries, and public transportation (what little there is) aren't located near the water. However, there's a new marina being built below the condos—maybe it'll bring in more services (Sunbay Marina).

February 10, 2006

Last night I went with the guys to Home Depot, which is about 30 minutes away. While they picked out plumbing fittings, I checked out the refrigerators. I managed to convince Marc that a temporary $150 refrigerator would save on the cost of ice and wasted food and—most important—would help guard against my future insanity. So, we are now proud owners of a 33-inch refrigerator.

The girls went to El Conquistador Resort for lunch today to celebrate Aunt Carolyn's birthday. The clifftop resort has spectacular views and gorgeous grounds.

El Conquistador Resort

Located just a few miles outside of Fajardo, this resort is set on a 300-foot cliff above the ocean. It has a golf course, water park, seven pools, seven tennis courts, private island beach, and 23 restaurants, bars, and lounges.

http://www.elconresort.com

We can see MARAVIDA from the condo. We leave the anchor light on, so we can also see it at night.

February 11, 2006

The guys got the generator running yesterday. Today they installed the stove, and then started work on a shelf for the refrigerator so it can be placed in the old fridge spot. We may make it permanent because there's room to surround it with the necessary 6 inches of foam insulation, and it could be converted to work with our 12-volt fridge compressor. We'll wait to see how we like it first.

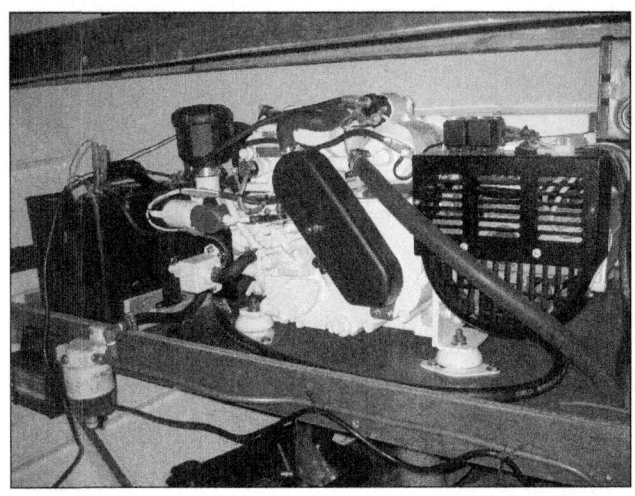

We plan to go back to Puerto del Rey Marina on Monday so we can pick up a shipment from the States. We also need to transfer the goods we bought on our shopping expeditions from the condo to the boat.

Mom, Carolyn, and John are leaving on Tuesday; we'll be sad to see them go. Once we're organized, we'll head to St. Martin via the U.S. and British Virgin Islands.

More later—
Sandy

Waiting for a Package

From: sandy_n_marc
To: Davis News Group
Subject: Davis News
Date: Sun, 26 Feb 2006

As planned, we docked in Puerto del Rey on Monday, February 13th, and our visitors left the next day. The first three packages had arrived on time, right before my family left, but the fourth package (watermaker part) got stuck in limbo. On Friday, it still hadn't come, so we checked out of the marina. Unfortunately, we couldn't fill our second water tank because the marina's water was temporarily shut off. We obtained permission to bring MARAVIDA back for a water top-up when our package arrived.

We moored at Palominos on Friday night. Since we were stuck waiting for our package until Monday at the earliest, we decided to go on a weekend outing. We moved MARAVIDA to Cayo Obispo anchorage on Saturday morning and rented a car that afternoon. Our destinations were the Arecibo Observatory and the Rio Camuy Cave Park.

Arecibo Observatory

The spherical reflector radio telescope at Arecibo Observatory was built in 1963. The collecting dish measures 1,000 feet in diameter and is the largest single-aperture telescope ever constructed. It is operated by the Stanford Research Institute in cooperation with the National Science Foundation. We recognized it from the movies *Contact* and *GoldenEye*.

> **Camuy River Cave Park**
>
> The Parque de las Cavernas del Río Camuy is the largest cave system in the Western Hemisphere and one of the largest in the world. The Rio Camuy, the third-largest subterranean river in the world, carved the cave system out of limestone. Over 10 miles of caverns have been mapped out, but many more are thought to exist.

Because both destinations were a couple of hours away, and it was already afternoon, we decided we'd have to spend the night somewhere along the way. However, we were unaware that it was President's Day weekend until we found hotel after hotel full. We looked in San Juan because we figured that was where the greatest number of hotels (and therefore the greatest number of vacancies) would be, but we finally gave up and switched our search to the area around the airport. Once again, we found nothing available. Eventually, we found a vacancy at Embassy Suites, but $300 was excessive. By this time, we were quite frustrated, and our jokes about sleeping in the car were upsetting Alex. We had one more place to try: Howard Johnson's. Luckily, it had a room available, which was easier to accept at $177.

Thank goodness we didn't drive past San Juan to search for lodging: We saw no motels or hotels on our drive to Arecibo the next morning. Our visits for the day were interesting but took longer than we thought they would, so we didn't get back in time to return the car for a one-day rental.

Since we had to pay for a second day on the rental car, we kept it overnight and made the usual stops at West Marine, Walmart, Kmart, and a grocery store. Our biggest purchase was a small television/DVD combo, which we discovered didn't work after we had returned the car. So, the next day we made the trek to Kmart with a little help from a trolley we encountered halfway there. We chose a different television, and this time we asked if we could plug it in and try it before leaving the store. Satisfied, we took a taxi back to the dinghy. Moral of story: Things get more complicated when you don't have easy access to transportation.

I was talking to Marc on Wednesday about the possibility of organizing the v-berth so that we could store some of the excess items lying around the salon. He went to the v-berth to assess the proposed project and returned with the radar dome. He said we should install it (up on the mast) to free up more room in the v-berth for storage. And so we started another project, which made an even bigger mess!

From our anchorage in Fajardo, we called the marina every day on the VHF radio, and every day they said our package hadn't come. Meanwhile, a throttle piece on our dinghy engine broke, and we ordered a replacement through the outboard repair guy at Villa Marina. He said he'd have it by Saturday. Finally, the watermaker guy said he had everything straightened out with FedEx and customs and our package would arrive at Puerto del Rey on Thursday or Friday. So, we took MARAVIDA to Puerto del Rey on Friday. Our top priority upon arrival was fueling up; starting a load of laundry was a close second. Then, we went to the office ... only to find that our package still had not arrived, and the next delivery wouldn't come in until Monday! Enough is enough! Marc e-mailed the watermaker guy and asked him to have FedEx return the package to the sender—we'd try again in St. Martin. We then filled our water tanks, hosed down the cockpit, and finished the laundry–leaving just enough time to get back to the Cayo Obispo anchorage before dark.

We didn't make it before dark, though, because we came across a stranded fisherman and towed his boat all the way to the anchorage. After anchoring, Marc towed him to the town dock with our dinghy.

Yesterday morning we took the dinghy to Villa Marina to pick up our outboard part and take showers—the marina people don't seem to mind, though we didn't ask for fear they'd say no. The outboard repairman wasn't at his shop, but Marc called him from the marina office and found out that we'd just missed him. We took him up on his generous offer to return at 1:00 p.m.

Definitely behind schedule but still determined to leave, we hauled the dinghy onto MARAVIDA's deck and took off for Culebra around 3:00 p.m. Because we arrived at dusk, we chose the easier anchorage on the west side of the town of Dewey.

This morning I insisted that we finish the last piece of radar wiring and replace the ceiling panels before going into town for drinks.

We'll stay here another night, then head around the corner to Bahia Almodovar, which our guidebook says is a scenic anchorage with good snorkeling.

Cheers—
Sandy

Puerto Rico to St. Thomas ... More than Once

From: sandy_n_marc
To: Davis News Group
Subject: Davis News
Date: Fri, 3 Mar 2006

February 27, 2006

Bahia Almodovar is almost too calm. I won't get my sea legs here, but I bet I'll get a good night's sleep. There are only two other boats anchored in this large protected bay and just a few houses hugging the hills.

We pumped up the small dinghy, threw it in the water with the oars and snorkeling gear, and went in search of coral. After finding only sea grass, we went back to the boat to recheck the guidebooks. We also installed the outboard engine because our progress had been painfully slow due to our pathetic rowing skills; anyone watching would have been entertained by our comedic performance. The second time out, we found coral. Marc and Madeline had a great time snorkeling, but I got too cold to stay in for long and Alex declined because he was still cold from the last time. Alex and I will be sure to wear our shorty wetsuits next time.

Back in Tortuga, Wayne from DAYDREAM had taught Madeline a secret method for fishing. She used this "secret weapon" to catch a small squirrel fish, which she brought back to the boat, cleaned, and then gave to the cats. Maria wasn't interested, but Emily ate the body of the fish and then played with the head.

February 28, 2006

A lazy day that included an afternoon snorkel. The wetsuits worked well, but the conditions weren't ideal. The water was choppy, which makes snorkeling a tiring endeavor. Nevertheless, Madeline used Wayne's "secret weapon" again and caught a small grouper. Later, she constructed a small weaving loom inspired by a piece in a *Martha Stewart* magazine we picked up in Dewey.

Alex has spent hours with his new Dungeons & Dragons books. He learned about the complicated role-playing game (RPG) from the Opp boys when they visited. His fascination with the game led him to purchase three of the D&D books and the dice at the Borders bookstore near San Juan and from Amazon.com. It cost him a whopping $70 but seems worth it—especially since it lures him away from video games.

In the evening, we played Mexican Train Dominoes, and then Alex and Marc went on deck to stargaze. Alex's grandfather sent him a star chart, which Marc and Alex have used several times.

March 1, 2006

We set out for St. Thomas at 1:00 p.m., but turned around after a miserable hour in heinous conditions. We left Culebra knowing the seas would be 7-8 feet but did not expect the other excessive conditions we encountered. The seas were not only high but also confused, jostling us so much that we couldn't go on deck to raise the mainsail for stability. Marc deserves praise because they say the best captains are the ones that aren't too proud to turn back.

Upon our return, we found the contents of the interior scattered all over the floor and were distressed to find that had we lost a water jug and our garden sprayer (freshwater shower), both of which had been tied on deck.

We'll wait for better conditions before setting out again. It's windy and rainy, so we're staying inside. The kids are continuing a comparison study of the new set of Star Wars movies versus the old set, Marc is studying weather, and I'm studying homeschooling books.

Homeschooling

March 2, 2006

I just finished reading, highlighting, and writing out notes from two homeschooling books that I ordered online when we were in Puerto Rico. The titles are *Homeschooling: The Teen Years* and *The Teenage Liberation Handbook*. I certainly have learned a lot about homeschooling in the past two years, and reading *The Teenage Liberation Handbook* has been a real eye-opener. Here are my current thoughts on homeschooling (as I stand on my soapbox).

Homeschooling, unlike traditional schooling, can give children the freedom to love, pursue, and be curious about learning again. We're born with an urge to learn, but schools (in general) require passivity; screen us from reality; condition us for the future—not the present; fill up our days with busy work; base teaching and learning on tests; give grades (which puts the wrong focus on learning—to make grades rather than to become educated); and drain our time and energy (and thus constrain us from exploring our interests and other learning opportunities, including travel, volunteerism, and other real-world objectives). Furthermore, traditional schooling often doesn't challenge the academically inclined nor help those falling behind.

Homeschoolers spend more time with all members of their family and, in the process, build strong relationships. Homeschoolers learn: independence, interdependence, initiative, resourcefulness, inventiveness, creativity, self-awareness, and socialization with all ages. In addition, they learn to ask questions, to like their parents and siblings, to communicate self-confidence, to search for intellectual achievement, to explore life to its fullest, and—most important—to love learning.

Madeline will work on "real math" while Alex works on "higher math." We'll introduce them to all the branches of physical science and let them focus on topics of their choosing. Such fields as astronomy, geology, meteorology, and nature studies will go well with our travels. The social sciences are also easy to incorporate as we travel. The children can map our routes, read travel guides, research history, discuss economies and political systems, visit museums and historical sites, listen to local music, and eat local foods. Both of the kids read constantly and are easily diverted to classical and historical novels. The more they read, the more they recognize how to write. (Everyone learns from example; thus, reading high-quality literature helps develop better grammar, vocabulary, and spelling.) After all the reading Madeline has done in the past year, I see a dramatic improvement in her spelling (more than I thought her dyslexia would allow). We'll encourage them to write in whatever genre they find most appealing—journals, reviews, reports, short stories, poems, plays and screenplays, articles for magazines, etc. And with the extra time not spent at school, independent living skills should come more easily: meal planning, cooking, cleaning, being a useful crew member on the boat, engine maintenance and repair, fishing, sewing, money management, and consumer skills. Ultimately, they need freedom to explore their interests and discover new ones. We want the world and life itself to be their teachers. How's that? More practical than radical when you think about it.

All the best—
Sandy

Onward

March 3, 2006

We left Culebra for St. Thomas this morning.

Cruising Guides

Pavlidis, Stephen J. *A Cruising Guide to Puerto Rico: Including the Spanish Virgin Islands and the Dominican Republic.* 3rd edition. Port Washington, WI: Seaworthy Publications, 2015.

Street, Donald M. *Street's Cruising Guide to the Eastern Caribbean: Puerto Rico, the Spanish, U.S., and British Virgin Islands.* Lincoln, NE: iUniverse, 2001.

Virgintino, Frank. *A Cruising Guide to Puerto Rico.* Kindle edition. Amazon Digital Services, 2012. **I haven't read this cruising guide.**

CHAPTER 7

U.S. & British Virgin Islands

U.S. Virgin Islands

> **U.S. Virgin Islands**
> During World War I, the United States purchased what's now known as the U.S. Virgin Islands from Denmark for approximately $25 million.

Water Island

> **Water Island**
> Water Island is the fourth U.S. Virgin Island—after Saint Croix, Saint John, and Saint Thomas. The 500-acre island is primarily residential, with 10-minute ferry service to Crown Bay on St. Thomas. Honeymoon Bay's man-made sandy beach with palm trees and a roped-off swimming area is Water Island's main attraction. Fort Segarra, constructed during World War II, is another popular tourist destination.

From: sandy_n_marc
To: Davis News Group
Subject: Davis News
Date: Sat, 12 Mar 2006

March 3, 2006

It took us four hours to motor from Culebra to St. Thomas. We anchored in crowded Honeymoon Bay (also called Druif Bay), off Water Island.

The next day we motored over to Crown Bay Marina's fuel dock to top off our water tanks for a mere $.14 per gallon (we had heard it was $1.00 per gallon in St. John). After a quick stop at the gourmet grocery store in the marina, we headed to St. John, which is only 4 miles away.

St. John

St. John

St. John has approximately 4,000 inhabitants on 19.62 square miles of land.

Because the Virgin Islands National Park owns 60 percent of the island, St. John stands in sharp contrast to the overdeveloped island of St. Thomas. The economy of St. John is supported by tourists who are attracted to its unspoiled natural beauty.

We picked up a $15 mooring ball *(costs more now)* in Caneel Bay, on the west side of St. John. The U.S. Park Service provides the mooring balls to protect the sea bottom. (Anchoring costs the same as mooring and is only permitted in a couple spots.)

Rules/Fees in St. John's Waters

Read up on current rules and restrictions for mooring and anchoring in St. John's waters. There's a limit to how long you can stay in St. John's waters: 30 nights in a calendar year and seven consecutive nights in one bay.

---

http://www.nps.gov/viis/planyourvisit/quick-mooring-information.htm

http://www.nps.gov/viis/planyourvisit/boating-information.htm

http://www.nps.gov/viis/planyourvisit/virgin-islands-marine-visitor-use-information.htm

We are surrounded by charter boats. I've heard that both the U.S. and British Virgin Islands are popular for charter vacations.

We're also surrounded by numerous islands of varying size—some close, some far—each an undeveloped hill of green. The combination of sparkling water and lush islands give us a stunning view.

We dinghied to Caneel Bay Resort to pay the moorage fee at the pay station next to the dinghy dock. We chose to moor in Caneel Bay rather than Cruz Bay Harbor because the latter gets rough from the ferry traffic that runs to St. Thomas and the British Virgin Islands.

> **Caneel Bay Resort**
>
> This low-impact luxury resort is set on its own 170-acre peninsula. In the 1950s, Laurance Rockefeller (the son of John D. Rockefeller, Jr.) began to buy up land on St. John, starting with the Caneel Bay sugar plantation. He opened the Caneel Bay Plantation Resort in 1956 and donated 5,000 acres to the Virgin Islands National Park.
>
> http://www.caneelbay.com

March 5, 2006

The morning after settling in, we dinghied over to the town of Cruz Bay (in Cruz Bay Harbor). The colorful town is touristy but quite pleasant, with many offerings from the island's artistic residents. We walked around a bit and then stopped at the Virgin Islands National Park Visitor Center, where we checked out the exhibits and chatted with the park ranger.

> **Maps**
>
> The National Park Service maps show the park boundaries and hiking trails on St. John:
>
> http://www.nps.gov/viis/planyourvisit/maps.htm

In the early afternoon, we rescued four Westin Resort patrons who had run out of gas in their dinghy. (The Westin covers 47 acres on Great Cruz Bay.)

In the late afternoon, we motored MARAVIDA to the north side of the island and picked up a mooring ball in Francis Bay.

Once settled in, we decided to check out Maho Bay Camps—an ecoresort that looks over the bay. From the beach, we hiked up countless wooden stairs and along many elevated wooden walkways that form the paths between the dozens of tent-cottages and bathhouses. Toward the top, we came to an open air restaurant. *(Maho Bay Camps is now closed.)*

March 6, 2006

We went on a long walk to the Annaberg Sugar Plantation and wandered among the ruins, reading the plaques that describe sugar production and plantation life. We also talked with the volunteer guide on site. The walk back was hot, so we jumped into the ocean as soon as we returned to the bay.

> **Annaberg Sugar Plantation**
>
> The Sugar Plantation's ruins date back to the 1700s. They are owned by the Virgin Islands National Park (donated by Rockefeller).

British Virgin Islands

> **The BVI**
>
> The British Virgin Islands are made up of more than 50 islands and cays. The largest are Tortola, Virgin Gorda, Anegada, and Jost Van Dyke. In total, the BVIs comprise 60 square miles and are home to 28,000 people, most of whom live on Tortola. The official currency of the BVIs is the U.S. dollar.

We left St. John at 3:00 p.m., because a large northerly swell was moving in. Two hours later, we arrived in Road Town Harbour, Tortola, and spent the next hour searching for a suitable anchoring spot in the large harbor (most of it is too deep for anchoring).

Tortola

> **Tortola**
>
> Tortola is the capital of the BVIs. It covers an area of 21 square miles and has over 23,000 inhabitants.

March 7, 2006

The next morning we dinghied around a huge cruise ship that had docked just 200 yards from where we were anchored. We headed to the dinghy landing next to customs to fill out paperwork and pay fees with immigration and customs. None of this was necessary in Puerto Rico, St. Thomas, or St. John because we are U.S. citizens; from now on, though, we'll have to deal with the chore of "checking in."

The cruise ship that had docked so close to us left while we were exploring the town. We bought a couple of tourist t-shirts, ate ice cream, and went grocery shopping. Later, another cruise ship came in and lit up our deck the entire night.

It seems that the busier and more commercial cruising destinations are the ones I like the least. I wasn't particularly impressed with Road Town, and I'll bet that other cruise ship towns will not be among my favorite stops. I suppose a drive around the island would broaden my perspective, but it's only 13 miles long and 3 miles wide.

March 8, 2006

The catamaran COOL RUNNINGS came into Road Town Harbour at 9:00 in the morning. We first met the family (Jim, Eileen, James, and Daniel) at Puerto del Rey Marina, where Alex got to play with the two boys for one evening and one morning before their departure. In Road Town, Eileen guided us to the Laundromat; we started our laundry and then went to a Chinese restaurant.

Norman Island

> **Norman Island**
>
> Only 7 miles from Tortola, Norman Island is a 600-acre private island with a storybook past. The so-called "pirate" island is said to have inspired Robert Louis Stevenson to write the classic *Treasure Island*.

In the afternoon, we took the boats to Norman Island. Alex rode with our friends on COOL RUNNINGS. We headed straight to The Bite, the most protected anchorage of the island. The anchorage is full of mooring balls, but only a few were open when we got there. We hooked up within the protected area (for a $20 fee), and later on, Jim, Eileen, James, and Daniel came over for spaghetti dinner.

March 9, 2006

At 6:00 a.m. the next day, we awoke to find the COOL RUNNINGS family on boat watch. We hadn't noticed that our boats had bumped a couple of times in the night (no damage, thank goodness). The problem was that wind eddies were causing the boats to circle their mooring balls at varying speeds and directions, especially boats as different as ours and theirs (30-ton steel monohull versus 10-ton fiberglass catamaran). This wouldn't be a problem if the mooring balls were spaced farther apart.

We decided against staying another night because of the bumper boat issue and because rough weather was approaching. The forecast was for strong northeasterly winds and 8- to 10-foot northerly swells. And so, it was time to move on to our next destination: North Sound on Virgin Gorda.

Virgin Gorda

> **Virgin Gorda**
>
> Virgin Gorda is approximately 8 square miles in size. The island is smaller and less commercial than Tortola. As of 2010, the population was 3,930.

We sailed most of the way, doubling the length of the trip to more than 5 hours. The 20-knot winds were good for sailing, but the 8-foot swells reduced our speed to 6 knots and made the passage uncomfortable.

North Sound, or Gorda Sound, is a huge lagoon protected from swells by the surrounding islands. Two of the three entrances into the sound are considered risky. Once inside, there are many different areas to anchor or moor, some a mile apart from each other.

We anchored near Leverick Resort, but out past the mooring balls. I hate the idea of a private resort or restaurant installing mooring balls and charging $20 to $30 per night for their use. How is it that they can claim rights to the water? I do understand that mooring balls are a good idea for inexperienced charterers out on vacation for a week or two: They can roll the mooring charges into the cost of their vacation; however, the fees add up too fast for full-time cruisers. This is one reason why I wouldn't come back to the BVIs unless I was on a charter vacation. At least the moorings put in by the Park Service in St. John pay for the park upkeep and services, and you're allowed to use their garbage containers. Here in North Sound, you have to pay garbage disposal fees in addition to the moorage fee!

March 10, 2006

Our first real showers in two weeks!

The winds here are constant, but the waves are not rolly. Riding in the dinghy is rough, though, because the water is choppy. We tried to use the small dinghy but got wet from the chop, so we lowered the large dinghy into the water. We decided to try the 4-horsepower engine on the large dinghy since Marc hasn't had time to install the new throttle linkage and do some maintenance on the 25-horsepower engine. Surprisingly, the smaller engine works fine on the large dinghy; it's just a lot slower.

We went to the pool at Leverick Bay with the COOL RUNNINGS family and then had dinner on their boat.

Leverick Bay Marina and Resort

The marina has a dock with 15 slips (110 and 220 volt electricity) and fuel. If staying overnight on one of their 36 mooring balls or in a slip, water (up to 100 gallons) and a bag of ice is free. They are open from 8 a.m. to 5 p.m. all week. Contact them on VHF 16. They also have a hotel, restaurant, grocery store, pool, showers, and laundry facilities.

http://www.leverickbay.com

March 11, 2006

In the afternoon, we dinghied across the sound to check out Saba Rock Resort and Bitter End Resort. Saba is a miniresort on a tiny island that's only reachable by boat. Bitter End, too, is only reachable by boat, but it's a huge complex with restaurants, gift shops, a small grocery store, beaches, a swimming pool, and a movie-watching area. We plan to return to use their wireless internet.

We met two other cruising boats—COOL CHANGE and TRADITION, both from the West Coast of the United States—that are also heading to St. Martin. All three of us will leave together on Tuesday or Wednesday when the weather calms down.

Saba Rock Resort

The resort sits on a single-acre island. The marina has 10 slips with 110 volt and 220 volt electrical connections (electricity fees charged) and free high-speed wireless internet access. They also offer 17 moorings that include up to 250 gallons of water and a free bag of ice. In addition to the yachting facilities, the resort has a few select rooms and suites, a restaurant, a bar, a beach, and tropical gardens. Access to the island is by ferry or boat only.

http://www.sabarock.com

The Bitter End Yacht Club

The resort sits on 75 acres and stretches along a mile of North Sound's shore. It offers boaters 35 slips with electrical hookups: 30 amp 110 volt; 50 amp 220 volt; and 100 amp (electricity fees charged). The resort also offers 70 moorings, provisioning, launch service, garbage drop off, fuel, and showers (for a fee). Accommodations consist of cabins set amid lush vegetation with large decks that overlook the water. Amenities and services are plentiful and include restaurants, a watersports center, shops, a pool, beaches, and kids' programs. Access to the island is by ferry or boat only.

http://www.beyc.com

March 12, 2006

We went back to Bitter End today and used their wireless internet while the kids played at the tetherball court. We then dinghied over to Saba Rock for french fries and more internet time.

That's it for now—
Sandy

On Our Way to St. Martin

From: sandy_n_marc
To: Davis News Group
Subject: Davis News
Date: Wed, 15 Mar 2006

Our weather window opened up, so we motored to Spanish Town—the capital of Virgin Gorda—to check out of the BVIs. We left for St. Martin at 3:00 p.m. and are currently en route.

I'll let you know when we get there.

All the best—
Sandy

The Baths

We didn't get to The Baths. Located on the southwest tip of Virgin Gorda, the famous beach is covered with huge boulders that hide pools, arches, tunnels, and grottoes. The BVI National Parks Trust provides daytime mooring buoys for visiting boats and a parking lot for landlubbers. (We hear it can get crowded between 10:00 a.m. and 3:00 p.m., when small cruise ships come in.)

My Favorites

My favorite islands of the U.S. and British Virgin Islands were St. John and Virgin Gorda. I'd even consider them for a land stay. Both have several beaches that sound interesting.

> **Other Virgin Islands**
>
> We didn't visit the U.S. Virgin Island of St. Croix because it was too far off our route.
>
> We also missed out on Jost Van Dyke and Anegada, and the various other small islands that comprise the BVIs.

Cruising Guides

Pavlidis, Stephen J. *A Cruising Guide to the Virgin Islands: Including the Spanish Virgin Islands, the United States Virgin Islands, and the British Virgin Islands.* 2nd ed. Cocoa Beach, FL: Seaworthy Publications, 2011.

Russell, Joe, and Mark Bunzel. *Cruising the Virgin Islands.* 2nd ed. Anacortes, WA: Fine Edge, 2009.

Scott, Nancy, and Simon Scott. *The Cruising Guide to the Virgin Islands, 2015-2016: The Complete Guide for Yachtsmen, Divers and Watersports Enthusiasts.* 17th edition. Dunedin, FL: Cruising Guide Publications, 2014.

Street, Donald M. *Street's Cruising Guide to the Eastern Caribbean: Puerto Rico, the Spanish, U.S. and British Virgin Islands.* Lincoln, NE: iUniverse, 2001.

Virgintino, Frank. *A Cruising Guide to the Lesser Antilles: The Virgin Islands.* Kindle edition. Amazon Digital Services, 2014. **I haven't read this cruising guide.**

CHAPTER 8

Six Weeks in Saint Martin

> **Saint Martin**
>
> The Dutch side of the island is called Sint Maarten and occupies 13 square miles; the French side of the island is called Saint Martin and occupies 20 square miles. Sint Maarten has a slightly larger share of the 77,000 inhabitants.
>
> The official currency of Saint Martin is the euro, while Sint Maarten uses the Caribbean guilder (as of 2012). They were still using the Netherlands Antillean guilder when we were there.
>
> Cruisers' net: Monday through Saturday, 7:30 a.m., on VHF channel 14.

We Made It

From: sandy_n_marc
To: Davis News Group
Subject: Davis News
Date: Thu, 16 Mar 2006

We left Virgin Gorda at 3:00 yesterday afternoon and arrived in Saint Martin at 7:00 this morning. It was not a pleasant trip, but we've had worse.

> **Predeparture Planning**
>
> Do your research before sailing to Saint Martin. Check the current clearance formalities for both the French side and the Dutch side of the island before deciding where you will anchor. They have changed since we were there and could change again.
>
> Sint Maarten – Dutch side:
>
> http://www.noonsite.com/Countries/SintMaarten?rc=Formalities
>
> Saint Martin – French side:
>
> http://www.noonsite.com/Countries/StMartin/?rc=Formalities#Clearance
>
> If you plan to enter the lagoon, decide ahead of time which bridge entrance you are going to use and be aware of the opening times. When anchoring in the lagoon, figure out where the invisible borderline is located and anchor on either the French or Dutch side—whichever you will use to check in. There isn't an obvious way to figure this out, though I've read that yachts anchored close to the "Witches Tit" are on the French side. At the very least, look at the courtesy flags on the boats already anchored and stick with the appropriate bunch.

We waited in Simpson Bay, Sint Maarten, for the 9:30 a.m. bridge opening that would allow us to enter Simpson Bay Lagoon. The lagoon is considered an ideal anchorage because it's well protected by surrounding land and has only two small entrances. Once inside, we were shocked to see hundreds of boats anchored in every available space. It looked like a humongous RV park. We went toward the back of the pack and set our anchor, but we soon discovered that we were situated at the end of the airport runway *and* in an established dinghy thoroughfare. Because it's such a large anchorage, dinghies run at full throttle on their way to the mainland—a huge change from the other anchorages we've been in, where it's common courtesy to keep the speed down to minimize wakes and noise.

Marigot

> ### Marigot
>
> Marigot is the capital of the French side of Saint Martin and has a quieter, more laid-back feel than the Dutch side's bustling capital, Philipsburg. The French town sits on beautiful Marigot Bay and is filled with boutique shops, bistros, and cafes that hint at being imported straight from France. My assessment of Marigot: The town wraps a European ambience in a Caribbean package with French confidence. C'est magnifique.

Once settled, we took the dinghy through the Sandy Ground Bridge passage to the town of Marigot to check in with immigration. This was easy and cost us nothing. We've heard that you have to pay if you check in on the Dutch side.

We explored the town and then sat at an outdoor cafe for coffee and sodas. Before returning to the boat, we stopped at a small grocery store (called US Supermarché) to pick up French goodies: wine, pâté, and baguettes. We'd been looking forward to the French islands and their authentic baguettes. We've never had a baguette in the States that compares to the taste and texture of one from France. And yes, the baguettes here are the real deal.

Diary

From: sandy_n_marc
To: Davis News Group
Subject: Davis News
Date: Thu, 23 Mar 2006

This group e-mail has become sort of a diary for me—it's not only the way I communicate with our family back home but also a permanent record of our cruising experiences. I'd much rather sit down and gather my thoughts in writing than make phone calls home from each port.

I've heard that a few people are forwarding these e-mails on to others. I hope my "readers" aren't getting frustrated with the sometimes-tedious account of our daily travels.

March 17, 2006

In the early morning, I awoke to loud and persistent duck quacks. I climbed up to the cockpit and saw a man on a nearby boat blowing a duck horn and pointing at us. Looking around, I didn't recognize any of the boats nearby; in fact, we seemed to be in an entirely different location. That's when I realized we were still in motion and heading toward shore. I yelled for Marc and we quickly started the engine, hauled up the dragging anchor, and motored behind an island at the back of the anchorage, where we discovered a whole new world—a huge area with only a few boats. It turns out the lagoon covers about 12 square miles. The large northern part of the lagoon we ended up in is on the French side, which is good: Having checked in to French Saint Martin, we had to move to that side anyway.

It's surprising how many cruisers we know here. So far we've bumped into: CENTIME, PSYCHE, WILLOW, HEART OF TEXAS, ALUMINE, GODIVA, INDIGO, and EVENTURE. We met them all down south in Trinidad and Venezuela.

Today we checked out the boat facilities and got a general lay of the land. We went to Budget Marine, Island Water World, and NAPA Auto Parts (same instantly recognizable bright orange and blue logo as the stores in the States). The first two are on the water and have dinghy docks. NAPA is a bit of a walk. Between the three places, Marc spent hours perusing their inventory, asking questions, and generally having a mighty good time.

> **Buying Boat Parts**
>
> Budget Marine has 13 chandleries in the Caribbean.
>
> http://www.budgetmarine.com/Store.aspx
>
> Island Water World sells boat supplies on four islands in the Caribbean.
>
> http://www.islandwaterworld.com/page.htm?PG=stores

March 18, 2006

We dinghied into Marigot and walked through the Saturday morning outdoor market. Then we picked up baguettes and French cheeses at a new (to us) grocery store.

In the evening, Marc and I dinghied to Ric's Place (on Airport Road), a restaurant and sports bar, to have a drink and use their free wireless internet. Our young waitress came to St. Martin from Idaho, and the owner of the restaurant is from California. She's about our age and has owned the place for only a couple of years.

> **Ric's is now...?**
>
> She doesn't own it anymore. Ric's was replaced by Bonita's Cantina, which has also closed. I wonder what's next?

March 19, 2006

We went to the Sunday morning cruisers' flea market at Shrimpy's bar/restaurant and bought a few fluorescent lights and solar garden lights. Marc returned to Shrimpy's in the evening to use their free Wi-Fi. He struck up a conversation with Mike, the owner, while he was there.

> **Shrimpy's**
>
> Mike and his wife Sally have since lost their lease at the facility on Airport Road but have moved Shrimpy's to a new location in the cut by the French bridge.
>
> http://www.shrimpys-saintmartin.com

March 20, 2006

In the morning, we went to Budget Marine, Island Water World, and Electec. We also picked up 10 gallons of water.

In the afternoon, we met up with friends (CENTIME, HEART OF TEXAS, etc.) at the Simpson Bay Beach for bocce ball and swimming. Even though Madeline and Alex were the only kids there, they had a great time and did well at the game. All the while they had their eye on an abandoned windsurf board (missing its rigging and cracked on the front point), so once everyone else left, we let them play with it. They had a blast and talked us into taking it back to the boat.

March 21, 2006

Madeline and I went into Marigot. We explored the town thoroughly, and then went to a French teahouse for coffee and Orangina soda.

Marc decided to rebuild MARAVIDA's main mast winch, but it broke when he took it apart. When we went to Budget Marine to order a replacement part, we discovered that the part isn't available for purchase. (We also picked up another 10 gallons of water while we had the chance.)

March 22, 2006

The kids stayed on the boat while Marc and I went in search of hex bolts for the broken winch and a machine shop to do the repair. We found a machine shop, but not the bolts that are necessary for the repair.

We also bought a pump for the watermaker and a pump for the new kitchen sink sump box that Marc plans to build from scratch. We're currently using a small plastic sump box with an internal submersible pump that might perform well enough for a bathroom sink, but isn't working for the kitchen sink. It gets plugged easily and then overflows into the bilge, leaving a nasty smell.

We ate a late lunch at a French cafe, then returned to the boat and took the kids to Simpson Bay for a swim.

Saint Martin is a great place for cruisers, with many places to anchor and lots of boat services. However, there are two drawbacks: One is that laundry costs US$10 per load (we hope to buy a washing machine here). The other problem is showers. It costs US$2.50 to take one at any of the marinas. That's US$10 for all of us, each time. We plan to move MARAVIDA into Simpson Bay where the water is clean enough for bathing. Then all we need is a garden sprayer for freshwater rinsing.

Philipsburg

> ### Philipsburg
>
> Philipsburg—the capital of Dutch Sint Maarten—is squeezed between Great Bay and Salt Pond, leaving enough room for only four parallel streets. Nevertheless, the streets run about a mile long, forming a long "shopping mall" for tourists taking advantage of this duty-free and sales tax-free cruise ship town. As expected, there are boutiques, restaurants, jewelry stores, souvenir shops, electronics stores, liquor shops, and an open-air market selling handicrafts.
>
> The boardwalk running the length of Great Bay beach was in its final stage of construction when we were there. I remember that the midday sun reflecting off the boardwalk's pink concrete was painfully bright. Evening might be a better time to visit, especially if the cruise ships have left for the day. Check out future cruise ship schedules at:
>
> http://www.portofstmaarten.com/schedule.htm

March 23, 2006

We took the dollar bus (large van) into Philipsburg to celebrate my 44th birthday. Of the cruise ship towns we've been to so far, I'd rate Philipsburg the best. It's nicely laid out and has reasonable prices.

Over the past few days, the kids and Marc have been watching DVD episodes of a BBC show called *Black Adder*. It's a comedy series set in early England. They love it. (Thanks, Robin and Rachel!) A few days ago, Marc and I finished watching the last episode of *24* (the second season). (Thanks, Wayne and Susan!) In addition to reading, most cruisers watch DVD movies and television shows to relax after a hard day of boat work. Not only does trading DVDs keep the entertainment coming, but it's a common way to get to know your neighbors in an anchorage.

Take care all—
Sandy

Getting Water

From: sandy_n_marc
To: Davis News Group
Subject: Davis News
Date: Wed, 5 Apr 2006

March 24, 2006

Last evening the outboard's propeller started to slip on its hub and we had to limp it back to the boat. Since buying a new propeller was the only solution to this problem, we headed to the Yamaha dealer in the morning, only to find that they didn't have any in stock ... and weren't able to order one because of "cash flow problems." But then, as we were leaving, one of the mechanics approached us and sold us a new prop for less than the dealer's price. A suspicious situation? Maybe, but we gladly paid without questioning his source.

We spent the early afternoon working on small projects (installed push button for generator and light on dinghy engine) while we waited to pull up anchor for the 4:30 p.m. bridge opening.

We pulled anchor at 2:30 and motored to Simpson Bay Marina's fuel dock to fill our water tanks, but a mega yacht was just docking. Knowing that the huge yacht would take more time to finish its business at the dock than we had available, we left and anchored temporarily near the bridge.

Our move to Simpson Bay was a bad decision. The anchorage in the bay was so rough and rolly that I got seasick, and the internet connection didn't work—despite our being told it would. Nevertheless, the kids and Marc played on the beach in the evening and had a good time.

March 25, 2006

I took a fast dip in the water before we pulled up anchor to return to the lagoon. We entered during the 9:30 a.m. bridge opening and headed for the fuel dock for water, but there were four boats ahead of us. How frustrating! We decided to give up on that idea and just continue to haul water each time we ran an errand. This time, we anchored in the middle of the huge pack of boats to shorten our dinghy transit time to the boat chandlers. Marc started on the fiberglass work to build the new kitchen sump box and a muffler for the generator.

Later in the day, we visited the chandleries and filled water jugs.

March 26, 2006

We spent US$70 at Shrimpy's flea market. Our justification is that we got a deal on things we needed to buy anyway. Madeline and I went for a long walk, southeast from Shrimpy's and back. Marc did more fiberglass work, and later we all swam in the bay. In case you haven't figured it out, we can't swim in the lagoon because it's too dirty and we don't want to pay US$10 for showers, so instead we go swimming in the bay. We have fun and get clean.

March 27, 2006

Boat errands and fiberglass work today. Errands: propane, water, and dinghy gas fill-ups, along with stops at Budget Marine, Island Water World, and the grocery store.

March 28, 2006

Madeline and I explored Philipsburg today until we were exhausted. On the way back, we stopped at Ric's for iced coffee, then walked to Shrimpy's, where we found Alex and Marc on the internet. Later on, we swam in the bay.

March 29, 2006

Marc and I did some shopping today. We took the bus to (1) Radio Shack (where we didn't find what we were looking for); (2) a large Ace Hardware (where we found a garden sprayer and other things); (3) Cost-U-Less, which is similar to Costco but doesn't require membership (we had to limit our purchases to what we could carry); (4) a cafe for lunch; and finally to (5) Le Grand Marché (where we once again had to limit our purchases). Le Grand Marché is one of the most impressive supermarkets we've ever seen. It has a huge variety of international products.

After dinner, we headed to Ric's to do some research on the internet. The kids also played foosball, air hockey, and met the owner, Tamara. The US$18 we spent on drinks and desserts was more than we would have spent at an internet cafe, but we had a nice evening.

March 30, 2006

We've been in Saint Martin for two weeks and haven't yet started on our original to-do list. It'll likely be another two weeks until we depart. We can't stay too long because we need to get started down the island chain to avoid being in the hurricane zone during hurricane season.

Marc and Alex went to Budget Marine and—you guessed it—picked up some more water.

March 31, 2006

Marc made a sale on the morning radio net: US$50 for Westerbeke generator parts he'd salvaged from the old generator. Madeline and I took the bus to Moho Bay. It's a resort and casino area with a few shops. We also rode the bus to the airport to pick up our package of bolts. In the late afternoon, Marc and I took MARAVIDA's jib sail to North Sails. Some stitching has come off, making it unusable without repair. (This actually was on the original to-do list!) Of course, we also picked up water.

Marc finished construction of the generator muffler today.

April 1, 2006

The once-a-month flea market at the Time Out Boatyard was held today on the French side of the lagoon near the Sandy Ground Bridge. We didn't find anything there but had better luck across the street at the French market. We came home with our favorite cheeses, pâtés, etc. In the afternoon, I took the kids to Ric's for internet time, drinks, and french fries while Marc finished and installed the new sump. Hopefully, no smelly bilge anymore. Marc and I went over to the boat called CLASS-I-CAT in the evening for drinks. The owners are also from Oregon.

April 2, 2006

We browsed Shrimpy's weekly flea market today and got back to the boat just in time for a whopper rainstorm. Because we have the large awning installed on MARAVIDA, we were able to run water off the canvas and into containers. We filled all our water jugs, and I started washing laundry by hand. We also put on our swimsuits and shampooed our hair in the rain. A couple of hours later it started pouring again, so Marc started to siphon water from a large plastic container into our water tanks. The kids emptied smaller containers of collected water into the large one, and I continued to do laundry. Can you believe it rained enough to fill both of the boat's water tanks? Before the storm, only about 30 gallons were left in the tanks; so, in total, we added approximately 220 gallons of rainwater. Now we don't have to worry about water for a while! By the end of the day, we were exhausted, exhilarated, and very proud of ourselves.

April 3, 2006

We dropped off the broken winch at the machine shop with the necessary bolts that had arrived from the U.S. on Friday (shipping cost a hefty US$20).

Marc spent most of the day working out the plumbing for the watermaker. This required trips to the plumbing store, Budget Marine, Island Water

World, and then back again. Once again, it was impossible to find the exact pieces needed for the job, so Marc had to reinvent the plan over and over until the available resources worked.

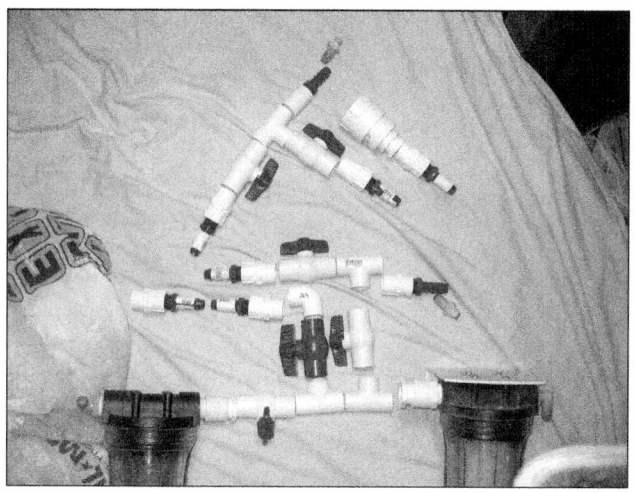

April 4, 2006

While Marc worked on the watermaker, Madeline and I went to Marigot. First we visited the boutiques, pretending we could afford the designer clothing. When we tired of that, we shopped at the locals' variety stores. Our favorite store is Forum. It has reasonably priced products from France. Madeline purchased fabric and a shirt, and I bought a Provencal-print plastic tablecloth and a bed covering.

COOL RUNNINGS has arrived in Saint Martin, though Jim has already flown off to the States to do some contract work. We spent some time today and yesterday with Elaine and the boys.

April 5, 2006

We've been experiencing strong gusts of wind, and at 1:00 a.m. today we realized we were dragging. Marc, Madeline, and I pulled up anchor, repositioned the boat, and dropped the anchor—all in the dark. This morning at 9:00 we started to drag again and had to reanchor. I'm hoping the wind will calm down soon. We're afraid to leave the boat, and I'm even nervous to go below, so I've been on deck washing laundry by hand and doing computer stuff. I'll read next.

From Marc: Sad News from Trinidad

From: sandy_n_marc
To: Davis News Group
Subject: Davis News
Date: Thu, 6 Apr 2006

I'm saddened to report that our friend Junior Heeralal was killed two weeks ago. Three masked men shot him near his home.

Some of you know Junior personally, others only from our newsletter. Junior was our main contractor while we repaired MARAVIDA in Trinidad. Without his help, the boat never would have been completed.

Junior could be aggravating at times, but he was generous, quick with a smile, and had a sharp mind. He also had a passion for animals and was always bringing a new one home. While we knew him, he had several dogs, a cat, hamsters, a donkey, and even alligators.

Junior's death is one more example of the crime problems facing Trinidad. I have no hope that his killers will be brought to justice or that the police will spend any significant time trying. With a population of only 1.25 million, Trinidad reels from the blow of a murder a day.

I don't think we'll return there.

Marc

Trinidad Murder Statistics

There was not much of a write-up about Junior's murder because he was only a small statistic in a growing epidemic. His murder was the 88th of 2006. The total for the year was 368.

"88) March 21. Junior Heeralal, 32, of Forest Drive, in Bagatelle, Diego Martin shot a few metres from his home. Gang-related."

http://www.newsday.co.tt/news/0,35198.html

Trinidad Murder statistics: *2004*—260; *2005*—386; *2006*—368; *2007*—395; *2008*—550; *2009*—509; *2010*—485; 2011—354; 2012—383; 2013—408; 2014—403; 2015—410.

http://www.ttcrime.com/stats.php

Miscellaneous Happenings

From: sandy_n_marc
To: Davis News Group
Subject: Davis News
Date: Mon, 24 Apr 2006

April 17, 2006

We haven't dragged since the last time I wrote, so I'm sure the anchor is set well this time. Yesterday, a boat near us was dragging and couldn't be hailed, so Marc and Madeline dinghied over to see if they could do anything. Luckily, the owner arrived.

Last Monday (April 10th), we went to Fort Louis, which was built in the late 1700s to protect the French settlement in Marigot. The hike up to the fort is worth it for the gorgeous panoramic view.

Alex played often with the COOL RUNNINGS boys until they left last week (on the 12th).

There's a U.S. Navy aircraft carrier here for a weekend of R & R. We went into Philipsburg on Saturday to see it, but it's way out in the bay. It doesn't look as big as it must be.

Besides the usual boat work and errands last week, we met the couple on the boat next door called GILANA. They are experiencing empty-nest syndrome because their daughter has just left to crew on a mega yacht. She's 17 and has been homeschooled on their boat since she was 10 years old.

There are more mega yachts here than we've ever seen in one place, all lined up at marinas at the front of the lagoon. We've seen a couple leave the lagoon and go out to sea, only to show up again a few hours later. We finally figured it out. The owners or charterers fly into Princess Juliana International Airport and then get picked up by their yacht's helicopter. The helicopter flies them out to their yacht and then the yacht makes a grand entrance.

Yesterday, Madeline and I collected several things from the boat to sell at the flea market—nothing of real value, but may be useful to someone. We had fun and netted US$24 (after spending US$8).

Meanwhile, Marc finally got the watermaker going. (The watermaker part that didn't show up in Puerto Rico arrived here on the 7th.) He was disappointed, though, at how long it takes to make water.

April 18, 2006

Marc jury-rigged our newly purchased washing machine yesterday. It works great and uses very little energy; in fact, it didn't even put a load on the generator (the microwave does). It did use 15 gallons of water, but next time I'll try the rapid cycle, which should use less. (*We purchased the Fagor washing machine in Marigot. Fagor is a well-known European brand, and the small front loader is common in Europe.*)

I don't think I ever told you that though our original intent was to cram a portable washing machine into the lazarette, that idea changed once we disposed of the old generator and installed the new one in the lazarette. Our new front load washing machine fits easily into the old generator space facing into the kitchen. We lost a cupboard, but it's worth it.

Now Marc has a large wiring task to complete. It involves wiring the washing machine and the shore power with the generator and an isolation transformer, and doing it so we don't have a problem with galvanic corrosion.

I'd hoped we'd be out of here this week, but it doesn't look good.

April 24, 2006

Marc finished what he's going to do for now on the electrical work and we started to clean up and organize. We took a break yesterday to do the flea market again. This time we sold US$38 and spent US$28. Not much of a profit, but it's a fun way to get rid of things. Madeline and Alex made cookies and sold them for US$.25 each. I think they made US$3.

Most of our cruising friends have left Saint Martin to make their journey down the island chain. Hurricane season starts in June and the prospect of its arrival weighs heavily on our minds. We want to have enough time to enjoy the islands as we head south, so it's time for us to leave, too. Marc and I are going to Cost-U-Less and Grande Marché today to stock up on food, then we'll finish cleaning and putting things away. We're accumulating a lot of trash to throw away. That's a good thing. Tomorrow, we'll check out of the country.

Leaving

From: sandy_n_marc
To: Davis News Group
Subject: Davis News
Date: Wed, 26 Apr 2006

This morning, we filled up with fuel and water at Island Water World and then left the lagoon during the 11:00 a.m. bridge opening. We are currently anchored in Simpson Bay and plan to wait until tomorrow morning to cross to St. Barts.

Emily fell into the water (here in the bay) but managed to swim to the dinghy and claw her way up and into it. She must have gotten too used to the calm water in the lagoon and wasn't prepared for the rolling waves out here.

> **Recommended?**
> Would we recommend visiting Saint Martin? By boat, definitely! You can't beat the great access to boat parts and French food. By land, I don't know ... maybe. We got to know the island well between the towns of Marigot and Philipsburg. The rest of the island is a mystery. We enjoyed our time in Saint Martin, but I'm not sure I'd recommend visiting a cruise ship island unless you're on a cruise ship. In that case, though, I would recommend it, especially over Tortola and St. Thomas.

Cruising Guides

Doyle, Chris. *2016-2017 The Cruising Guide to the Northern Leeward Islands*. 14th edition. Dunedin, FL: Cruising Guide Publications, 2015.

Pavlidis, Stephen J. *A Cruising Guide to the Leeward Islands: Anguilla, St. Martin, St. Barts, Saba, Statia, St. Kitts, Nevis, Montserrat, Barbuda, Antigua, Guadeloupe,*

Iles des Saintes, Marie Galante, Dominica. 2nd ed. Cocoa Beach, FL: Seaworthy Publications, 2012.

Virgintino, Frank. *A Cruising Guide to the Lesser Antilles: The Leeward Islands*. Kindle edition. Amazon Digital Services, 2014. **I haven't read this cruising guide.**

CHAPTER 9

Island Hopping Down the Chain

St. Barts

> **Saint Barthélemy**
>
> St. Barts—also known as Saint Barthélemy, Saint-Barth(s), and the St. Tropez of the Caribbean—is a fashionable retreat for the rich and famous. Like half of St. Martin, St. Barts is an overseas collectivity of France.
>
> The small island covers only 8 square miles and has a population of 8,800 (2008). Because the island lacks arable land, it did not support slave plantations like most Caribbean islands did in the 17th through 19th centuries; thus, most of the inhabitants are white and of European origin.
>
> The highest point on St. Barts is a 938-foot-tall mountain known as Morne du Vitet. The climate on the island is arid tropical, with a temperature range from 72 to 86 degrees Fahrenheit.

From: sandy_n_marc
To: Davis News Group
Subject: Davis News
Date: Sat, 29 Apr 2006

We arrived in St. Bart's at noon on Thursday, after a three-hour motor (14 miles). We are now anchored at Anse a Corossol, just outside of Gustavia harbor. Gustavia is the capital and main harbor of St. Barts.

A 4-euros-per-day anchoring fee *(costs more now)* is charged for the inner and outer harbors of Gustavia. It's a good way to keep stored or abandoned boats from filling up the anchorages. The fee also provides yachtsmen with restroom/shower facilities and garbage disposal.

We ran into a snag at check in. The port authority officer looked through our paperwork and noticed we hadn't provided our boat insurance information. He explained that insurance is required for any boat anchoring in the port area—including Anse a Corossol. He then asked how long we planned to stay. I asked if we could stay a couple of hours while we worked out a new destination. He said it was okay to stay a few days this time, but to be sure to have boat insurance next time. At first I felt ashamed, but then I remembered that the French love the idea of rebellion and most would respect us for not having insurance and thus not being "legal" in the anchorage. After all, they love a good argument and often protest by going on strike (which we've experienced firsthand in France).

Yesterday morning, Madeline and I decided to check out the town of Gustavia. The red-roofed buildings are filled with restaurants, boutiques, and galleries. It's a duty-free port, but not a place to look for deals since it caters to the wealthy. Nevertheless, Madeline and I enjoyed our thorough investigation of the town.

In the afternoon, Marc and I walked to the beach town of St. Jean. To get there, we walked up the hill behind Gustavia, then down to the other side of the island. The road running downhill to St. Jean parallels the island's short airstrip. Small airplanes *(those that carry 20 or fewer passengers)* descend over the hilltop and land on the downward slope of the airstrip that ends at the beach. Departing planes also take off on the downward slope, right over the heads of sunbathers. *(Pilots must have specific flight training to land on the short (2,133 feet) and tricky airstrip.)* Being an airplane enthusiast and pilot, Marc watched every plane that came and went as we sat on the beach.

Early this morning, we saw racing sailboats come into the harbor. Each boat was festooned with sponsor graphics and was escorted in by various watercraft filled with cheering fans. *The sailboats had just finished the Transat Ag2r race from Concarneau, France. (They left on April 9th.)* By evening, the race boats were lined up on the main dock in Gustavia, awaiting award ceremonies and festivities.

That's all for now—
Sandy

From: sandy_n_marc
To: Davis News Group
Subject: Davis News
Date: Wed, 3 May 2006

We left St. Barts at 6:30 a.m. on April 30th. There was no wind, so we motored the entire eight hours to Nevis (52 miles), passing up St. Kitts on the way.

Nevis

> **The Federation of Saint Kitts and Nevis**
>
> Nevis and St. Kitts are sister islands that were formerly ruled by the British but are now united as one independent nation. They are volcanic in origin, and each has a large central peak covered in rainforest. Both islands were once dominated by sugar plantations but now rely on tourism, as most Caribbean islands do. The climate is tropical marine, with the average temperature ranging from 75 to 80 degrees Fahrenheit. Even though they are only 2 miles apart, the islands are very different from each other. St. Kitts is 65 square miles with a population of 35,000 (2011). Nevis is 36 square miles with a population of only 11,000 (2011). Development is increasing on St. Kitts, while Nevis, so far, is hanging back as the quieter more relaxed island.

We anchored within dinghy distance of the small capital town of Charlestown. We're alongside Pinney's Beach, which is a 3-mile-long beach lined with palm trees. About halfway down the beach is the Four Seasons Resort, which is the island's largest employer (see http://www.fourseasons.com/nevis). *(The resort was severely damaged in October 2008 by Hurricane Omar but reopened in December 2010.)*

Like many Caribbean islands, the majority of the population on Nevis is of African descent, and we stand out as tourists because we are white. Nevertheless, the locals are laid-back and friendly, and we feel comfortable in this pleasant, relaxing place.

This anchorage is less rolly than the anchorage in St. Barts, but that could be because the wind has died down. The only disruption to the calm waters comes from the ferry that travels between St. Kitts and Nevis.

Though Monday was a holiday *(Labour Day)*, we were able to check in with immigration, customs, and the port authority. In the afternoon, Marc and I went to the Double Deuce Beach Bar (right across from our boat) and chatted with the couple that owns the bar and a customer who works for the local telephone company. The couple enthusiastically told us about the Vancouver 32 sailboat they rebuilt after salvaging it as a wreck off a reef here. They take it out often and love sailing. We'll have to keep Madeline away from their place because the owners are fostering three abandoned kittens, and we don't want her getting the itch to add to her menagerie. It was amusing to watch their three-year-old female dog follow the newly mobile kittens around, licking them and acting as if she's their mother (see http://www.doubledeucenevis.com).

While exploring Charlestown on Tuesday, we stopped in at the library. When I noticed how lovingly worn the books were, I realized that I'd found a home for our overflowing box of already-read children's books—most in perfect shape. When we took the books to the library today, the two librarians were grateful and requested our names so that they could write them in the books. *(Interesting fact: St. Kitts and Nevis have a literacy rate of 97.8 percent.)*

After the library, we had coffee at Cafe des Arts, went grocery shopping at Superfoods (a medium-sized, modestly stocked grocery store), and then checked out at customs.

The anchorage has been rolly today.

Sandy

Montserrat

> **Montserrat**
>
> Montserrat is a British territory that measures 10 miles by 7 miles at its longest and widest points, covers a total of 40 square miles, and has 25 miles of coastline.
>
> From 1995 to 1999, a series of eruptions from the Soufrière Hills Volcano destroyed the southern part of this "up and coming" island, and the charming capital of Plymouth was totally destroyed. The mountain still spews ash from time to time and had another explosion and more lava flows in 2010. Check current volcanic activity at http://www.mvo.ms. The 1994 pre-eruption population was 13,000. Many people left the island after the destruction and few have returned, leaving a population of only 4,900 (2012 estimate). There are still lush tropical forests and quiet beaches on the northern half of the island. The average year-round temperature is between 76 and 88 degrees Fahrenheit.

From: sandy_n_marc
To: Davis News Group
Subject: Davis News
Date: Thu, 4 May 2006

We left Nevis today at 6:30 a.m. and anchored in Rendezvous Bay on Montserrat Island at noon (about 35 miles away). Once again, we had to motor because there wasn't any wind. We plan to fly our yellow Q (quarantine) flag and won't get off the boat. That way, we don't have to check in and pay fees. We've decided not to stay for two reasons: Montserrat's anchorages are poorly protected from swell, and we want to cover more distance on our journey south. However, this overnight stop has benefits: we'll avoid a night passage, and we'll get to pass by the southern part of Montserrat in the daylight, which will give us a glimpse of the active volcano and its devastation.

Sandy

Maritime Exclusion Zone

From: sandy_n_marc
To: Davis News Group
Subject: Davis News
Date: Fri, 5 May 2006

Last night the anchorage conditions were miserable. The wind and waves came straight into the bay from the west, and MARAVIDA was bucking like a bronco. Marc and I hardly slept. Needless to say, we were ready to get out of there this morning.

We left Rendezvous Bay at 7:30 a.m. and slowly motored past the Montserrat volcano and the ruined town of Plymouth. I'm sure we were within the maritime exclusion zone, but we wanted to take the opportunity to get a close-up view from the sea.

Guadeloupe

> **Guadeloupe**
>
> Guadeloupe is an overseas region of France. Comprised of seven inhabited islands, it covers 629 square miles and has a population of 405,000 (2008). The economy depends on tourism, agriculture, French subsidies, and French imports.

We entered the protected bay of Deshaies at 2:30 p.m. (The distance from Plymouth to Deshaies is 36 miles). Deshaies is a quaint fishing village located on the northwest coast of Basse-Terre Island, Guadeloupe. The town and bay are edged with lush green hills and mountains.

We immediately spotted Gail and Ken, whom we'd first met in Trinidad on their boat SANGREAL. We joined them later in town for drinks. They are the most self-sustaining cruisers we've met. They have a very small boat with minimal electronics and no refrigeration.

The customs office was closed so we decided to skip checking in and leave in the morning. I'm sure this pleasant French fishing village (with sidewalks even!) would be worth a stay, but I'm itching to get to Terre-de-Haut and spend a few days there.

To see our location on a map, go to http://www.winlink.org/userPositions and click on our call sign KE7BZI. *(Marc has since upgraded his call sign to AE7UV because he now has an Extra Class License.)*

> **Winlink**
>
> One of the best features of Winlink (the radio-based e-mail system we use on MARAVIDA) is its ability to let people know where you are. The Winlink system sends your computer-generated e-mails through a modem and out over Amateur radio. If a GPS is connected to the computer, your position can be sent out each time you send and receive e-mail. This information is then posted automatically to a web page.

We are cut off from news of the world. We didn't even know about Katrina hitting New Orleans until three weeks after it happened. So, please feel free to fill us in on current events.

Sandy

Moving On

From: sandy_n_marc
To: Davis News Group
Subject: Davis News
Date: Sun, 7 May 2006

We left Deshaies yesterday at 8:00 a.m. and spent most of the day motoring alongside the green, mountainous island of Basse-Terre. We had to weave through numerous fish traps along the way, but it was worth the effort for the close-in views of the verdant island. Once we had passed the island, we were able to sail the final two hours with the engine off.

You may have noticed that we've been motoring a lot because of a lack of wind. At this rate, we're making little progress in improving our sailing skills. Sometimes we wonder if we should have bought a trawler. Besides having a more efficient engine, they don't have the extra costs involved with sails, rigging, etc. Nevertheless, when we finally do get the sails up and turn off the engine, we relax and enjoy the quiet ride.

The Saints

> **The Saints**
>
> The Îles des Saintes—also called Les Saintes—are an archipelago of islands that include Terre-de-Haut (2 square miles with a population of about 2,000), Terre-de-Bas (3.65 square miles with a population of about 1,000), and seven smaller, unoccupied islands. All nine islands belong to Guadeloupe. The highest peak on Terre-de-Haut is Morne du Chameau, at 1,000 feet.

We anchored in the large bay off the village of Bourg-des-Saintes at 3:00 p.m. (a trip of approximately 32 miles). This charming town is on the island called Terre-de-Haut, the only island in The Saints with hotels and restaurants.

We cased out the town and immediately fell in love with it. Touristy? Yes, but understandably so, since tourism is the only industry on the tiny island. Most tourists come on ferries from Guadeloupe. Though there's an airstrip on the island, we saw little air traffic—a contrast with St. Barts, which has constant activity on its short airstrip.

The town has typical French bakeries and sidewalk cafes. Little old ladies sit on benches and children run in every direction. The red roofed houses come in many colors—I couldn't resist taking lots of pictures of the quaint shuttered windows and colorful doors.

We spent a leisurely two hours eating dinner at an outdoor restaurant called Le Mambo. The reasonably priced restaurant is one of many located on the main street that parallels the waterfront.

All four of us were pleased with our food choices. Alex had pizza. Madeline had a mixed salad and cod fritters. Marc had a tomato salad, grilled fish, and fries. I had eggplant fritters, grilled fish, and rice. We ate homemade ice cream for dessert, which seems to be an island specialty.

While at the restaurant, we watched the tourist shops close at 7:00, though the pedestrian-only street stayed active. The rest of the island's narrow streets keep busy with scooter traffic. There are only a few cars on the island, but there are hundreds of scooters.

Today the kids wanted to stay on the boat, so Marc and I went for a hike without them. The hike we followed is called "Trace des Cretes." We walked along a paved road to the popular swimming beach called Pompierre, located on the northeast side of the island. From there, we hiked up a trail into the hills, following white dots and arrows painted on rocks. The beautiful views from the top of the hills made me feel like Maria from *The Sound of Music*, up in the Austrian Alps, ready to burst out singing "The Hills Are Alive." We descended to Grande-Anse Beach, which is at the end of the island's airstrip. Unlike Pompierre Beach, this one was deserted, probably because swimming is *interdit* (French for "forbidden") due to dangerous surf. We lingered at the beach and then headed inland, passing La Cimétière Rose, which was full of white tombs decorated with shells and black and white tiles. The complete hike formed an oblong circle, covering the central part of the island. There are two other hikes that would allow us to see other parts of the island, but I don't think we will stay long enough to take them.

More later—
Sandy

From: sandy_n_marc
To: Davis News Group
Subject: Davis News
Date: Wed, 10 May 2006

The four of us hiked up to Fort Napoleon yesterday morning. The steep climb to the 400-foot bluff above the town was exhausting but worth it for the panoramic views and the botanical garden (Jardin exotique du Fort Napoléon), specializing in succulents and iguanas. The fort itself has been turned into a museum about the Saints.

At 4:00 p.m. the same day, we said goodbye to the beautiful town of Bourg des Saintes. We sailed overnight to Martinique, passing up the island of Dominica. Yes, we got to sail again (for 10 of the 16 hours). The winds varied from 0 to 20 knots and our speed was between 3.5 and 7 knots.

Martinique

> **Martinique**
>
> Martinique is another overseas region of France. It is the largest single island of the French West Indies, covering 435 square miles. The island is mountainous; the highest peak is Mount Pelee at 4,583 feet. Most of the roughly 400,000 inhabitants are descended from enslaved Africans.

We arrived at the town of St. Pierre at 8:00 a.m. (approximately 72 miles) this morning, staying just long enough to check in and eat a quick lunch before motoring down island. Now we're anchored off of Fort-de-France in the Baie de Flamands, about halfway down the west side of the island. The Baie de Flamands is a bay within the larger Baie de Fort-de-France.

Anchoring is not an exact science, and we often find that after we've dropped the anchor and backed down on it, we aren't positioned as we had hoped. So, we reanchor. This happened to us here, but when we went to pull the anchor back up, it wouldn't budge. We tried to back down on it, drive over it, and pull it up with the windlass from directly above, but nothing worked. In desperation, Marc got his scuba equipment out and dove down to check on the situation. It turned out the anchor was hooked on the main sewer line for the town! Marc says it's a 12-inch-diameter pipe supported 2 feet off the bottom. Marc had Madeline release some anchor chain so he could unhook the 110-pound anchor from the huge pipe. We were mortified to realize that the yanking and pulling we'd been doing with our 30-ton boat could have broken the town's sewer pipe. Needless to say, when we reanchored, we chose a spot well away from the pipe.

Fort-de-France is a big town and Madeline is excited to go shopping—especially since her birthday is in two days and she knows she gets to pick out her own presents. However, it doesn't look like it's a good restaurant town, so we may move to another anchorage for her birthday dinner. *(We were anchored off the downtown business area, most of which closed up in the evenings. This seemed to include restaurants. The large town didn't have the same French ambience as Bourg-des-Saintes, Gustavia, and Marigot. We didn't even see any sidewalk cafes.)*

Sandy

Diary of Last Week

From: sandy_n_marc
To: Davis News Group
Subject: Davis News
Date: Tue, 16 May 2006

May 11, 2006

Madeline and I shopped in downtown Fort-de-France. Later in the day, Marc and I went to Sea Services Chandlery and Leader Price grocery store.

May 12, 2006

Madeline's birthday. We took a public van to La Galleria Mall and Hyper U grocery store. Around 4:00 p.m., we drove MARAVIDA across the Baie de Fort-de-France to Les Trois-Ilets. It took two hours.

May 13, 2006

Marc and I went on a walk to La Pagerie, a sugar plantation that was the birthplace of Josephine Bonaparte (Napoleon's first wife, born in 1763). To get there, we passed through the small town of Les Trois-Ilets and turned west on Avenue de L'Imperatrice Josephine. We passed by a golf course and then turned inland on D38, headed southeast, and came across the

Parc des Floralies, a botanical garden, which was closed. I'd guess we walked about a mile.

What's left of Josephine Tasher de la Pagerie's childhood estate is a crumbling sugar mill building, the original kitchen outbuilding, and the stone foundation of the original residence. We didn't go into the museum, which is housed in the kitchen cottage, but we did wander through the beautiful grounds and explored the ruins of the sugar refinery.

May 14, 2006

On our passage to the south end of the island, we made a brief stop at Anse Mitan, then motored to Anse-a-l'Ane, arriving at 2:00 p.m. Both anchorages roll when the ferry comes by, but we were just passing through and planned to leave Anse-a-l'Ane first thing in the morning.

May 15, 2006

We left at 8:30 a.m. and motored against 20-knot winds to Saint-Anne. It took four hours. The anchorage is large and open, though protected well from the east. Once settled, we visited the charming French village and then hiked up the zigzag trail (depicting the Stations of the Cross at each turn) to the Catholic Church and its beautiful views.

May 16, 2006

We made the 2-mile dinghy trip into the large and crowded bay of Le Marin, a huge yachting center, visited the chandleries there, and then went on a long hike.

Keep in touch—
Sandy

Leaving Baguettes

From: sandy_n_marc
To: Davis News Group
Subject: Davis News
Date: Sun, 21 May 2006

May 17, 2006

We stocked up on French groceries at the Leader Price grocery store in Le Marin, filling two shopping carts. You'd think that after the tremendous amount of time and money we'd spent stocking up in Puerto Rico and then again in St. Martin, we'd be done with provisioning for a while. But no, some items we've gone through fast and others are new to us. Our biggest purchases here were milk (best price on boxed UHT milk anywhere—and Marc says better tasting), French wines (also best prices), and toilet paper (they have compact toilet paper that has more paper on a roll and, therefore, is better for storage—not very cushy, though).

May 18, 2006

After making purchases at two chandleries, buying four baguettes, and checking out, we left Martinique, our last French island. Our destination: Rodney Bay, St. Lucia, 21 miles away.

St. Lucia

> **St. Lucia**
>
> St. Lucia is a British Commonwealth. The 672-square-mile island is mountainous; Mount Gimie, the highest peak, measures 3,120 feet. Most of the 166,526 (2010) inhabitants are descendants of African slaves who once worked on the island's plantations. Tourism is the primary industry, though agriculture and manufacturing are also important.

May 19, 2006

We sailed the entire trip without the engine! We pulled anchor and sailed off at 1:00 p.m. Four hours later, we reached the anchorage of Rodney Bay, St. Lucia.

Rodney Bay Marina is an official port of entry with its own immigration and customs office. We met with four different officers in the confined little room and paid EC$40 (East Caribbean dollar) in fees. We'll now use EC currency down the island chain through to Grenada. The exchange rate is US$1 = EC$2.70.

The 253-berth marina feels like a ghost town, but it isn't always this empty. I hear it's packed when the ARC rally finishes here. *(The annual Atlantic Rally for Cruisers is a 2,700-mile voyage of more than 200 boats, taking an average of 14 to 21 days to complete. It begins in Spain's Canary Islands in November and ends here with celebration and award parties. Many stay on for Christmas.)*

The marina compound houses many businesses. Island Water World Chandlery is the most important to us. There are also a couple of restaurants, an electronics shop, a bank, a market, a car rental agency, a charter company, a fuel dock, and a boatyard (see http://www.igy-rodneybay.com).

We took a public van (EC$1.25 each) to a small shopping center called JQ Mall. We had high hopes for the bookstore in the mall (Sunshine Bookshop), since we're now on an English-speaking island. It panned out for Madeline, but not for the rest of us. She found the last three books in the five-volume "Outlander" series she's been reading. She's thrilled. Books are like gold to cruisers. They're the number-one source of entertainment (DVDs are the second). Because of this, most marinas and cruiser hangouts have book swaps. However, if you're looking for specific books, you've got a challenge.

> **JQ Mall**
>
> JQ Rodney Bay Mall has more than 50 stores, including a large supermarket. It's located near the southern part of Rodney Bay Lagoon. You may be able to dinghy there if a dinghy dock is available. It'd be worth asking about at the marina.
>
> http://www.shopjqmall.com
>
> There is a new mall next door to JQ Mall. It's called Baywalk Shopping Mall and has over 70 stores and restaurants.
>
> http://www.baywalkslu.com

May 20, 2006

Marc and I went into downtown Castries (capital of St. Lucia) to check out the Saturday morning market and another bookstore. I wish we'd brought our camera; the market was big and colorful, with an old-world feel. We purchased cinnamon bark, nutmeg pods, and saffron.

We find the St. Lucians to be friendly, helpful, and honest. Although we've had only a fraction of the time to get to know these islands compared to our lengthy experience in Trinidad, I think this is another island that is happier and safer than both Trinidad and Venezuela.

> **Safety**
>
> Unfortunately, a month later, a boat in Rodney Bay was boarded by three locals who assaulted, raped, and robbed the couple on board—so maybe it wasn't so safe after all. I believe those assailants were caught, but once again I want to emphasize that before going to an island you should assess the current safety problems by doing some research.
>
> http://www.safetyandsecuritynet.com
>
> http://www.noonsite.com/General/Piracy
>
> https://www.facebook.com/groups/341518759227037

I found only one book at the downtown bookstore (for Madeline), but we came upon several classics for Alex at a school supply store (*Tom Sawyer, The Three Musketeers, The Wizard of Oz,* and *Gulliver's Travels*). We were told about another Sunshine Bookstore on the island and stopped there on our way back to Rodney Bay (in Gablewoods Shopping Center). I picked up copies of *Great Expectations, A Midsummer Night's Dream,* and *The Hunchback of Notre Dame.* Overall, our goal of buying books on the island was successful, and we'll continue to be on the lookout for bookstores when we visit other English-speaking islands.

May 21, 2006

We are anchored in Rodney Bay rather than Rodney Bay Lagoon, where the marina is. Many cruisers prefer the lagoon because it's closer in, but we're fine out here with clean, calm waters and nice views. We're anchored off of Reduit Beach, in front of the Royal St. Lucia Resort. Over to the side of us is a Sandals Resort. After Marc changed the generator and engine fuel filters, we dinghied over to the beach to play in the water.

That's all for now—
Sandy

Into the Grenadines

From: sandy_n_marc
To: Davis News Group
Subject: Davis News
Date: Fri, 26 May 2006

May 23, 2006

We checked out at the customs office after doing last-minute errands at the hardware store, grocery store, and chandlery.

News of recent yacht boardings on the island of St. Vincent—by robbers with machetes, no less—was enough to make us skip a stop there. Too bad ... it would be interesting to see where *Pirates of the Caribbean* was filmed *("The Curse of the Black Pearl" and later, "Dead Man's Chest").* I'm not overly disappointed, though, because I hear the island has "boat boys" who harass cruisers incessantly.

We left at 5:00 p.m. for our overnight sail to Bequia (70 miles away) and managed, once again, to sail off our anchor without the engine. The crossing was smooth on the leeward side of St. Lucia and St. Vincent but rough between the islands. We ran out of wind and had to turn on the engine for the final three hours of the passage.

Stars Above and Stars Below (From Marc)

While sailing in the lee of St. Lucia, we had a very cool experience. I was on watch and it was well past dark. The new moon was about to set and the stars were out in full force. The water was so clear that I could see phosphorescence stream off the back of the keel and watch the autopilot move the rudder, making "stars" stream out from behind the boat in large S-shapes. From the cockpit, I heard a loud exhale of breath and knew that we had visitors. I went up to the bow and watched as the dolphins played in the bow wake. The path of each animal was highlighted with stars. It was like underwater fireworks. For a minute, they would disappear under the boat. Then one would shoot out from under and away from the boat, leaving a trail. The next one would zoom in to swim in the bow wake for a bit. From time to time, one would surface with a "phoof" and dive back down. I called the family and we sat on the bow to watch. It was quite a show, with the new moon setting, sails towering above us, and stars above and stars below.

Bequia

St. Vincent and the Grenadines

Bequia is a part of Saint Vincent and the Grenadines, a group of 32 islands and cays. Together, they belong to the British Commonwealth and cover 389 square miles with 109,991 inhabitants (2011). The economy is dependent on agriculture and tourism.

Bequia

The 7-square-mile island of Bequia, the largest of the Grenadine Islands, has a population of about 4,300. The island has a strong whaling history and "is one of the few places in the world where limited whaling is still allowed by the International Whaling Commission. Natives of Bequia are allowed to catch up to four Humpback Whales per year using only traditional hunting methods of hand thrown harpoons in small open sailing boats.... They rarely catch their limit and some years do not catch any."

May 24, 2006

We arrived in Admiralty Bay, Bequia, at 9:00 a.m. I'm surprised to read that it has 4,000 residents because the hilly and rugged landscape doesn't look hospitable for development.

We napped, then lifted the dinghy off the boat and went into Port Elizabeth to check in. It's a sleepy village with a few small restaurants and shops. We found a DVD rental shop off the main road and rented two of their (copied) DVDs.

May 25, 2006

Madeline and I dinghied into town to rent more DVDs. We only stayed in town long enough to browse through a couple of shops and get Madeline a drink. She was in a hurry to get back to the boat because she was too hot. She thinks that the heat and humidity are increasing as we get closer to Trinidad. She may be right, but I've been hot since we left St. Martin.

The catamaran COOL CHANGE came in today. We first met the friendly couple in Virgin Gorda. Gina is American and Ted is South African. They plan to do crewed charters on their new Leopard 47 catamaran and will base out of Bequia.

> **Charter with COOL CHANGE**
>
> Gina and Ted have a *cool* website for their charter business: http://www.sailcoolchange.com.

May 26, 2006

We returned the DVDs and stopped in at the grocery store, then cleaned up the boat. We're having Gina and Ted over for dinner tonight.

Tomorrow we leave for Mustique.

Sandy

From: sandy_n_marc
To: Davis News Group
Subject: Davis News
Date: Wed, 31 May 2006

May 27, 2006

After hearing that the crossing to Mustique is good for catching tuna, we went to the tackle shop in Port Elizabeth to buy new fishing line. On our way, we bumped into the couple from CALIENTE (we first met them in Trinidad) and the couple from TRAMONTANA (a boat that had been on the hard next to MARAVIDA for a short time when we were in Trinidad). Marc is fond of Phil, and his wife is super nice. They are from Australia/New Zealand. We'll probably meet up with them again in Grenada, if not before then.

We finally got going at 11:30 a.m.

Moonhole

As we motored away from Admiralty Bay, we made a point of looking for the trippy Moonhole rock houses on the southwest peninsula. It is a 40-acre eco-community that was started in the 1960s. Five of the Moonhole houses can be rented by the week or month.

http://www.moonholecompany.com

We decided to motor since we'd be heading straight into the wind, and the distance to travel was only 12 miles. The trip took three and a half hours because we went off course to find the best fishing route. We trailed two 80-pound fishing lines and appeared to be on the same path as the seabirds—but we caught nothing. Later at anchor, though, Marc caught a bar jack with our small fishing pole.

Mustique

> ### Mustique
>
> Mustique is also a part of St. Vincent and the Grenadines. The 2.2-square-mile island is privately owned by the Mustique Company, which is comprised of the island's property owners. Development is limited to 100 villas, one 17-room hotel, one 7-room guesthouse, employee housing, and a fisherman's village. The year-round population is about 500; the peak season population gets up to 1300.
>
> http://www.mustique-island.com

Mustique only allows yachts in Britannia Bay, requires use of a mooring ball, and charges a mandatory mooring fee. For a boat of MARAVIDA's size, it cost us EC$75 for a three-consecutive-night stay. *(The conservation fee may have risen since we were there.)*

We had been warned that the heavy steel mooring balls are hard to hook to because they don't have a line attached. Luckily, the dinghy was already in the water because we had decided to trail it behind MARAVIDA for the short trip rather than haul it onto the deck. So, as soon as we arrived, Marc was able to throw a line into the dinghy, hop in, motor over to the ball, tie the line on, and hand it up to Madeline on MARAVIDA. Their teamwork looked impressive, despite their inexperience with that kind of maneuver.

After dinghying to the dinghy dock near Basil's Restaurant/Bar, we checked out the two petite grocery stores, and then hiked up the steep hill to the Mustique Library. On the way, we encountered a couple of turtles. They were about 6 inches wide and 9 inches long and didn't tuck into their shells until we got really close. Madeline was concerned about the one in the road—though there wasn't any traffic—and moved it off to the side. Once at the library, Alex settled down with a *Fantastic Four* comic book, Marc started to read cruiser magazines, Madeline thumbed through cookbooks, and I looked at the Mustique coffee table books.

May 28, 2006

We decided to walk to Macaroni Beach, supposedly the most beautiful beach on the island and frequented by famous people. (I understand that employees aren't allowed to use it; apparently, they have access to their own separate beach.) We headed out, following the directions we'd received the day before from the librarian. After walking and walking, we finally realized we must have taken a wrong turn at some point.

I took many pictures on our walk, including some of an impressive estate we could see from the road. Later, on another trip to the library, I found pictures of the very same villa in a coffee table book. It said the place was called "Palm Beach" and was Tommy Hilfiger's estate. He had knocked down two houses to the east of Mick Jagger's place to build it.

We finally stopped a "mule" to ask for directions. Mules are the most common vehicle on the island–similar to a golf cart. The occupants were surprised at how far away we were from our destination and gave us directions to get there. We trudged on, trying to remember the complicated directions, but eventually had to stop another mule for directions. (There was very little traffic on the roads.) They, too, were surprised by how far off course we were. We continued our walk until a third mule came down the road and stopped, asking us if we wanted a ride. We gratefully accepted. I'm sure someone in one of the two previous vehicles had sent him to us. Thank goodness, because we were still some distance away from the beach. Before he left us, we asked for directions back to Britannia Bay.

All our effort to get to Macaroni Beach was worth it. We were rewarded with a beautiful white sand beach, turquoise waters, and perfect surf for jumping waves. The beach was fringed with palm trees and scattered with a few round picnic tables with palm leaf canopies. I've read that you can reserve the picnic huts on the beaches through the Mustique Company, and a recommended highlight of staying on the island is to have your hotel or villa pack you a picnic meal to take to the beach. There were no picnickers while we were there. In fact, we had the beach to ourselves; no one famous to share it with—like Bill Gates, whom we'd been told had been there the previous day. The walk back to Britannia Bay was much shorter than the wayward route we took to get to Macaroni Beach.

Because the villas on the island are spread apart for maximum privacy, there's a lot of public acreage. The Mustique Company must employ loads of gardeners; when we walked along the roads, all the grounds that we could see were perfectly landscaped. And there was zero litter; we noticed that covered garbage cans were placed in convenient locations all over the island.

Some might be sickened by the utopian feel of the place, but not me. This is a place where you can let your guard down and not worry about crime, poverty, or corruption—a place where you can totally relax before getting back to the real world. I can see why it's a perfect retreat for celebrities who can't go anywhere public without intrusion.

May 29, 2006

We went to the library again, minus Madeline this time. We wanted to use our laptop with their wireless internet (donation requested), but the wireless wasn't working. The charge to use the internet on their computers was EC$5 per 15 minutes. That's expensive for us, so we kept it to a half hour.

In the afternoon, Madeline and I checked out the three boutique shops, then purchased a few items at the grocery store.

Marc worked on the generator's fuel supply problem. He decided to install an additional, coarser fuel filter that will catch larger sediment.

This is our last paid night, so we'll leave tomorrow for the Tobago Cays, which are only 19 miles away.

Tobago Cays

> **Tobago Cays**
>
> The Tobago Cays are five tiny uninhabited islands located in the southern Grenadines (Petit Rameau, Petit Bateau, Baradol, Petit Tobac, and Jamesby). In 1999, St. Vincent and the Grenadines purchased the area to be a national park. The Tobago Cays National Marine Park now has a user-fee system that includes a daily fee for visitors and a daily yacht-mooring fee.

May 30, 2006

We sailed off the mooring buoy at 1:15 p.m. and continued to sail—skipping the islands of Canouan and Mayreau—until we were ready to turn east into the reefy area of the Tobago Cays. We dropped sail and motored to a spot off Horseshoe Reef, arriving at 5:45 p.m. (That's three and a half hours of sailing and one hour of motoring.)

There are lots of boats here. We're anchored next to JJ and can see TRAMONTANA a few boats away. At night, it looks like there's a little town here, but the lights are only on boats.

This is supposed to be one of the world's prime snorkeling spots. We'll see...

Sandy

Diving in the Grenadines

From: sandy_n_marc
To: Davis News Group
Subject: Davis News
Date: Sun, 4 June 2006

June 1, 2006

Yesterday, we tied up to one of the dinghy mooring buoys along the reefs and went snorkeling. Yes, it is a marvelous snorkeling spot. The water is crystal clear and the fish are plentiful, varied, and colorful. I'm sure the reason for the abundant fish life is that fishing is forbidden here.

Marc went scuba diving today with Jim, from JJ, and Dave, who's a guest on EXCALIBUR. There's a choice spot outside of the reef where you descend along a wall. Marc said it was a great dive.

At 5:00 p.m., we dinghied over to Baradal Island for a potluck picnic on the beach with the folks from JJ and EXCALIBUR. EXCALIBUR brought fresh conch meat they had hammered thin, then breaded and fried. It was delicious.

June 2, 2006

Alex and Marc went snorkeling in the morning and then Marc went diving with Jim in the afternoon. Marc was excited when he returned to the boat, reporting that they'd seen a nurse shark, a southern stingray, a large grouper, and many smaller fish. I haven't been doing much because I've picked up a bout of travelers' diarrhea.

June 3, 2006

Marc and the kids played in the water, jumping off and swimming around the boat. Then Marc gave Alex a short scuba lesson. They went down about 15 feet.

We dinghied over to tiny Jamesby Island in the early evening. Three of us hiked to the top while Madeline made a small fire. She loves to play with fire—a pyro at heart.

June 4, 2006

In the late afternoon, we dinghied over to Jamesby Island again. This time we took chairs, drinks, and our bocce ball set.

If we leave here tomorrow morning as planned, we will have been here five days and six nights. Between 20 and 30 boats have been here during our stay at this anchorage. I hear that in-season, there are as many as 80 boats anchored at a time (many of them charter boats). That's too many. Even though this is a beautiful and uninhabited place, it's definitely been discovered. The Venezuelan islands that we've been to (and will soon go to again on our way west) are just as beautiful and not as crowded.

Tentative Itinerary

Our next stop is Union Island to check out of St. Vincent and the Grenadines. From there we'll go to Carriacou and then Grenada (the end of our southern passage). We'll probably stay in Grenada and work on the boat until the end of June. Then we'll head west and work our way to the ABC islands (Aruba, Bonaire, and Curacao). Our friend Elliot and his son, Neil, may join us the first week of August in Curacao. After that, we have to decide if we're on the fast track or the slow track to the Sea of Cortez in Mexico (the fast track is crossing the Panama Canal in September; the slow track is waiting until March).

Take care—
Sandy

Union Island

> **Union Island**
>
> Union Island is the southernmost island of St. Vincent and the Grenadines. It is 3 miles long and 1 mile wide and has a population of about 3,000. The highest point is Mount Taboi at 999 feet, and the climate is semi-arid.

From: sandy_n_marc
To: Davis News Group
Subject: Davis News
Date: Thu, 8 Jun 2006

June 5, 2006

We departed at 11:00 a.m., later than planned because Marc had to do unexpected repairs to the windlass. It turned out there was no need to rush, though. After an hour-long motor (4 miles) over to Union Island, we found out that it was a holiday *(Whit Monday, a Christian holiday)*, and we wouldn't be able to check out with customs and immigration until the following day.

After we anchored next to JJ, Marc and I took a walk through the closed-up town of Clifton, stopping to talk to a few young men trying to repair a Peavey amplifier. Marc, being Marc, was interested in their project and gave them some tips. We then found an open grocery store and made a couple of purchases. The cashier couldn't break my 20-dollar bill but took all my change, stating that I could pay back the remaining dollar later. How trusting!

On our way back to the dinghy dock, we decided to stop for drinks at the Bougainvilla Hotel and Restaurant.

Bougainvilla Hotel

The Bougainvilla Hotel has 12 rooms and 15 boat slips.

http://www.grenadines-bougainvilla.com

As we were leaving the restaurant, we were stopped by a somewhat intoxicated British man who shook Marc's hand and said, "I know you; you're the one with the white boat." I found this quite funny since most boats are white, but then I recognized him as the owner of DUET, a boat that had been anchored in front of us in the Tobago Cays. His entrance into the anchorage piqued my interest not only because the boat was a Taiwanese pirate-style sailboat, but also because—out of the four gray-haired men in the boat—only one was actually operating it (both steering and anchoring). It started to rain and the group of men invited us to come back into the restaurant for a drink. We found out the captain is a single-hander with three friends visiting. They were a crack-up to hang out with.

Happy Island

On the reef, next to the anchorage, there's a tiny man-made island called Happy Island. A man named Janti Ramage built it with conch shells left on the beach by fishermen (along with some concrete and sand). He runs a bar and BBQ on his unique island; no shoes required.

https://www.facebook.com/happyislandgrenadines

Carriacou

> **Carriacou**
>
> The two islands called Carriacou and Petite Martinique are dependencies of Grenada. Carriacou is 13 square miles and hilly. The highest peak is called High Point North (at 955 feet). The tropical climate averages between 80 and 85 degrees Fahrenheit. Most inhabitants are of African descent.

June 6, 2006

First thing in the morning, we stopped in at the grocery store to pay our debt and check out with customs and immigration. We left Union Island at 9:15 a.m. and arrived in Hillsborough Bay, Carriacou, at 10:45 a.m. (it's only 7 miles away). Marc stayed on the boat—the anchor wasn't holding well—while Madeline and I went into town to check in. This was the first time I've signed in as Captain. We left at noon and arrived in Tyrell Bay, 4 miles and an hour later. There are many cruisers anchored in quiet Tyrell Bay, but I liked Hillsborough better, maybe because there's more infrastructure there—more to see and do. Oh well, we weren't planning to stay longer than overnight anyway, because our primary destination is the island of Grenada.

Grenada

Grenada

Grenada is a British Commonwealth comprised of the large island of Grenada and eight smaller islands in the Grenadines chain: Carriacou, Petit Martinique, Ronde Island, Caille Island, Diamond Island, Large Island, Saline Island, and Frigate Island.

The main island covers 133 square miles; Mount Saint Catherine, at 2,756 feet, is the tallest of five volcanoes on the island. The tropical climate is tempered by northeast trade winds, with temperatures between 75 and 87 degrees Fahrenheit.

A sixth of the land is preserved as national parks and wildlife sanctuaries, and there are many hikes in the rainforest that lead to waterfalls. Grenada is known as the spice island and has more spices per square mile than any other place in the world. Nutmeg, mace, cinnamon, cloves, allspice, ginger, turmeric, and cocoa are all exports. One-third of the world's supply of nutmeg is produced in Grenada. We hope to visit at least one of the working spice estates before we leave—and maybe a rum distillery—since we haven't had a chance to see any of these on the other islands.

Most of the island chain's 103,328 (2011) residents live on the large island of Grenada, and a majority are descendants of African slaves. The economy relies mostly on tourism, especially since Hurricanes Ivan and Emily did great damage to the agricultural sector, particularly to the nutmeg and cocoa cultivation.

In 2004, Hurricane Ivan damaged 90 percent of the buildings on Grenada, leaving more than half of its people homeless. The rainforest was also damaged. But Grenada has bounced back. Both the people and the environment have made tremendous strides in their recovery. The large churches downtown, however, remain an obvious reminder of Ivan's power. They sit in their damaged state without roofs. One local told us that the government hasn't kept up with private enterprise in rebuilding.

> If you've heard of the 1983 U.S.–led invasion of Grenada, this is the island where it took place. In 1979, the revolutionary leader Maurice Bishop seized power in Grenada and established a leftist government with ties to the communist nations of Cuba and the Soviet Union. Four years later, a faction within the Grenadian Army organized a coup to overthrow Bishop and form an even more extreme Marxist government. The leaders of this military splinter group arrested Bishop and his aides and executed them. The U.S. and six Caribbean nations then invaded Grenada, restoring power to a democratic government.
>
> Cruisers' net: Monday through Saturday, 7:30 a.m., on VHF channel 66.

June 7, 2006

The next morning, we left for Grenada at 10:30 and arrived in Martin's Bay—off the town of St. George's—at 3:30 p.m. (30 miles away). Though the sailing was good (up to 8.2 knots of speed in 25 knots of wind), we had a string of bad luck. When leaving, we managed to break a mast step and bend the bimini supports. (The bimini is the canvas roof that covers the cockpit area.) At sea, the only thing we caught on our two fishing lines was a sea bird. Sorry bird. Upon arrival, we tore the mainsail, then had to anchor three times before we achieved acceptable holding. Later, we realized that we'd forgotten to bring in the fishing lines before anchoring. Consequently, they got wrapped around the propeller and we lost both expensive lures. Aargh!

On a more positive note, we have decent reception of two television channels here. The kids are excited about this and are watching now.

We plan to stay in Grenada for a while and get a few projects done on the boat.

Sandy

The Last Couple of Weeks in Grenada

From: sandy_n_marc
To: Davis News Group
Subject: Davis News
Date: Tue, 20 Jun 2006

June 8, 2006

We dinghied into St. George's Lagoon to visit Island Water World and Ace Hardware, then headed to the Carenage to use an ATM, eat lunch at the popular Nutmeg Restaurant, and visit a bookstore. Later on, we returned to the lagoon to buy groceries at Foodland but didn't get to downtown St. George's.

June 9, 2006

We decided to move to the south side of Grenada to be near Budget Marine. Higher winds and seas were on the way, so we needed to do it right away. The trip took two and a half hours. Our destination was Hartman Bay because we had friends there and it's calm compared to Prickly Bay; but as soon as we passed Prickly Bay, we realized that the sea was too rough to pass from one bay to another by dinghy. We decided to turn back to Prickly because that's where Budget Marine is located—and we expect to be frequent customers. (The distance from St. George's to Prickly Bay is about 7 miles.)

The cruising guide was right. Prickly Bay got so rolly that things were falling off the shelves. Marc hooked up a bridle to the anchor to make us face into the swell so we wouldn't roll. This helped until we ran out of wind. There are 40 or 50 boats in this anchorage–I can't believe so many put up with the roll. Maybe, like us, they've decided to choose convenience over comfort.

We made a list of all of the necessary boat projects and then prioritized the jobs according to safety considerations. Marc insists that everything has to be done before we leave Grenada at the end of the month, but I'm the realist, and I know that we'll only get to a fraction of the items on the list by then.

June 11, 2006

The generator stopped working. When Marc investigated, he found the impeller in pieces. We already have 500 hours on the generator, so maybe impellers only last that long. Marc went to check how much power we were getting from the wind generator and discovered it wasn't working either. We spent the evening worried about power, since we didn't know whether the local chandleries would have the impeller in stock.

June 12, 2006

We lucked out and found a Johnson impeller that would work in the generator's Jabsco pump. Marc replaced it but then realized the generator was out of antifreeze, so we had to go back to Budget Marine (again). Once the generator was working, we took the torn mainsail to the sailmaker's loft that's behind Budget. We bumped into Jan and Jim from JJ and had them over for lunch.

In the afternoon, we had another breakdown. The watermaker pump (bought in St. Martin) failed. So many things have failed that I'm afraid we won't get to any of the items on our to-do list.

Meanwhile, the wind died down again and the rolling increased dramatically. We decided to move to the northwest side of the bay, where there's a small anchorage with a few boats—and luckily room for one more. The move was successful—this spot is much calmer.

June 13, 2006

Marc and I took a minivan bus to Island Water World to buy a new pump for the watermaker, then stopped by the Ace Hardware and a stationery shop next door. Next we went to the Grande Anse area for lunch and groceries. Back at the boat, Marc discovered that the new pump wasn't strong enough to pump the water up to the watermaker.

June 14, 2006

We went back to Island Water World to exchange the new pump for a different type. Marc installed it, and it worked well. Next, we removed the staysail and bimini and took both to the sailmaker for inspection and repairs. After that, we put up the large awning so that we'd have protection from the rain. Then ... back to Budget Marine to buy an antenna.

June 15, 2006

Corpus Christi holiday—everything is closed today. Marc removed the pushpit for welding (it's not safe because it has a broken spot) and then drew up a blueprint for the welder to build a custom piece to hold the two GPS antennas. I worked at polishing off the rust on the stainless steel tubing that holds up the bimini, and the kids scrubbed the topsides of the boat.

> **Pushpit**
> The safety railing at the stern (back) of a boat. It is sometimes referred to as the stern pulpit.

> **Pulpit**
> The safety railing at the bow (front) of a boat. It is sometimes referred to as the bow pulpit.

Soon after we settled down to bed, Marc heard one of the cats in the water. It was Maria. I think that makes it three times for her and two for Emily.

Maria doesn't have a typical cat personality. She's more like a puppy. She is constantly getting into trouble and getting dirty. You aren't supposed to give cats baths because they clean themselves, but Madeline usually ends up giving Maria a bath every couple of weeks because she needs it. The other day is a good example. She got drenched in the rain and then lay down in the litter box while she was still soaking wet. (It drives us crazy that she likes to hang out in the enclosed litter box.) She emerged an hour later, her fur matted with cat litter. Madeline whisked her to the kitchen sink for a bath. Madeline loves to give her baths and Maria is used to it; I don't think she enjoys it, but she doesn't fight it either.

June 16, 2006

Madeline and I went to downtown St. George's while Marc and Alex took the dinghy over to Clarkes Court Bay to find the welder. The conditions were calm, so he felt comfortable making the passage.

Downtown St. George's is similar to many large Caribbean towns—a somewhat frenzied and chaotic atmosphere, lots of small shops, and a big focus on the cruise ship business. The two bookstores we'd been told about turned out to be schoolbook suppliers. The highlight of our trip was when we discovered two smoothie shops in a new building down by the cruise ship docks. Our expectations were heightened by the long line of people waiting to buy the fresh fruit smoothies, despite the absence of any cruise ships in port. We weren't disappointed.

Later in the afternoon, Marc worked at gouging out the dry rot in the windshield.

That night, Marc and I went over to the dinghy dock where "Da Big Fish" restaurant is located *(now Timbers Restaurant and Bar)*. We had a drink and listened to the band.

June 17, 2006

Marc worked at grinding and sanding off the rust in the pushpit area and then primed it. I continued to polish the bimini's stainless tubing. We made a last-minute trip to Budget Marine before it closed at noon for the weekend. We like the employees at this Budget. They are friendly, helpful, and serious about their jobs. And the store is better organized than any chandlery we've visited. Also, the girl who works at Turbulence Sails is a gem. From what we've seen, the work ethic in Grenada is better than in Trinidad.

In the late afternoon, Marc and I took a minivan bus into Grande Anse to buy groceries at Foodfair. They handwrite their prices on each item!

June 18, 2006

Once again, Marc started to chip away at the windshield's dry rot, but then gave up and cut out the whole section. Oh no, another small job evolving into a large project!

I applied ospho to various places on the deck. It's a rust remover (made with phosphoric acid) that was recommended by the couple on the steel boat next door to us—ALLELUIA. We visited their immaculate boat in the late afternoon to swap books.

June 19, 2006

Marc purchased wood for the windshield project and worked on that today. Madeline and I walked to the True Blue Pharmacy to get Zantac for my stomach pain. I've been stressed about the quantity of work to do, our schedule, and Madeline's constant badgering about going to Portland. Marc had mentioned the possibility of her visiting Oregon this summer, and she's taking it very seriously. There's no turning back now.

We had Mark and Natalya, from the sailboat FREE SPIRIT, over for dinner. They are a charming young couple from England.

June 20, 2006

Marc got our wireless internet connection to pick up more reliably by using a wok lid. So I spent the day researching airline schedules and fares for Madeline, while Marc worked on the windshield. *(Marc set up the wok lid to be used as a parabolic antenna. He placed a USB Wi-Fi adapter at the focal point to focus the reception/transmission energy, thereby extending the range to reach many times what it would normally be. This only worked when the wok lid was pointed directly at the access point and thus became tricky when we swung at anchor.)*

Some of you may be seeing Madeline soon! We'll let you know.

Sandy

Our Last Week in Grenada

From: sandy_n_marc
To: Davis News Group
Subject: Davis News
Date: Wed, 28 Jun 2006

June 21, 2006

The kids from KELANI came over to our boat.

June 22, 2006

We walked to the airport (a 6-mile roundtrip) to pay for Madeline's airplane ticket—they wouldn't let us pay over the internet. We hadn't planned to go to Trinidad, but the flights that leave from there are much cheaper and less complicated, and Trinidad is only 85 miles from here. Marc also wants to pick up paint and some other items while we're there.

June 23, 2006

Marc and I took the dinghy over to Clarkes Court Bay to pick up the finished pushpit. Our timing was terrible. The conditions in the open water between the two bays became so rough that Marc could barely handle the dinghy, and to make things worse, the rain started to pound down on us. We were soaked through by the time we arrived and still had the return trip ahead of us.

The weather calmed down later in the day, and Marc attached the new radio antenna onto MARAVIDA.

We went to an evening potluck at Clarkes Court Bay Marina. The marina's owners provided transportation for cruisers anchored in Prickly Bay.

> **Clarkes Court Bay Marina**
>
> Clarkes Court Bay is a small marina with friendly owners. The location isn't handy to services, but it's in a scenic bay and they have big plans for the expansion of the marina and its services. *(Now called Clarkes Court Boatyard and Marina. Ownership has changed hands and development is still progressing.)*
>
> https://www.clarkescourtmarina.com

June 24, 2006

Madeline and I took a minivan bus to Spiceland Mall, while Marc sanded and painted the new section of the windshield.

We had dinner at Mark and Natalya's apartment. They've put FREE SPIRIT on the hard at Spice Island Boatyard and have rented an apartment until they leave for home. There's a lot to do to get a boat ready for long-term storage and the possibility of hurricanes.

June 25, 2006

More coats of paint. We used the internet at Mark and Natalya's apartment.

June 26, 2006

Repeat of yesterday.

June 27, 2006

Painted, sanded, installed Plexiglas windshield, and once again used the internet at Mark and Natalya's. Nice people!

June 28, 2006

Final paint.

Leaving Grenada

From: sandy_n_marc
To: Davis News Group
Subject: Davis News
Date: Thu, 29 Jul 2006

We spent the entire day getting MARAVIDA ready for passage, a process that involved taking down the awning, reinstalling the canvas bimini and the mainsail, clearing off the deck, and straightening up downstairs. We left Grenada at 6:45 p.m., bound for Trinidad.

On our way—
Sandy

Cruising Guides

Doyle, Chris. *2015-2016 Sailors Guide to the Windward Islands: Martinique to Grenada*. 17th edition. Dunedin, FL: Cruising Guide Publications, 2014.

Doyle, Chris. *2016-2017 The Cruising Guide to the Northern Leeward Islands*. 14th edition. Dunedin, FL: Cruising Guide Publications, 2015.

Doyle, Chris. *2016-2017 The Cruising Guide to the Southern Leeward Islands*. 14th edition. Dunedin, FL: Cruising Guide Publications, 2015.

Nyns, Roland. *Sailing from Guadeloupe to Martinique: A Pilot Book*. Kindle Edition. Amazon Digital Services, 2014. **I haven't read this cruising guide.**

Pavlidis, Stephen J. *A Cruising Guide to the Leeward Islands: Anguilla, St. Martin, St. Barts, Saba, Statia, St. Kitts, Nevis, Montserrat, Barbuda, Antigua, Guadeloupe, Iles des Saintes, Marie Galante, Dominica*. 2nd ed. Cocoa Beach, FL: Seaworthy Publications, 2012.

Pavlidis, Stephen J. *A Cruising Guide to the Windward Islands: Martinique, St. Lucia, St. Vincent & the Grenadines, The Tobago Cays, Carriacou, Grenada, Barbados, Trinidad and Tobago*. 2nd edition. Port Washington, WI: Seaworthy Publications, 2013.

Street, Donald M. *Martinique to Trinidad: Including Martinique, St. Lucia, St. Vincent, Barbados, Northern Grenadines, Southern Grenadines, Grenada, and Trinidad & Tobago*. New York: iUniverse.com, 2001.

Van Sant, Bruce. *The Gentleman's Guide to Passages South: The Thornless Path to Windward*. 10th ed. Charleston, S.C.: CreateSpace, 2012. **I haven't read this cruising guide.**

Virgintino, Frank. *A Cruising Guide to the Lesser Antilles: The Leeward Islands*. Kindle edition. Amazon Digital Services, 2014. **I haven't read this cruising guide.**

Virgintino, Frank. *A Cruising Guide to the Lesser Antilles: The Windward Islands*. Kindle edition. Amazon Digital Services, 2014. **I haven't read this cruising guide.**

CHAPTER 10

Southern Caribbean Islands

Back in Trinidad

From: sandy_n_marc
To: Davis News Group
Subject: Davis News
Date: Sat, 1 Jul 2006

June 29, 2006

We pulled up anchor and left Grenada at 6:45 p.m. The seas were calm. After a while, the wind picked up enough to raise the mainsail but not enough to turn off the engine.

June 30, 2006

We dropped anchor in Chaguaramas Bay at 12:15 p.m. After checking in with customs and immigration at the CrewsInn Hotel and Yachting Centre, we walked over to the marina office to ask about slip availability. None. Oh well, it was worth a try—even though we hadn't expected any openings during hurricane season. (In addition, Grenada is no longer viewed as being below the hurricane belt after the recent poundings from Hurricanes Ivan and Emily, and Venezuela is experiencing increasing crime problems).

We dinghied over to Coral Cove Marina. It felt weird to be back on our old stomping ground. Nothing much had changed. The same marina employees—Gregory, Winston, Calvin, Cow, Lao, etc.—greeted us warmly. We also chatted with old friends from WANDERING STAR, CHESHIRE CAT TOO, and DOROTHY ELLEN. We even ran into Karl and made plans to get Tyler and Alex together.

As expected, Coral Cove didn't have any slips available either so we topped off our visit with an early pizza dinner at Joe's, then dinghied back to the CrewsInn complex to shop at the Hi-Lo grocery store before returning to the boat for an early bedtime.

How do we perceive Trinidad a year later? On the negative side: There's still a lot of garbage in the water, the murder rate is up, and we were told to lock up our dinghy at night because of a new rash of thefts. On the positive side: The hills are beautiful, green, and lush; the marinas are nicer than most in the Caribbean; and food is cheap.

All in all, we're happy that we stopped here, however briefly. But we are sad—sad to be in this place that will never feel right without Junior.

Sandy

Coral Cove

From: sandy_n_marc
To: Davis News Group
Subject: Davis News
Date: Thu, 6 Jul 2006

July 1, 2006

We dinghied to Coral Cove and talked the office staff into letting us stay in the travel slip from 2:00 p.m. Saturday until Monday morning (during the marina employees' weekend). This allowed us to hook up to shore power to get the batteries equalized and fill up the water tanks to do laundry.

Summary of our first full day back in Trinidad: We moved MARAVIDA from the anchorage to Coral Cove, Marc dealt with a tricky electrical hookup, we took our first "real" showers in four months, ate hot dogs from the mini grocery store in Coral Cove, and then took a maxi-taxi to West Mall.

July 2, 2006

Marc hauled the dinghy up onto the dock to scrape off barnacles and scrub it clean while I did laundry and cleaned cupboards. Tyler came by to hang out with Alex. In the evening, we joined in on the Sunday night Coral Cove BBQ potluck.

July 3, 2006

We planned to take MARAVIDA back out to the rolly anchorage Monday morning, but the boat that had Monday reservations for the spot next to the travel slip postponed their arrival until Thursday. So, we were able to move over to their slip and stay at Coral Cove for a few more days.

Madeline and I went to immigration to sign her off the boat, and then we went to Jesse's office ('Members Only' Maxi-Taxi Service) to arrange for a taxi to the airport the next morning.

In the afternoon, Marc and I walked to Budget Marine to check their stock on items we hadn't been able to find at other chandleries in the last few months. For better or worse, we returned to the boat with US$1,000 of boat goods.

Madeline and I dinghied over to CrewsInn to grocery shop and use the ATM.

For dinner, we went to Joe's with Karl, Tyler, Lily, Lily's brother, and Lily's five-month-old baby girl, Meyla. Yes, we were surprised to find out that Lily had been pregnant when we left Coral Cove last August. Now, Karl has a boy and a girl with two different Trinidadian women. Just a reminder, Karl is German and has a fiberglass repair shop in Chaguaramas. Alex spent many hours with his son, Tyler, when we were here last. Karl and Marc had become good friends, and Madeline and I had befriended his girlfriend, Lily.

July 4, 2006

Marc and Madeline left for the airport at 4:00 a.m. After many flight delays and changes, Madeline finally arrived in Portland at midnight (3:00 a.m. Trinidad time).

That same morning, Alex and I joined Jesse's weekly shopping trip to Long Circular Mall. We found a fantasy-themed store where Alex found a few books to buy.

Back at the boat, I continued to do laundry, clean, and copy a friend's movies to DVDs.

In the evening, we were invited to a spaghetti dinner with Karl, Lily, Meyla, Tyler, and Tyler's mother, Olivia.

July 5, 2006

This morning, we went on another of Jesse's weekly trips, this time to PriceSmart, where we filled three shopping carts! Trinidad is a good place to stock up on food because their prices are a little cheaper than the U.S. and a lot cheaper than elsewhere in the Caribbean.

Marc went to Mariner's Haven Compound to purchase Jotun paint from Echo-Marine. He also picked up epoxy and supplies from the shop next door to Echo-Marine.

Once again, we took advantage of handy and affordable Joe's for dinner. We save by eating dinner off the lunch menu (hamburgers are US$2.50 and a large pizza to feed four is US$10).

July 6, 2006

Tyler is here again this morning—the boys have been together nonstop since we arrived in Coral Cove.

We plan to leave for Chacachacare Island this afternoon. We'll meet up with CHESHIRE CAT TOO at the island before heading off to Los Testigos together. The ham (SSB) radio hasn't been working, so we won't be able to send out e-mail once we leave here, or at least not until Marc figures out how to fix the problem. It's possible that we won't be able to e-mail again until we reach Curacao toward the end of July.

Talk to you again when I can—
Sandy

Los Testigos—Again

Venezuela's Offshore Islands

Venezuela's offshore islands are Federal Dependencies of Venezuela. The 600 islands and formations are sparsely populated and have a combined total area of 132 square miles. They stretch along the coast for 559 miles.

From: sandy_n_marc
To: Davis News Group
Subject: Davis News
Date: Sat, 8 Jul 2006

July 8, 2006

We arrived in the beautiful Los Testigos islands at 2:30 p.m. yesterday. We are anchored off Playa Real beach.

It's been almost a year since we were last here—a year of travel and meeting new people, while working on the boat—a typical year in a cruiser's life.

Once we got settled, Marc worked on the wiring for the radio, television, and battery monitor. Now I can send e-mail.

To backtrack a little: On the 6th of July, we checked out of Trinidad, refueled, and then anchored next to CHESHIRE CAT TOO in Morris Bay. We slept a little before pulling up anchor at midnight. The wind was too light to sail, but we raised the mainsail to help temper the rolling seas. Unfortunately, we forgot to bungee the refrigerator door closed, so most of the contents spilled onto the floor after a particularly strong roll. Marc made the best of the situation, though, by saving the broken eggs until we anchored and using them to make a double batch of lemon bars.

The Plan

We had a hard time finalizing the itinerary for this trip because we couldn't decide whether to stop in Margarita. We had to make up our minds before leaving Trinidad because we would either fill up with 200 gallons of fuel in Trinidad at US$1 per gallon, or fill up in Margarita at 30 cents per gallon. In the end, we decided to choose the safer route, skipping Margarita and not officially checking into Venezuela. These days, anchoring anywhere near civilization in Venezuela is a risk. Tales abound of boats being boarded and robbed by "pirates." (CHESHIRE TOO left for Margarita this morning, so we'll be on our own.)

We'll keep to the far offshore islands as long as we don't get rerouted to Margarita by authorities. Late tonight, we'll leave Los Testigos to go to Blanquilla (92 miles), then to Los Roques (116 miles), from there to Islas de Aves (30 miles), then on to Bonaire (45 miles), and finally to Curacao (30 miles). We have exactly three weeks to reach Curacao for the arrival of our friend Elliot and his son, Neil, though we hope to beat them there by a few days. We'll see. How long we stay at each anchorage will depend on weather and our stamina to push on.

Talk to you later—
Sandy

Blanquilla

> **Blanquilla**
>
> The Venezuelan island, Blanquilla, is fan-shaped, 72 square miles in size, and is uninhabited, except for visiting fishermen and the coast guard.

From: sandy_n_marc
To: Davis News Group
Subject: Davis News
Date: Tue, 11 Jul 2006

July 9, 2006

We left Los Testigos at 2:00 a.m. and dropped anchor 15 hours later at Playa Yaque anchorage on the western shore of Blanquilla. Because of low winds, we sailed only four and a half hours without the motor. The wind did pick up temporarily when a squall came through, hitting us when we were sailing wing-and-wing (jib sail hauled out on one side of the boat and mainsail hauled out on the other side). The wind jumped to 30 knots, the staysail unfurled, and all three sails thrashed about violently. It was too dangerous to go on deck to get control of the sails, which added to the stress of the moment as we worried they would tear. Meanwhile, we could hear things crashing below. It was scary, but the whole episode lasted only about 10 minutes and the rest of the passage was calm. We even caught a yellow fin tuna a mile from our destination.

July 10, 2006

A few squalls came through the anchorage today. Fortunately, we're not in the open ocean. All three of us jumped in the water this morning, and then Marc scraped the bottom while I scrubbed the waterline. It felt good to get exercise, and swimming here is definitely a workout because the current is strong.

The National Guard came by just as we were getting out of the water. We had been nervous about this happening because the Venezuelan coast guard in Los Testigos told us that we had to go to Margarita to check in to the country before going to Blanquilla. We decided a half-truth was justified for our safety and thus stated that we had come straight from Trinidad, were headed to Bonaire, and needed to rest. The men welcomed us and said we could stay a maximum of three days.

July 11, 2006

The three of us swam to the beach today. There are large granite boulders on the island and granite pebbles on the beach.

Life is quieter and simpler without Madeline, but not ideal. She's an important part of our foursome and is missed. We have an offer from Ron Opp to help with our Panama Canal crossing (probably late September). It's possible Madeline will fly back with him. (She has an open ticket because we didn't know where we'd be in September.)

We plan to leave today around 4:00 p.m. That will get us to Los Roques tomorrow at about noon, which is the best time of the day to navigate through the reefs.

Sandy

Los Roques

> **Los Roques**
>
> Los Roques archipelago consists of approximately 350 islands, islets, and cays with a total area of 15 square miles. The largest and only inhabited island is El Gran Roque, with a population of about 1,400 (2011). Los Roques was declared a national park in 1972 and receives approximately 70,000 visitors per year by boat and small aircraft. Most come from Caracas, which is 100 miles away.

From: sandy_n_marc
To: Davis News Group
Subject: Davis News
Date: Wed, 12 Jul 2006

Marc made an unfortunate discovery early in the passage to Los Roques. The gooseneck, on the starboard side of the boom where it attaches to the mast, is completely broken off, and the port side is twisted. The damage must have occurred during the squall on our last passage. We quickly brought the mainsail down to lessen the load on the boom. We were shocked to realize that the boom could have separated from the mast completely, broken the sail, and then crashed down on us as we sat underneath it in the cockpit. We'll have to make our way without the mainsail until we can get the break fixed in Curacao.

Our entrance into the archipelago of Los Roques was a bit unnerving. We had to be extra careful as we entered the pass of Sebastopol because our electronic charts didn't seem to be accurate in this area. Just around the corner from Boca de Sebastopol was our destination, Buchiyaco anchorage. We arrived at 10:00 a.m., after an 18-hour passage (four hours without the engine). We had 7-foot seas and 20-knot winds for most of the way.

It's beautiful here. Our only neighbor is an old wreck stuck on the outer reef.

I want to remind everyone that we *love* to receive e-mail. Some days we check for e-mail multiple times in the hopes of something new. Luckily, my mother, Marc's father, and some cruiser friends e-mail us often, but we'd love to hear from others, too. Some say that their lives aren't exciting enough in comparison to ours, but we want to hear about you and life back home. Just chat at us, if nothing else.

Sandy

Buchiyaco to Cayo de Agua

From: sandy_n_marc
To: Davis News Group
Subject: Davis News
Date: Mon, 17 Jul 2006

July 13, 2006

We plan to stay one more night in the Buchiyaco anchorage. We're at the far southeastern corner of the Roques islands. There are hundreds of small islands here that are protected by two barrier reefs, one to the east and one to the south. The water gets up to 60 feet deep and is perfectly clear with the most brilliant shades of turquoise imaginable.

In the late afternoon, Marc blew up the little dinghy, attached the motor, and we headed toward the southern side of mangrove-covered Buchiyaco Island. The engine died halfway to the island, so we had to row the rest of the way. We walked along the ancient exposed reef in our water shoes and marveled at the aggregation of conch shells covered with coral. We also snorkeled, but Alex and I weren't particularly impressed. Marc, however, snorkeled farther out than we did and claims he saw a variety of large and beautiful fish. The return trip was easy; we just lounged in the dinghy and let the current take us back to MARAVIDA.

July 14, 2006

We pulled up anchor at 10:00 a.m. and tiptoed our way through the reefs, heading first to the northern part of Los Roques and then toward the far western side. We made a point to avoid the island of *Gran Roques* so that we wouldn't have to check in with the authorities. The wind averaged 20 knots, and we sailed with the jib only (no motor) for four of the five hours. The anchorage of Cayo de Agua isn't as still as Buchiyaco, but that's okay: The motion will get us acclimated for the next passage.

July 15, 2006

This may be my favorite anchorage. On the nearest island is a single palm tree on top of a 15-foot-high white sand dune. An enticing path leads up to the top of the dune and must continue down to the other side of the island.

In the morning, I was restless from lack of exercise, so I convinced the guys to go on a visit to the beach. Marc added air to the little dinghy (always necessary) and attached the motor. We crossed our fingers that he'd been successful with his repairs to the engine, and yes, thankfully, it started. So, we motored over to land. I led the way up the path to the top of the rise, took in the view of the other side, and then walked over to that single palm tree I mentioned earlier. Satisfied with my inspection, we continued our walk along the beach in the softest and finest sand I've ever felt. Later that day, I noticed my calloused feet had become baby smooth.

For this trip from Trinidad to Curacao, we've tried to take a day of rest between passages. We read, check for e-mail (hint, hint), beachcomb, snorkel, and watch movies. The passages are tiring, and we've been mentally exhausted from our constant push since we first left Trinidad a little over a year ago. Add to that the numerous maintenance problems and, of course, the projects hanging over us still undone.... Marc says he's never worked so hard in his life as he has on a day-to-day basis on MARAVIDA. I still have high hopes that someday we'll finish putting her back together and then just have the normal maintenance headaches that come with boat ownership.

July 16, 2006

We pulled anchor at 10:00 a.m. and motored out carefully through the reefs. Once out, we put up the jib sail and turned off the motor. We had no problem sailing; the winds have been at a steady 20–25 knots for the past few days. But the passage was rolly. You'd think that after experiencing so many rolly crossings in the past, we'd have everything tucked away securely downstairs. But no, there's always something new to dislodge and crash to the floor. It must be from the varying angles and speeds of the rolls

Las Aves

> **Las Aves**
>
> The Venezuelan archipelago of Las Aves is made up of 21 islands and islets divided into two atoll-like reef systems: Aves de Barlovento and Aves de Sotavento. These islands cover about the same square miles as Los Roques but aren't as "discovered." There's no airstrip and no one lives there (at least not permanently).

At 4:00 p.m., we picked our way through the reefs to get to Isla Sur anchorage in the Aves de Barlovento. The island next to us is thickly forested with mangroves.

Las aves means "the birds." There are hundreds, if not thousands, of them here. Many species of boobies predominate, though there are plenty of other types as well. Unfortunately, when we were a couple of miles out, the birds came to greet us and mistook our trolling lures for fish. So, once again—before we could even think about it—we caught birds on the hooks. And once again, we felt terrible.

July 17, 2006

Marc and Alex went snorkeling. I stayed on the boat with a migraine. Yes, migraines are possible even in paradise.

Take care—
Sandy

Aves de Barlovento

From: sandy_n_marc
To: Davis News Group
Subject: Davis News
Date: Tue, 25 Jul 2006

July 18, 2006

The wind calmed down today. We went beachcombing, and then moved MARAVIDA to a spot away from the island, out next to the open reef. With any luck, this will enable an easier exit early tomorrow morning when reef visibility is not so good.

July 19, 2006

The wind blew hard the entire night and didn't let up in the morning. At the same time, the water was breaking on the reefs harder and higher than we'd seen when we arrived. We decided to put off our departure.

July 20, 2006

Conditions improved, so we left at 7:00 a.m. Despite having repositioned the boat for an easier departure, we managed to bump a reef on the way out—our first grounding. We weren't worried about MARAVIDA (remember, she's made of steel), but we felt bad about the reef.

The 20-knot winds increased to 30 knots as we came up the west side of Bonaire. The strong winds combined with protected seas made for an exhilarating sail.

Bonaire

> **Bonaire**
>
> Bonaire is the "B" in the ABC islands. (Aruba and Curacao represent the other letters.) Bonaire became a municipality of the Netherlands in October 2010. When we were there, however, it was a part of the Netherland Antilles, which has now been dissolved. The population is 16,541 (2012).

> Bonaire's total land area is 113 square miles. The entire coastline is a marine sanctuary. Though there are few sandy beaches, the island is ringed by a coral reef that entices tourists to scuba dive and snorkel. It's known worldwide as a diver's paradise.
>
> The island's average air temperature is 82 degrees Fahrenheit, the water temperature is 80 degrees Fahrenheit, humidity is 76 percent, and rainfall is 22 inches—a very comfortable place to be.

Bonaire is 24 miles long and only 3 to 7 miles wide. Salt is harvested on the flat, southern part of the island. We spied the many hills of salt as we passed by on our way up the west side of the island, heading for the moorage off the capital town of Kralendijk.

We tied up to a mooring ball at 6:00 p.m. Anchoring isn't allowed: You must tie to a designated mooring buoy at a cost of US$10 per night.

July 21, 2006

After saying hello to our friends on INDIGO, we went to check in. There are no fees to check in to Bonaire, which is good since we plan to stay for only three nights. Kralendijk is a small sleepy town with many restaurants. Alex loves the large grocery store because it has a blow-up jumping cage for kids.

It's odd that almost every boat lined up on the moorings is American. This is unusual for the Caribbean and probably just a coincidence.

In the afternoon, we dinghied to the marina to pay our moorage fees and dispose of our garbage. We greeted HEART OF TEXAS on our way back to the moorage.

July 22, 2006

We introduced ourselves to Lourae and Randy on the sailboat PIZAZZ. We were told that they wrote a series of articles in *Caribbean Compass* magazine about sailing along the coast of Colombia. They gave us a CD with the Colombia info, and we purchased their used collection of books, charts, and notes that cover Costa Rica up to the Sea of Cortez in Mexico.

We checked out today so we don't have to do it in the morning.

Curacao

> **Curacao**
>
> Curacao is a constituent country within the Kingdom of the Netherlands. It has a land area of 171 square miles and a population of 154,843 (2011). The economy is based mainly on tourism, petroleum refining, and offshore finance.
>
> The highest point is 1,230-foot-tall Mount Christoffel. The semi-arid climate has an average temperature range between 78 and 88 degrees Fahrenheit.
>
> Cruisers' net: Monday through Saturday, 7:45 a.m., on VHF channel 72.

July 23, 2006

We left Bonaire at 9:00 a.m. and arrived in the main harbor of Willemstad (Curacao) around 4:00 p.m., having sailed without the engine for half the trip. Bright pastel colonial buildings line up along the inlet to the harbor. We were immediately impressed with this beautiful harbor town.

> **Willemstad**
>
> Willemstad's historic city center and harbor was awarded UNESCO World Heritage status in 1997.

I had prearranged by e-mail for us to side-tie MARAVIDA along Curacao Marine's pier on Sunday afternoon so that the welder could start work on our boom first thing Monday morning. We drove into the inner harbor but found no spots to tie up to and no one to talk to at the marina.

We radioed Willemstad's port captain and asked if we could temporarily tie up or anchor someplace in the harbor for the night, but he said no. He said our only choice was to anchor in the bay called Spanish Waters. We were annoyed because it was 5:00 p.m.—quite late to journey to an unfamiliar anchorage, but now that the port captain knew we were here and had a direct view of us from the control tower up on Fort Nassau Hill, we knew we had to leave. Back in the open water, we kept close to the coast and examined the various resorts along the way as we fought the current and rough seas on our way to Spanish Waters.

Spanish Waters: THE place to anchor in Curacao

We kept a careful watch on the map and depth gauge as we weaved our way through Spanish Waters' entrance; it's a long, narrow and twisty channel. Inside is a large protected body of water with many capes and small islands. The surrounding land offers rocky cliffs, hills of green brush, and trees intermixed with cacti. Some of the area is populated and some is not. Table Mountain (Tafelberg), at 637 feet, towers over the entrance. *(It's been mined for phosphate in the past and may still be mined, but to a lesser extent.)*

We arrived in the harbor at 6:30 p.m., totally beat, and parked MARAVIDA as near as possible to the dozens of other anchored boats. In no time at all, we were asked to move over because we had anchored in the windsurfing school's training area.

> **Spanish Waters' Anchorages**
>
> There are five designated anchorages in the large bay. The harbor authority should have maps; I recently (as of 2012) found a map of the anchorages online, but don't know if it's current:
>
> http://www.noonsite.com/PDF_Files/SpanishWaterAnchorages/view

July 24, 2006

I sent an e-mail to Gijs at Curacao Marine (he's one of the owners of the boatyard) explaining our setback last night. We'll wait to hear from him with a guarantee of dock space before we go back.

Our goal for today was to get ourselves to Willemstad to check in to the island. This simple endeavor, however, became a challenging chore. We took the dinghy to the fishermen's marina and walked out to the road. Our guidebook wasn't specific about where the bus stopped, but it didn't matter because first we needed to find a place to get change for our 100-guilder note (the exchange rate is 1.77 Netherlands Antillean guilders to the U.S. dollar). We turned right and walked until we came to a restaurant, but it was closed. We turned around, went back the way we came, and then walked up the hill to what looked like a main road, but that didn't seem very promising, either. We turned left and trudged along for about a mile in the hot sun until we came to the Jan Thiel Resort complex. Immediately, we plopped down on the bar stools at the beach bar and paid for much-needed drinks with the large bill. We then asked about the bus and were told that it came only once an hour and was always late, if it showed up at all. So, we went back to the road and waited and waited. Alex was VERY unhappy by this time.

Finally, the bus showed up, we made it downtown, and we fortified ourselves the fastest way possible—McDonalds. Satiated, we walked the couple of blocks to the big white customs building along the harbor inlet. The friendly customs officer granted us the maximum six-month visit and gave us directions to immigration.

Getting to immigration involved crossing from the Punda side of the inlet to the Otrabanda side. We crossed by ferry because the pedestrian bridge was closed for repairs. (Originally built in 1888, the Queen Emma pontoon bridge operates on a hinge.) Once on the west side of the bay, we headed north, following the water down to the other side of the huge highway bridge. We were hot and tired from too much sun and walking ... and dismayed by the thought that we'd have to walk back up the hill for our return.

Immigration granted us a three-month stay. But we weren't done yet; the immigration officer informed us that we must go next door to the harbor authority for an anchor permit.

The purpose of the anchor permit is to keep track of boats so they can watch for drug smugglers. This is well intentioned, but we soon found out it makes cruising around the island difficult. The young lady at the harbor authority office said she'd give us an anchor permit for Spanish Waters, but that was it. She said we had to return to the harbor authority office to get a new anchor permit each time we wanted to go to a different anchorage. I'm not sure how they expect us to do this, since we are anchored in one place when we apply for the next place; surely that means we should be allowed to hold two permits at once. We gave her a hard time until she went to the back and consulted with her manager. In the end, we finagled two anchor permits out of them. The first permit had to be for Spanish Waters, where we're anchored now. Picking the exact location and dates for the second permit was a bit tricky because we had to make an on-the-spot decision and weren't prepared, but I didn't want to have to come back anytime soon. I remembered reading about an anchorage called Santa Cruz, so we picked it for August 4th through 8th, which falls during the time Elliot and Neil will be here. When we return from Santa Cruz we'll have to return to the harbor authority for a new anchor permit for Spanish Waters. They make "cruising" almost impossible here. No wonder there are so many boats in Spanish Waters—they're being held captive.

Even though we've had various problems since our arrival, I've decided that I like Curacao. I'm especially pleased with the climate that provides us temperatures in the 80s along with constant trade winds.

I think Curacao's capital, Willemstad, is one of the nicest towns in the Caribbean. It's clean, safe, and beautiful. The 17th- and 18th-century Dutch colonial buildings, painted with cheerful bright colors, display an architectural style that could be described as Caribbean Colonial or Tropical Amsterdam.

Curacao feels more developed than most Caribbean islands, but foreign nonetheless. Though the European, African, and Jewish cultural heritages have had a great impact on the island, there are plenty of other influences, too. When I searched the internet for a list of ethnic groups in Curacao, I was surprised to find there were dozens; no wonder the dominant language of the island, Papiamento, is a mixture of many languages (Spanish, Dutch, Portuguese, English, and French, with some Arawak Indian and African influences). Dutch is the official language, but English and Spanish are also widely spoken. Needless to say, we've had no problems with communication.

July 25, 2006

Marc and I took the 10:00 a.m. free shuttle bus from Sarifundy's to the large Vreugenhil grocery store and Budget Marine. Vreugenhil provides the shuttle service daily. We're thrilled with the store's large variety and reasonable prices. *(This shuttle now leaves from the roundabout near the fishermen's marina and I believe there may be other free shuttles available.)*

Sarifundy's is a floating restaurant that caters to cruisers. They have a dinghy dock, a book exchange, and give out a cruisers' information sheet with all kinds of helpful information, including the public bus schedule, which we picked up one day too late.

(Sadly, Sarifundy's burned down in 2008. I'm not sure what cruisers do now that they've lost such a valuable resource. The best way to find out about the area is to listen and ask questions on the daily net. I also found useful info here:
http://www.noonsite.com/Countries/Curacao/SpanishWater.)

That's all for now—
Sandy

Getting Ready for Guests

From: sandy_n_marc
To: Davis News Group
Subject: Davis News
Date: Sat, 5 Aug 2006

July 26, 2006

We emptied the contents of the lazarette out onto the deck to continue the shelf-building project we started last fall in Venezuela. Our motivation is to cram more stuff into the lazarette before the arrival of our guests, Elliot and his 13-year-old son, Neil.

July 28, 2006

The shelves aren't done yet, but we need to sideline the project because we're running out of time. Instead, we reorganized the contents of the cabinets under the port side v-berth bed and managed to empty the starboard side so our guests would have some storage space. We also moved the US$1,000 worth of deck paint (that we bought in Trinidad) out of Madeline's room.

July 29, 2006

We picked up a rental car in the morning and took off for Cost-U-Less. It was another one of those "big trips." We jammed the small car full of food, a microwave (it's smaller than the one we busted and uses less power), and a telescope that Marc couldn't pass up (it was discounted to US$30 because it had the wrong eyepiece).

Marc left at 8:00 p.m. to pick up our guests at the airport.

Guests in Curacao

July 30, 2006

Elliot, Neil, Mark, Alex, and I spent the afternoon exploring Spanish Waters in the dinghy. First, we motored over to Seru Boca Marina, which is tucked back into a concealed cove. It's a quiet and scenic location for a marina, but perhaps a little too isolated for us (see http://www.santabarbaraplantation.com).

Next, we motored around the corner of the cove and came to an area thick with mangroves. The mangrove roots were covered in small mussels, but we didn't pick them because we weren't sure if they're safe to eat. We spotted an inconspicuous opening in the trees and decided to row back along a narrow path. When we came to a secluded clearing within the trees, we joked that we'd just discovered a pirate hideout; however, upon realizing it might be a spot for drug exchanges, we made a quick exit.

Back in open water, we continued to explore the large bay and landed the dinghy in an area that appeared less problematic for exploring. We walked around on the cracked dry earth that was littered with small snail shells and got some close-up views of various cacti. Back on the water, we moved along, slowing as we passed below one of the old plantation houses looking down on us. At this point, we were getting hungry, so we headed back to MARAVIDA, having only covered a fraction of the bay.

> **Landhuizen**
>
> The *landhuizen*—Dutch for "plantation houses"—on the island date back to early island colonization in the 17th and 18th centuries. Because the island's climate was too dry for farming, the plantations served primarily as a status symbol for the wealthy Dutch settlers. There were about 100 of these country houses originally, but now only about half as many. The remaining *landhuis* structures are government buildings, private residences, and restaurants, others are in ruins.
>
> http://www.curacao.com/en/directory/do/landhuizen

July 31, 2006

Elliot and Neil are still struggling with jet lag and consequently slept until 1:30 this afternoon.

Marc started epoxying the shelves for the lazarette.

August 1, 2006

Marc finished the shelves this morning.

In the afternoon, we took the dinghy to the mouth of the bay to go snorkeling. The snorkeling was good, but the wave action made it tiring.

The boys went swimming off the boat after dark. They discovered that the water is bioluminescent, though not to the same degree as the water in the bay in Puerto Rico.

We started a nightly ritual of playing Mexican Train Dominoes.

August 2, 2006

We installed the shelves and restored the original gear, and more, into the lazarette.

August 3, 2006

After pulling anchor at 9:30 in the morning, we motored to Curacao Marine (see http://www.curacaomarine.com). It took about an hour and a half to get there. Marc expertly parallel parked the boat between two other boats at the dock, and we got to work detaching the boom. Erick (the welder) promptly showed up to take it to his shop, which is located in the rear of the marina complex.

Marc, Elliot, and I dinghied into downtown Willemstad. We found an ATM for Elliot, then purchased Stugeron motion sickness medicine (for future crossings), shoes (for me), and some groceries.

August 4, 2006

We reinstalled the boom and left Curacao Marine at 1:00 p.m. Since we hadn't taken the time to install the mainsail, we used only the jib. After a three and a half hour passage with winds up to 30 knots, we arrived at Santa Cruz Bay, a small bay on the northwest side of the island with a sandy beach, palm trees, picnic tables with thatched umbrellas, and a dive shop. Marc and Neil snorkeled around the boat.

August 5, 2006

After lunch, Marc and the boys took the dinghy to go snorkeling. Later in the afternoon, we dinghied to the beach for fries and sodas at the dive shop's restaurant.

We'll stay here until the 8th (at the latest) and then head back to Spanish Waters. Elliot and Neil leave on the 12th.

Sandy

Santa Cruz Anchorage, Continued

From: sandy_n_marc
To: Davis News Group
Subject: Davis News
Date: Sat, 19 Aug 2006

August 6, 2006

All four of us took the dinghy out around the corner from Santa Cruz Bay to search for the entrance to the "Blue Room." Once we located the small opening to the hidden cave, we anchored the dinghy and snorkeled through the tiny gap in the cliff. It leads into a sea cave (about the size of a large room), in which you can swim or stand on a small rise of sand. Because the only light source is from the small opening, the room has a turquoise glow. Very cool.

Back at the boat, the coast guard came to check our papers and make sure we had an anchor permit.

August 7, 2006

The coast guard helicopter flew over us once in the morning and once in the afternoon. This isn't the first time we've been buzzed; they checked us out on our initial entry into Curacao waters and on our way to Curacao Marine the last time. They are very serious about catching drug traffickers.

Marc worked on the boom. He had to replace the outhaul block and tackle because the old one was undersized and shattered.

We went snorkeling again and Marc went scuba diving.

Back in Spanish Waters

August 8, 2006

Our anchor permit runs out today, so we packed up the boat and left just before noon. We motored into the wind, in choppy seas, without sails. Elliot and Neil didn't get seasick—probably thanks to the meclizine I gave them before leaving. We anchored in Spanish Waters at 5:00 p.m. and Elliot treated us to dinner at Sarifundy's.

August 9, 2006

All five of us took the 10:00 a.m. Vreugenhil grocery store shuttle.

In the afternoon, Marc and Neil went out to the mouth of Spanish Waters to snorkel.

August 10, 2006

Elliot rented a car and we drove into Willemstad. We visited the oldest operating Jewish synagogue in the Western Hemisphere. It was dedicated in 1732 and has a floor made of sand. There are a few explanations for the sand floor: One is that it's a reminder of Moses leading his people through the desert, and another is that it's to muffle footsteps.

We watched Alex and Neil gobble down greasy KFC for lunch, and then walked over to DeliFrance for a more dignified adult lunch.

We stopped at a grocery store on our way back to the boat and later took off again for a Radio Shack run. The SSB radio has been giving us trouble, and Marc wanted to try freeze spray on it.

August 11, 2006

Did a bit of sightseeing today, beginning with a drive to the Curacao Liqueur factory located in the Chobolobo plantation house. The liqueur is made from the peels of laraha oranges and various spices. Most people know it as a blue liqueur, but it's sold in many colors here.

Next, we drove up into the northern part of the island. We didn't see anything too interesting, just a sparsely populated desertlike landscape. We did discover a huge run-down church in the middle of nowhere. It fascinated me; what was such a big church doing in this remote location? Unfortunately, it wasn't open, so we couldn't see the inside.

Back in downtown Willemstad—this time on the Otrabanda side of the harbor—we walked around and then ate lunch at Subway. (Yes, we have a new appreciation for American fast-food restaurants after being away from them so long.) After lunch, we happened upon a numismatic museum, which thrilled Elliot. I'd never heard of numismatology before and wasn't particularly interested once I found out it meant the study of coins, but since admission was free, it was worth a look. I left impressed with the high quality of the exhibits and the docent's remarkable ability to keep us engaged.

Since we were near the harbor patrol office, we stopped in to get a new anchor permit for Spanish Waters (I was happy not to have to walk there this time). Now, we're legal again.

August 12, 2006

Elliot and Neil left at 6:30 a.m. for the airport.

Since we're settled into the anchorage for a while, we've signed up for wireless internet service. Hans, on the boat SOL, provides it to cruisers for a reasonable price.

I did three loads of laundry, a job that required Marc's help in carting water from Sarifundy's. In the evening, we had hors d'oeuvres and drinks on the boat NORSEWIND and exchanged DVD movies for duplication.

Getting Parts

August 15, 2006

I took the bus downtown by myself and treated myself to some much needed—albeit cheap—clothing.

August 17, 2006

Marc is frustrated because every project he comes up with requires parts from specialty shops and the cheap rental car isn't available right now. We'll have to try to get it next week. In the meantime, he decided that snorkeling would calm his frustration, so we tried a place on Caracas Bay we'd heard about recently. Not far from a swimming beach on the bay is the wreck of a sunken tugboat. It's been there for more than 20 years and is a popular dive site. Sure enough, the tug provided us with a great snorkeling adventure. It was only about 15 feet below us, covered in many types of coral, and teeming with numerous varieties of fish. I wish we'd known about the site when Neil and Elliot were here.

August 18, 2006

Marc ordered boat parts from Defender in the U.S. That ensures we'll be here for another couple of weeks, at least. Though, to be realistic, our to-do list is so large that we hadn't planned to leave yet anyway.

August 19, 2006

Alex has been playing with Bastien, a Dutch boy living on the boat named SOL. He goes to a local school and speaks perfect English.
We took the grocery shuttle and picked up our replacement battery

monitor from Budget Marine. The one we'd purchased from Budget Marine in Trinidad was defective. Budget Marine in Curacao kindly sent it back to the manufacturer and ordered us a new one. In the afternoon, Marc installed the monitor and then installed hinges on the engine control panel.

Love to all—
Sandy

Windsurfing

From: sandy_n_marc
To: Davis News Group
Subject: Davis News
Date: Wed, 30 Aug 2006

August 20, 2006

Alex went sailing on a sunfish with his friend Bastien. They had fun, though Alex got knocked off the boat once by the boom. Marc and I went to Kima Kalki Marina to play Mexican Train Dominos with other cruisers. We were the only players, at our table of seven, that weren't Dutch. That's not a problem, though, since every Dutch person we've met speaks almost perfect English.

August 21, 2006

Marc and Alex took a 90-minute windsurfing lesson today. Even though it was difficult, they've decided to continue with the full package (three more lessons). We're anchored near the windsurfing school/rental facility and always have windsurfers flying by the boat.

We went to Sarifundy's for Happy Hour. The bar/restaurant hosts a Happy Hour on Mondays and Thursdays; it gets quite crowded with cruisers doing what they do best—socializing.

Watermaker

August 22, 2006

Marc took the watermaker apart to see why it's leaking. We need to decide whether to invest in a new one while we're here. The old one has to run at the same time as the generator and only produces four gallons an hour; certainly not enough to keep up with the laundry.

There's a guy here who sells a simple, high-yield watermaker kit. The cost compares to purchasing the pieces yourself from scratch. We're hesitant, though, because US$3,800 would make a large dent in our funds.

August 23, 2006

According to Marc, the watermaker has a cracked high-pressure vessel, the solid stainless steel hoses are leaking, and the pressure regulator is faulty. He doesn't feel it's worth the money and time to fix it, so we'll have to get a new one. I can't imagine going all the way to Mexico without a reliable water source.

We picked up the US$25 rental car and drove to three home improvement stores. I liked Kooyman the best because of its home decor department; it's like a cross between IKEA and Pottery Barn. We also went to a hydraulic shop, a bookstore, and Goisco grocery store. Curacao has a lot more shopping choices than most of the other islands we've visited. I think it's because the island is large and has one of the highest standards of living in the Caribbean.

Alex's reward for being dragged around on errands was to eat chicken nuggets and play at the huge playland outside of McDonald's with lots of kids of all ages. The equal number of black kids and white kids in the playland (the latter usually having blonde hair and blue eyes) seems typical for the island.

August 24, 2006

We took the morning grocery shuttle and went to Budget Marine, NAPA Auto Parts, and the hydraulic shop. All three are a short walk from the grocery store.

I watched the guys at their windsurfing lesson and observed that Marc fell a lot more often than Alex did. I guess youth trumps age.

August 25, 2006

We made several trips to Sarifundy's for water.

August 26, 2006

Did laundry with the water we hauled yesterday.

Alex got frustrated while windsurfing today because the wind direction kept changing. Since both the confused winds today and the zero wind yesterday are unusual for Curacao, I'm guessing the reason is that hurricane Ernesto is passing north of us now.

A new boy, Jelle *(pronounced Yell-ah)*, came over to play with Alex.

August 27, 2006

The family from AQUAMARINE stopped by to visit in the late morning.

Jelle (age 10 from the boat DUNYAM) and Louis (age 13 from the boat TIMELLA) came over to play with Alex. They were here for six hours. Jelle is Dutch and Louis is Scottish.

Marc cleaned the filthy bilge and drilled larger drain holes (they're always getting plugged). He went scuba diving in the afternoon.

August 28, 2006

We took the grocery shuttle to NAPA Auto Parts and Budget Marine.

I painted the new holes in the bilge and some others that Marc drilled for routing new wires.

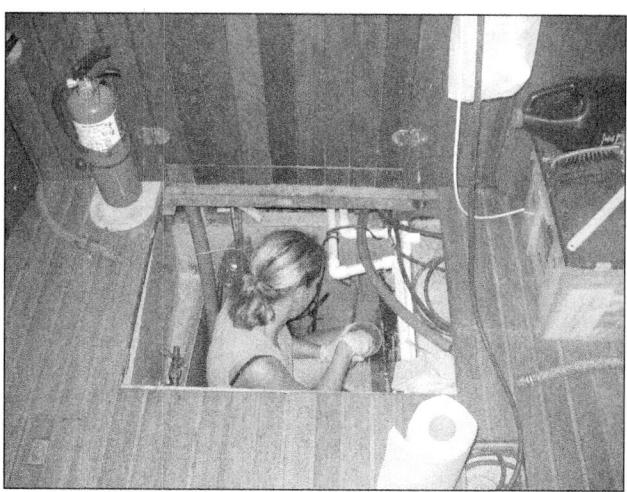

I took pictures of the guys windsurfing when they sailed close to MARAVIDA. Alex was doing great, but Marc was using a new style of board and fell a lot. In the end, he banged up his knee pretty badly. Luckily, it was the final lesson.

August 29, 2006

Marc has been limping around today but managed to install the new GPS wires through deck pass-throughs. He finished up the project by reinstalling Alex's cabin ceiling and the salon wall that covers the radio equipment.

Alex and Louis spent the day going back and forth between MARAVIDA and TIMELLA.

August 30, 2006

I took the grocery shuttle by myself today. We've been using the service about every other day. It's a good excuse to get off the boat.

Marc's knee is a lot better, thank goodness.

Today we approved Madeline's request to stay an additional month in Portland and booked her flights for October 6th. It's just as well, since we have another month of work to do here and the best time to make the crossing to Colombia and Panama is in October. (Hey Bill and Benita, we'll still be in Curacao when you come back to get your boat!)

Alex had three boys over this afternoon.

Sandy

Three More Weeks in Curacao

From: sandy_n_marc
To: Davis News Group
Subject: Davis News
Date: Tue, 19 Sep 2006

August 31, 2006

Marc sumped the keel fuel tank, then put biocide in all three fuel tanks to treat obvious algae growth.

Louis and Siebe *(Pronounced See-beh)* came over in the afternoon. Siebe is Jelle's younger brother.

September 1, 2006

Marc cut and epoxied a wooden board to go in the bilge. It will support two bilge pumps, a fuel pump, and two fuel filters.

Most afternoons, after school, we have one to three extra boys on MARAVIDA.

We had Louis, Sharon (Louis's mom), and Cameron (Sharon's boyfriend) over for dinner. Sharon raved about MARAVIDA's size. Their boat, TIMELLA, is only 30 feet long. They sailed from Ireland and are on their way to Cameron's home, Australia. Sharon and Louis are from Scotland. The first time I heard Sharon speak, I couldn't understand a word she said. I'm getting accustomed to her accent, but when she talks fast, my comprehension goes back to zero.

September 2, 2006

Barry from WITCHCRAFT (the guy I mentioned earlier) came over to talk about the watermaker. He and his wife live on their boat in Curacao and sell watermakers and watermaker kits. *(Their website wasn't working the last time I checked: http://www.watercraftwatermaker.com. Perhaps they have retired.)*

Marc attached the pumps and filters to the new board.

September 3, 2006

Marc worked on the website today. We hope to get a revamped website up soon that will include the pictures from our trip down the Caribbean island chain.

Siebe and Louis came to MARAVIDA, then the three boys went to Sarifundy's to swim (off the dock I guess), then to DUNYAM, then back to MARAVIDA. Alex has a busy social life these days.

September 4, 2006

Grocery shuttle, website work, Louis over to play with Alex in the evening.

September 5, 2006

We rented a car from Limestone Resort and took Alex and Louis with us to run some errands, the most important of which was refilling our propane tanks. They've been empty since we first arrived in Curacao. While we tried to figure out where and how to fill them, we used up our tiny BBQ tanks and then had to borrow a tank from a fellow cruiser. The problem is that Sarifundy's stopped their propane service a while ago, and then the closest gas station to Spanish Waters also stopped selling propane. We finally ascertained the location of the only place on the island that fills propane tanks; unfortunately, it's not close or convenient to reach by public transportation.

September 6, 2006

We've had a hard time finding oil filters for MARAVIDA's Mercedes diesel engine, but that changed when Marc discovered that we can order them through NAPA here in Curacao. As soon as we got back from picking up the filters today, Marc got to work on an overdue oil change. Unfortunately, he had already drained the oil from the engine when he realized that the new oil filter was too small. Luckily, after some online research, Marc pinpointed the problem: because our Mercedes engine is a marine version, it uses the larger turbo filter. Of course the oil is out of the engine now, so we hope we won't need to move the boat before we get our hands on the proper filters.

We had Steve, Pat, and Neil from NORSEWIND over for dinner.

September 7, 2006

We returned and reordered the correct oil filters at NAPA. However, we were not successful in finding a one-half-inch thimble at any of the marine stores. We need one to install the new topping lift because the old line is damaged from chafing.

> **Topping Lift**
>
> A topping lift is the line that extends from the top of the mast to the end of the boom. It holds up the boom when the mainsail isn't in use.

The generator is getting too much air in the line. Marc thinks it's a problem with the fuel pickup, so he stuck a hose down into the fuel tank as a temporary fix.

Marc installed the board of pumps in the bilge.

September 8, 2006

While swimming behind the boat this morning, I was stung by a jellyfish—at least we think that's what caused the rash that covered the right side of my stomach and my right arm. I was miserable until Marc suggested I take an antihistamine pill. It worked great; not only did the pain go away, but about half of the rash disappeared, too.

Marc went ahead and stole the thimble off the spinnaker halyard this afternoon (we haven't been using the spinnaker sail). He used a Samson rope splicing kit to aid him in performing a double braid eye splice to attach the thimble to the new topping lift. It looks great!
http://www.samsonrope.com/Documents/Splice%20Instructions/DblBrd_C1_Eye_Splice_WEB.pdf.

Louis was over most of the day.

September 9, 2006

My rash was itchy again today. I've never had a poison oak or poison ivy rash, but I think this might be similar. Aside from the discomfort, I'm frustrated about being so behind on laundry: We can't seem to cart enough water to the boat to keep up with it! I'm looking forward to getting the new watermaker.

Marc and I went to Sarifundy's for drinks with Sharon and Cameron of TIMELLA and were joined by Brigitte and Jo from DUNYAM. All four boys stayed on MARAVIDA to play electronic games.

September 10, 2006

I winched Marc up the mast yesterday, and again today. The new topping lift is now installed, though we're still unsure of the cause of the chafing.

September 11, 2006

Barry from WITCHCRAFT delivered the watermaker parts.

I worked at linking blogs to pictures for the website.

We found cockroaches on the boat today. Ugh! I've read that they stow away via cardboard packaging.

September 12, 2006

There's a taxi driver named Irvin who has started taking cruisers around in his 13-passenger van. This is similar to what Jesse does in Trinidad, and it's a welcome service here. We went with Irvin today for a free trip to the Centrum grocery store.

Lots to do on the watermaker...

September 13, 2006

The kitchen foot-pump has been leaking on my foot when I do dishes. Marc rebuilt it a while ago, but I guess it's time for another overhaul. Since Marc's busy working at installing the new watermaker, he has temporarily rerouted the new pressure waterline from the back deck (for showers) through the kitchen hatch so we can use it for the kitchen faucet.

Louis has come over three afternoons in a row. We don't mind at all; we have a bigger boat for the boys to hang out on, and Alex loves the company.

We had the family from DUNYAM over for dinner this evening.

September 14, 2006

I took the grocery shuttle to Vreugenhil; Marc stayed home to work on the watermaker.

Three boys came over in the afternoon.

Madeline's return flight to Curacao has been complicated by an airline rule stipulating that unaccompanied minors can't be booked on overnight flights. This is a problem because all flights from Portland, Oregon, to Curacao are overnighters. Luckily, I was able to solve the problem by rerouting her to visit the Erreras in Connecticut for a week. She'll leave Portland on September 30th and arrive in Curacao on October 7th. We miss her; three months is a long time. Once she's settled onto the boat, we'll wait for a weather window and then leave for Colombia.

September 15, 2006

Marc is still working on the watermaker installation.

Alex went over to DUNYAM.

September 16, 2006

Barry came over to help with the final watermaker installation.

Louis and Alex spent the morning on DUNYAM and the afternoon on MARAVIDA (Saturday—no school).

September 17, 2006

We had Sharon, Cameron, and Louis over for morning waffles.

Barry came over in the afternoon to help with the initial watermaker startup. By evening, we were able to fill the empty water tanks at a rate of about 45 gallons per hour! We celebrated by taking long freshwater showers on the back deck.

September 18, 2006

Laundry, Laundry, Laundry. Yay! Topped off with Happy Hour at Sarifundy's.

Cheers—
Sandy

September 19, 2006

The website now has our pictures of the Caribbean islands (see http://www.maravida.org).

Sandy

The Continuing Saga in Curacao

From: sandy_n_marc
To: Davis News Group
Subject: Davis News
Date: Wed, 6 Oct 2006

September 20, 2006

I took the bus downtown.

Rather than fix the kitchen water foot-pump again, Marc installed pressure water to the kitchen sink. What a luxury!

September 21, 2006

Took the grocery shuttle to pick up the oil filters from NAPA.

Put up the awning.

A large red sailboat named ADRIATICA anchored next to us. I'm told the occupants are Italian celebrities filming a live TV show of their sailing trip around the world.

We joined ADAMAS on TIMELLA for dinner.

September 22, 2006

I jumped in the water today and scrubbed the waterline. The boat accumulates a lot of growth at the waterline when it's anchored in protected waters.

Marc foraged for items to sell at the flea market tomorrow.

September 23, 2006

We sold a few things at Sarifundy's flea market and didn't make any purchases. Good for us.

Louis, Jelle, and Siebe played with Alex on MARAVIDA.

September 24, 2006

I woke up this morning with a painful bladder infection. Ugh. I started Bactrim—an antibiotic in our first aid kit.

Marc spent a few hours on TIMELLA helping set up their new SSB radio.

September 25, 2006

Pulled out boat supplies, divided into categories, and put in lazarette. There's much more to go through...

September 27, 2006

Marc installed the oil filter on the Mercedes engine and filled it up with oil. Now we can start the engine if necessary. He also rewired the generator fuel pump today.

September 29, 2006

We rented a car so we could go to a copy shop and then take Alex and Louis to the Seaquarium for Alex's birthday. The aquarium was fun but expensive. We saw dolphin and sea lion shows, sea turtles being fed, nurse sharks being fed, and we even got to pet the nurse sharks.

September 30, 2006

Alex got a mini remote control car from Radio Shack for his birthday. Madeline will bring some other gifts. This was a low-key day.

October 1, 2006

I cleaned windows while Marc did epoxy work, then we did more deck cleanup.

In the afternoon, we had all the boys over for birthday cake and sodas. No ice cream when you're on a boat, since it's rare for boats to have freezers that freeze hard enough.

October 4, 2006

I went for an afternoon stroll with Sharon on the road that loops through the undeveloped peninsula between Caracas Bay and Spanish Waters. There's rarely any traffic there, so it makes for a peaceful and scenic walk.

After many additions, the website is back up. Marc put a lot of work into it over the past few days.

That's all for now—
Sandy

Madeline Returns

From: sandy_n_marc
To: Davis News Group
Subject: Davis News
Date: Wed, 18 Oct 2006

October 7, 2006

Madeline's flight was scheduled to arrive at 1:35 p.m. We picked up the rental car in the morning so we could shop at Radio Shack, Kooyman, and La Curacao before going to the airport. The car's air conditioning died, which was unfortunate because Madeline wouldn't be accustomed to the heat, and it's always worse in a car. She came out of the arrivals gate late, looking distressed; it turns out her luggage had been lost. The flights went fine and she was happy to see us, but she was tired from lack of sleep the night before and, of course, upset about her luggage. We asked the airline personnel to deliver the luggage to Sarifundy's when it came in, then left and took Madeline to eat.

If bad luck comes in threes, then this was the day for us. First the air conditioning in the car, then the lost luggage, then our dinghy was stolen.

Yes, Marc woke me up at 1:30 a.m. and said, "Sandy, get up, the dinghy's gone." He hurried to the lazarette and removed the spare dinghy. Once he pumped it up with air, he mounted the small outboard motor onto its transom. I got the flashlights and joined him. We started to search the shore behind us in case the line had chafed and broke. No luck there, so we continued the search, making our way over to the fishermen's marina. An old fisherman on his boat at the edge of the marina motioned us over to talk with him. He wanted to know what we were doing. He couldn't speak English, but we managed to communicate the situation to him. He took us to the security guard who let us use his phone to call the coast guard. They said they couldn't do anything about it that night, but we should also call and report the theft to the police. We thanked the guard and the fisherman, and continued our search on past the marina. The dinghy turned up in an area of derelict boats, tied to a pole. The outboard was gone. Since there was a road nearby, we presumed the engine had been taken away in a vehicle. Both the outboard security device and padlock were intact (so we aren't sure how the thieves got it off). The painter (dock line) was cut close to its attachment point under the front end of the dinghy and thus must have been cut by a swimmer.

October 8, 2006

Dinghy Theft

We hadn't been locking up the dinghy at night for two reasons: (1) There had been no reported thefts in Spanish Waters for a couple of years, and (2) we were lazy.

We reported the theft on the Spanish Waters radio net and on the Caribbean Safety and Security Net. The Caribbean Safety and Security Net is a high frequency radio network of cruising yachts that meets each morning on SSB frequency 8104.0 at 1215 UTC to exchange safety and security concerns in the Eastern Caribbean. They posted it on their website:

> CURACAO / SPANISH WATER / 7-Oct-06 /
> THEFT / DINK & O/B / NOT LOCKED / BTWN
> 10 P.M. & 1 A.M., DINK RECOVERED ABOUT 2
> A.M. NEAR FISHERMEN'S MARINA, 35HP
> YAMAHA GONE (it was 25 HP.)

We mounted the 4-horsepower outboard on the large dinghy. It moves very slow compared to the 25-horsepower engine, but it gets us where we need to go—eventually. Although we considered buying a new outboard, we've decided to conserve funds for now.

We called the airline twice about the lost luggage (from the pay phone at Sarifundy's).

Madeline and I went for a long walk with Sharon.

Jelle and Louis spent the night after we made certain that Madeline wouldn't be overwhelmed by such a full house. She was fine with it. I think she likes the excitement of having lots of people around her.

October 9, 2006

Madeline and I took the grocery shuttle. She was thrilled with the Dutch food choices.

Marc made shelves for the cupboard in Madeline's cabin.

Madeline's lost luggage showed up at Sarifundy's in the evening during Happy Hour. Very happy, indeed!

October 11, 2006

All four of us went on the grocery shuttle, and in the afternoon, Madeline, Sharon, and I went with Jenny on WITCHCRAFT to bead shops. Jenny and Barry have a car since they live here year-round.

Marc is redoing the engine electrical panel and wiring.

October 12, 2006

Bill and Benita of ALCHERINGA II are here now. We haven't seen them in almost a year. Our plans to head to the beach with Sharon, Louis, Siebe,

Bill, and Benita were almost dashed because our outboard wouldn't start, but we ended up hitching a ride. Marc decided to stay behind to try to figure out what was wrong with the outboard—turned out to be a dirty carburetor. *(The beach we visited is on the open-ocean end of the peninsula that lies between Caracas Bay and the inlet to Spanish Waters. We later discovered that it's a good spot for snorkeling and exploring coral and sea life. Definitely worth the trip.)*

October 13, 2006

I osphoed the rusty spots in the cockpit area. While wearing gloves (the rust remover is a skin irritant), I poured a little at a time in a plastic cup and applied it with a brush. It definitely improved the appearance of the cockpit.

This time, Marc joined in on an afternoon trip to the beach with Bill, Benita, Louis, Siebe, and Jelle. Louis and Siebe spent the night.

October 15, 2006

We had five kids on the boat for the afternoon. That's a lot of people on board when the boat is taken apart in the midst of a project, but I think all cruisers have had to adjust to living in a construction zone at one time or another. It's normal to have to step over and around tools, opened walls, floors, etc.

We finished work at 4:00, then loaded the kids in the dinghy and went to the beach.

October 16, 2006

Marc and the kids went to the dentist. I stayed on the boat because my bladder was bothering me again. Later on Marc and the kids went to the beach with Sharon, Cameron and Louis.

October 17, 2006

Madeline and I took the grocery shuttle so I could go to a doctor near the grocery store. Jenny picked us up from the doctor and drove us to the lab and then home. Thanks Jenny.

Marc, Madeline, Alex, and Louis went to the beach in the afternoon. I'm glad this has become a routine. Playing in the water should be a priority in the Caribbean.

October 18, 2006

Madeline has settled back into the cruising life. She uses the words "I'm bored" multiple times per day and enjoys picking on her brother. Nevertheless, she's still saying she's glad to be back. She approves of Curacao and would like to stay longer.

Marc finished the wiring today. The new panel looks great.

Went to the beach in the late afternoon again.

Now we need to decide which projects and fixes are most important so we can finish them up and be on our way to Colombia. There's been a perfect weather window for the past week, and we're hoping it'll hold out until we can get to Cartagena.

We'll let you know when we get on our way—probably a week or so from now.

Take care—
Sandy

Our Last Week in Curacao

From: sandy_n_marc
To: Davis News Group
Subject: Davis News
Date: Thu, 26 Oct 2006

October 20, 2006

Marc took Madeline, Alex, and Louis to the sunken tugboat to snorkel. On the way back, Marc caught the kids throwing manchineel tree apples and stopped them immediately. It was too late, though: All three kids had skin rashes that evening.

Manchineel

Manchineel is a poisonous fruit tree native to beaches in the Caribbean.

October 21, 2006

Went to flea market.

Major cleanup of boat.

Had Jenny and Barry over for dinner.

October 22, 2006

Marc hooked up a new engine fuel filter.

In the late afternoon, TIMELLA was pushed by dinghy over to MARAVIDA. A couple of weeks ago, Marc had tried to help out with engine repairs, but Timella's engine is still not working. She's now rafted up to us, charging her batteries.

We shared dinner and watched a show with our new neighbors.

October 23, 2006

All four of us went downtown on the 1:15 bus. We checked out of the country with customs and immigration, went to a museum, ate ice cream at Haagen-Dazs, and purchased cheap shorts for Marc and Alex.
Happy Hour at Sarifundy's.

October 24, 2006

We had Cameron, Sharon, and Louis over for waffles. (They are still rafted up to us.) After breakfast, Marc worked on TIMELLA's engine. Our goal is to leave for Colombia on the 27th.

Sandy

We're on Our Way to Colombia

From: sandy_n_marc
To: Davis News Group
Subject: Davis News
Date: Fri, 27 Oct 2006

We had a nerve-racking departure. Before separating the boats, we pulled up MARAVIDA's anchor while TIMELLA's was put down. We messed up the next part by choosing the wrong lines to let loose first. The two boats crunched back corners, scratching paint and breaking the bracket on our barbecue. Marc rushed to cut the spring line in order to speed the separation.

We left Spanish Waters, Curacao, at 1:30 p.m. and we're now on our way to Colombia.

More later—
Sandy

Cruising Guides

Doyle, Chris. *Cruising Guide to Venezuela and Bonaire*. 3rd ed. Dunedin, FL: Cruising Guide Publications, 2007.

Van Sant, Bruce. *The Gentleman's Guide to Passages South: The Thornless Path to Windward*. 10th ed. Charleston, S.C.: CreateSpace, 2012. **I haven't read this cruising guide; the cover says it has sailing directions from Florida to South America.**

Waterson, D. & D van der Reijden. *Gotto Go Cruising: The ABC Islands*. Guernsey, UK: Compass Consultants Ltd., 2006. **We used this guide but it doesn't seem to be in circulation anymore.**
Virgintino, Frank. *A Cruising Guide to the ABC Islands*. Kindle edition. Amazon Digital Services, 2012. **I haven't read this cruising guide.**

CHAPTER 11

Three Months in Colombia

> **Colombia**
>
> Colombia covers 440,831 square miles of the northwest corner of South America. It abuts Venezuela, Brazil, Ecuador, Peru, Panama, the Caribbean Sea, and the Pacific Ocean. The climate is tropical along the coast and eastern plains and cooler in the highlands. Though the Andes mountain range crosses through Colombia, the highest point in the country is part of the Sierra Nevada de Santa Marta, called Pico Cristobal Colon (18,950 feet). Colombia is one of only 17 megadiverse countries that harbor the majority of the Earth's species and thus are considered the most biodiverse.
>
> Colombia's Spanish-speaking and ethnically diverse population totals over 48 million (2015), making it the second most-populated country in South America, after Brazil.

On Our Way

From: sandy_n_marc
To: Davis News Group
Subject: Davis News
Date: Sat, 28 Oct 2006

We left Curacao at 1:30 p.m. yesterday. Our plan is to stop and rest in Five Bays, Colombia, on our way to Cartagena. Since Five Bays is about 275 miles from Curacao, we figure we'll be at sea for two nights.

We are following four sailboats that are also headed to Cartagena: CALIENTE, ZIP-A-DEE-DOO, HANALEE, and PALDAMAR. We hope to catch up with them at Bahia Guayraca (one of the Five Bays) before dark tomorrow.

The seas are light (2–4 feet), and the winds are medium (10–20 knots). One heavy squall come through last night, but we were so busy dealing with it that we failed to take note of the wind speed.

I'll send another e-mail when we get to Five Bays—
Sandy

Five Bays

From: sandy_n_marc
To: Davis News Group
Subject: Davis News
Date: Mon, 30 Oct 2006

On our second night at sea, the wind died to nothing and we were forced to motor the rest of the way. The calm seas allowed us the rare opportunity to spend time down below without getting sick.

We arrived in Bahia Guayraca at 5:30 p.m. yesterday, after 52 hours at sea. The other sailboats were already settled into the anchorage.

The bay is surrounded by majestic mountains with green-forested slopes. There are a few primitive houses and fishermen's shacks along the shore.

The other four boats left this morning, bound for their next anchorage; they plan to make two stops before Cartagena. We've decided to stay here one more night and then head out mid-morning tomorrow for an overnight, nonstop crossing to Cartagena. More anchor stops would use up more diesel, and since there's a chance of having to motor the whole way, we want to conserve our fuel.

We didn't fuel up before leaving Curacao because we found out the fuel dock was only open between 2:00 p.m. and 5:00 p.m. It didn't seem wise to take the chance of waiting another day and having our weather window close up. In hindsight, though, we should have considered that we might have no wind for part or all of our trip and thus should have waited to fill up on fuel. We don't have an accurate method to measure the fuel tanks, but Marc guesstimates that we may have only 25 hours of diesel left. Since Cartagena is still 117 miles away, and we will be running against countercurrents, we are on the edge of having enough diesel to get there.

We accomplished a few important tasks today: Marc jumped in the water to clean the barnacles out of the raw water intake hose, I did a load of laundry, we all took showers, and then Marc ran the watermaker to refill the water tanks. We know we won't be able to run the watermaker in Cartagena because the water in the harbor is too dirty.

We'll let you know when we get to Cartagena!

Sandy

Safety in Five Bays

We picked Bahia Guayraca because our intel from PIZAZZ described it as a quiet and safe harbor. But safety conditions can change, so it's important to get the latest information from other cruisers and from posts made on http://www.safetyandsecuritynet.com and http://www.noonsite.com. My recent research uncovered the following two posts:

"SECOND YACHT ATTACK IN THREE MONTHS IN COLOMBIA'S FIVE BAYS - French cruising sailor Brice Lequertier, sailing on yacht Piolan has reported an attack in Bahia Guayraca, the third (middle) of five bays in the Five Bay area of the Caribbean coast of Colombia.... On May 28 this year (2010), while the crew was sleeping, two men boarded the yacht armed with a gun. They attacked and beat up the crew, then stole all they could from the boat, including passports, money, the GPS, the dinghy, computer, even paper supplies.... The locals confirmed to Lequertier that the area was 'not safe anymore' and that there had been another attack within the last three months..."

Knudsen, Nancy. "Second Yacht Attack in Three Months in Colombia's Five Bays." *Sail-World.com*. 3 June 2010. Web.

http://www.sail-world.com/Cruising/international/Second-yacht-attack-in-three-months-in-Colombias-Five-Bays/70316

"FIVE BAYS—NOW A PROHIBITED ANCHORAGE." Well it was for a while but now "5 Bays is no longer a prohibited anchorage, just restricted. If you are on a zarpe with destination Santa Marta, the Coastguard will force you out of 5 Bays to go and check-in, and then you can come back to 5 Bays! If you are on a zarpe to Cartagena, it seems you can stay at least one night before being forced to move on. Some cruisers have been able to get people in 5 Bays to take them to Santa Marta to check-in."

> Jacana, Dan and Yolanda. "Five Bays—Now a Prohibited Anchorage." *Noonsite*. 29 July 2010. Last modified: 5 April 2012. Web. http://www.noonsite.com/Members/sue/R2010-07-29-3
>
> This last update led me to a new-to-me yahoo group for cruisers: http://groups.yahoo.com/group/Cruisers_Network_Online/

Cartagena

> ### Cartagena
>
> Cartagena de Indias (Cartagena of the West Indies) is located on the north coast of Colombia, with the Caribbean Sea to its west and Cartagena Bay to its south. It was named after Cartagena, Spain, when founded in 1533. Cartagena's colonial walled city and fortress, built in the 17th century, are designated a UNESCO World Heritage Site. National and international tourists are drawn to the old walled city and to the beach and hotels of Bocagrande (located on a peninsula between the Caribbean Sea and Cartagena Bay).
>
> The tropical climate averages 90 percent humidity with an average high of 89 degrees Fahrenheit.
>
> Cruisers' net: Monday through Saturday, 8:00 a.m., on VHF channel 68.

From: sandy_n_marc
To: Davis News Group
Subject: Davis News
Date: Wed, 1 Nov 2006

We motored into Cartagena Bay at 10:30 a.m. Though the trip from Five Bays took 24 hours to complete, we didn't run out of fuel—thank goodness. However, our passage was slowed by currents running against us and uncooperative winds (either nonexistent or coming on our nose). Still, the seas were only about 2 feet high, which was fortunate because the route between the ABC islands and Cartagena is considered one of the more dangerous crossings in the world. To be honest, we'd been dreading it. We took the Bocagrande ("Big Mouth") entrance into huge Cartagena Bay. Upon reaching the inner bay, we passed by the monument of the Madonna and Child. It stands on a shoal in the middle of the harbor, a reminder that we were entering a Catholic country.

Dozens of other boats were already anchored around Club Nautico Marina, and soon after we dropped anchor, Chris and his daughter, Yvette, from AQUAMARINE dinghied over to give us a cruiser briefing of the place. Tired but anxious to get off the boat, we dinghied over to the restaurant at Club Nautico Marina to start the check in procedure with David, one of the agents who hangs out at the marina. Sitting with him at a table overlooking the docks, we discussed our plans (or lack thereof) and admitted that we weren't really sure if we'd be staying for a week or a couple of months. He recommended we sign up for the three-month maximum stay.

Next, we set up a tab with the marina. For US$2.50 per day, we are given access to their dinghy dock, garbage facilities, water, showers, and other amenities. The facilities appear a bit dilapidated from time and use, but not neglected—they're serviceable and clean. (See http://www.clubnauticocartagena.com.)

Having left Club Nautico through a gateway that opens onto the street, we saw a yellow taxi and a couple of rickshaws parked by the curb, the drivers talking as they waited for potential passengers. They looked at us questioningly, but we nodded our heads no, pointing instead toward the street that we were told would lead to a nearby grocery store. We crossed the street and walked a block and a half inland to the Carulla market. The immediate area and the store itself are modern. Carulla's is smaller and offers less variety than the megastores in Curacao, but its polished appearance and cool air are welcoming.

After purchasing a few items, we returned to Club Nautico, where we were approached by a fellow cruiser who delivered some startling news: MARAVIDA had been hit by another boat in the anchorage. As we headed over to see the extent of the damage, Chris on AQUAMARINE flagged us down and told us what he knew about the collision. Apparently, the offender hadn't been paying attention and was going 6 knots when his boat, DOMANI, hit MARAVIDA square on the side.

The man—his name is Bruno—and his girlfriend had left the accident scene to go anchor their boat, but they returned to MARAVIDA in their dinghy. They were surveying MARAVIDA's damage when we arrived. The kids and I cried when we saw our wounded boat; we knew from experience how much work would be required to fix it. Marc's immediate reaction was pure anger. The couple was distressed and apologetic, and when Marc calmed down, they were able to discuss a plan of action. Neither of us has insurance. *(Note: Many cruisers don't have boat insurance because they can't afford it, or because they plan to venture into areas not covered. I believe Colombia is on the prohibited list of most insurance carriers.)*

MARAVIDA will have to go to a boatyard. A bathroom window was damaged beyond repair (we will have to order a replacement), and the buckled topsides surrounding the window need to be reshaped somehow. The 2-inch steel toerail is busted and bent with pieces of the wooden boat wedged into it–a few feet of this will have to be cut out and replaced with new steel. Two stanchions are bent almost in half. If she weren't made of steel, MARAVIDA would have been destroyed. It's a good thing neither boat is made of fiberglass; otherwise, one or both of them might have sunk.

Marc has dinghied over to DOMANI to examine its damage and to give the owner, Bruno, a bottle of French wine to apologize for his harsh words.

Sandy

Impressions of Cartagena

From: sandy_n_marc
To: Davis News Group
Subject: Davis News
Date: Fri, 3 Nov 2006

Though the water in Cartagena Harbor is muddy and polluted, the scenery from the anchorage is captivating. Our 360-degree view consists of: high-rises in the business district on the Bocagrande peninsula to our west; ships docked at the Colombian Naval Base to our northwest; the old walled city to our north; the residential high-rise area called Manga to our east (where we alight from our dinghy at Club Nautico); Cartagena's busy shipyards to the southeast; and finally, the mouth of the bay directly south of us.

With a population of more than a million, Cartagena is the largest city we've traveled to with MARAVIDA. Inland travel, outside of Colombia's metropolitan areas, is not recommended, but Cartagena is considered a safe city.

It's definitely hotter and less windy than Curacao.

Emily fell off the boat at 3:00 a.m. yesterday. Marc scooped her out of the brackish water with the fishing net and gave her a bath in the kitchen sink.

In the late morning, we showered at the marina and then took MARAVIDA to Ferroalquimar boatyard (see http://ferroalquimar.com). We followed DOMANI there, heading southeast from the anchorage for about 5 miles, then we anchored off the busy boatyard and waited for Bruno to transport the welder to MARAVIDA for an assessment of the damage. They made a plan for us to return on Monday at 8:00 a.m. for the repairs. I think they've decided they can do the work from the dock and thus save the cost of hauling MARAVIDA out of the water.

We left Bruno and DOMANI at Ferroalquimar to return to the anchorage. Not far from the yard, though, we hit bottom and came to a complete stop. Fortunately, a tugboat passed by and the driver helped us maneuver off the shoal by pointing us in the right direction. After using full engine power, we broke free from the mud, but it wasn't long before we hit again. (Too bad the shallow spots aren't marked!) Thanks to a strong engine and propeller, though, we finally got away from the shoaly area. We're certainly not looking forward to the return journey on Monday.

After reanchoring near Club Nautico, we walked to the old city; it took about 20 minutes to get there. We were immediately impressed with the walled town: Ancient buildings embellished with wrought iron balconies and cascading flowers shade the narrow cobbled streets. Some of the old churches, public squares, and colonial structures are crumbling with washed-out pastel facades; others are pristinely renovated—painted with vivid colors proudly announcing their restoration. The romantic ambiance of Old Town makes it a perfect place for a leisurely stroll.

Our mission was not only to see the town but also to locate a tourist office to get our hands on a map of the city. In addition, we hoped to find a shop that sold cheap Colombian flags because we don't have a courtesy flag for Colombia. A small courtesy flag is flown out of respect to the country that is being visited. *(I don't think I mentioned this before, but while we were in Trinidad, a fellow cruiser recommended a place in Asia that made cheap flags. So, we took our best guess of which countries we would visit and had the flags made.)*

We didn't find a tourist office or any Colombian flags, but we did stumble upon a gourmet ice cream shop with cones for 2,800 pesos. (I think the current exchange rate is about 2,300 pesos to the dollar.) After that, we walked and walked and eventually became too hungry and tired to go any farther.

We ducked into a restaurant called American Broasted Chicken and had ... a pizza. *(I have no memory of the food itself, but I do remember a lot of red and yellow neon signs, a sticky floor and table, and an angry daughter.)* Madeline was livid with us for not finding a more traditional restaurant, but at the time, the rest of us couldn't walk another step. Once our hunger was relieved—even if it wasn't with authentic Colombian cuisine—we gladly spent 5,000 pesos on a taxi ride back to the marina.

The long day was topped off by fireworks at midnight. Though Independence Day isn't until November 11th, it seems the celebrations start early in Cartagena.

Bruno came by this morning to tell us that he'll ride with us to the yard on Monday and help direct us past the shoals. He'll pay for the repairs and the replacement window, but we'll have to be patient while we wait for the window to get here from the States.

After borrowing a city map from the couple on CABARET, we took a taxi to Old Town. Since it was lunchtime, our first destination was a highly recommended restaurant called El Bistro (see http://www.el-bistro-cartagena.com). We each dined on a three-course, 8,000-peso "menu" that consisted of soup, salad, and a main dish.

The delicious meal renewed our energy, and we wandered around the town for a couple of hours taking pictures. When we came upon a restaurant called "Crepes y Waffles" that served ice cream, we decided we were ready to sit down, rest our feet, and have a treat. The high ceilings, tall windows, and elegant décor seemed a bit excessive for an ice cream and waffles place, but the dessert menu—filled with enticing pictures of frozen masterpieces—was just as impressive as the shop itself. After much contemplation, we each ordered an elaborate ice cream dish (ranging from 3,300 to 5,500 pesos). Then we walked around a little more before taking a taxi back to the marina, our hands empty but our stomachs full. *(Note: We ran into many cruisers in Cartagena who had already discovered Crepes & Waffles and raved about it. I didn't know this at the time, but there are Crepes & Waffles franchises in many Spanish-speaking countries, including Brazil, Chili, Colombia, Ecuador, Spain, Mexico, Panama, Peru, and Venezuela. Colombia has the most locations, which makes sense considering the chain originated there. See* http://crepesywaffles.com.*)*

There's a refreshing breeze this evening. We're out on deck, enjoying it and hoping the boat will cool down better tonight.

Sandy

Diary of the week

From: sandy_n_marc
To: Davis News Group
Subject: Davis News
Date: Fri, 10 Nov 2006

November 4, 2006

We were invited to go on an outing to Fort San Felipe with a group of cruisers and their kids from the boats AQUAMARINE, MENKE, YOMANA, and DUCHESS. All great people, though unfortunately, their kids' ages don't match well with Madeline and Alex's ages. To get to the fort, we walked east from the marina for about 20 minutes. The location is obvious, since the massive castle is set on a hill overlooking the entire city and harbor. It's filled with an extensive system of underground tunnels that the kids enjoyed exploring.

> **Fort San Felipe**
>
> El Castillo de San Felipe de Barajas was originally built in 1536, then expanded further—first in 1657 and again in 1763. It was Spain's largest fortification in the New World. Now a UNESCO World Heritage Site, the castle is often used for cultural events.

November 5, 2006

Madeline and I wanted to explore the Bocagrande area, so Marc drove us over and dropped us off at a public dock. We were surprised to see that the buildings are residential high-rises, not business high-rises as we'd thought. Though beautiful when lit up at night, some are getting old and I wouldn't trust their stability in an earthquake. We walked the few blocks across the peninsula to the Caribbean Sea, which is lined with crowded beaches and tourist shops. It didn't take long for us to finish our examination of the Bocagrande neighborhood and turn our sights toward our preferred part of town. The trek to Old Town was tiring, but we rewarded ourselves with ice cream at our new favorite spot, Crepes & Waffles.

For the journey back to the marina, Madeline and I opted for a different mode of transportation: the bus. After making sure the bus was headed to Manga, we jumped aboard. It was crowded and we had to stand the entire trip, which was long because the route was indirect and the stops frequent. In the end, we agreed that riding the bus in Cartagena was too long and exhausting to be worth the 1,800 pesos. *(From then on, we either walked to and from Old Town or spent the 4,000 to 5,000 pesos for a taxi ride home, utilizing the latter especially when we were hauling heavy purchases or just too tired to walk any farther.)*

November 6, 2006

We discovered that today is an official holiday and everything is closed, so we'll go to the boatyard tomorrow. The fuel dock is open, though, so we motored over to fill our fuel and water tanks (325 gallons of diesel). At US$2 per gallon, diesel costs twice as much here as it does in Trinidad and a lot more than in Venezuela, but it's still cheaper than in the U.S.

November 7, 2006

We tied MARAVIDA up to Ferroalquimar's dock at 9:00 a.m., and the welders immediately got to work. Marc supervised and Bruno came by often.

Bruno is German, around our age, and separated from his wife. He has a volatile relationship with his Colombian girlfriend, who is in her twenties. I guess they were arguing when DOMANI hit MARAVIDA.

We ate lunch at the boatyard cafeteria where the boat workers eat. It was cheap, filling, and good: soup, rice, chicken, pasta, salad, and drink.

I spent the day cleaning MARAVIDA's interior and doing three loads of laundry, taking full advantage of the unlimited water source.

By the end of the workday, the workers had cut out a four-foot piece of the toerail and welded in a new one. They also bent the window area back into shape, making it as straight as possible. Since they didn't have time to work on the two broken stanchions, they kept them to do later.

At 5:00 p.m., Marc filled the water tanks, then sprayed the mud off the boat (from the collision—probably from DOMANI's anchor). We then motored back to the anchorage next to Club Nautico and anchored in the dark.

On our passage to Colombia, we passed through a time zone. At about the same time, the U.S. changed to daylight savings time, so I think that means we still have a three-hour time difference from the West Coast of the States. The difference for us is that instead of getting dark at 6:30, it now gets dark at 5:30.

November 8, 2006

Marc's 44th birthday. We had breakfast at the marina restaurant and then took a taxi to Home Mart and Olympica. Once the kids heard that Home Mart is the closest thing to a Home Depot here, they decided to stay back at the boat. Not surprising, since they've had more exposure to Home Depot in their lives than most kids, and they're not fond of it. It turned out, however, to be just an upscale variety store with a tool section. Olympica is a grocery store adjacent to Home Mart that we wanted to try, but it's not worth a trip back. Carulla's is handier and offers just as much variety.

The grocery store food selection in Colombia is comparable to mainland Venezuela—simple, with limited choices. We were surprised that grocery prices in Colombia aren't cheaper than in Curacao. From what I've heard, Panama will have the lowest prices.

In the late afternoon, Marc and I went to an internet café that's located between the marina and Carulla's. We wanted to check our finances and send e-mail messages.

A little later I left Marc at the marina's Happy Hour and dinghied to MARAVIDA to check on the kids. They were fine and had a plan for dinner, so I returned to Marc and we walked down the block to a restaurant called Danna's House. Most of its seating is outside in the back garden area. There are trees, twinkle lights, and a large grassy area with children's play equipment; a quiet and pleasant place to relax. We both chose a meal of shish kabobs, baked potatoes, and salad for only 6,500 pesos each.

November 9, 2006

Marc spent most of the day helping Bruno work on his generator. Madeline took a beading class at the marina where she learned to crochet beads into a necklace. Some of the women in the class had trouble with it, but Madeline caught on fast.

November 10, 2006

We took a taxi to Exito and Castellana Shopping Mall, which are across the street from each other. We had no problem getting Madeline to join in when she heard the word *mall*, and Alex knew he needed to get off the boat to stretch his legs, so he didn't complain about going.

Exito is similar to a Walmart. Castellana is a large outdoor mall with movie theaters and crowds of people shopping and socializing. To get there, the taxi took a major roadway called Pedro de Heredia that heads southeast from Old Town. The avenue runs through a large portion of Cartagena and is congested with businesses and traffic. On the way, we passed two large stadium complexes, one a bullring and the other a *futbol* stadium. They stood out because they were so big and new compared to the old and run-down businesses along the way. The taxi ride cost 7,000 pesos, which seemed reasonable since the distance was probably 5 or 6 miles compared to the mile between Club Nautico and Old Town.

We ate lunch at the Vivero grocery store that's at the mall—all the large grocery stores here have cafeterias.

That's it for now—
Sandy

Another Couple of Weeks

From: sandy_n_marc
To: Davis News Group
Subject: Davis News
Date: Thu, 23 Nov 2006

November 11, 2006

We started work on MARAVIDA's injuries today. To get her back to her former state, we must grind, sand, prime, fill, sand, prime, sand, and then finally top coat the repaired areas. This process is not overkill: It's necessary to prevent rust on a steel boat. Today Marc did some grinding and sanding, and then I primed the area. It's miserable work in this hot and humid climate.

November 12, 2006

We sanded and painted all morning. Later on, when we went to the marina to take showers, we had to bypass an event taking up the entire bar and restaurant: It was a beauty contest for young girls. The girls, probably between the ages of 6 and 14, were wearing swimsuits and full makeup. The concept was disturbing to us but customary for the people of Colombia.

Colombian women are very beautiful and obviously take great pride in their appearance. They wear eye-catching makeup, high heels, and sexy clothing, while maintaining the respect that a devout catholic woman and her family expect.

November 13, 2006

Marc made a few dinghy trips to the marina to fill the water jugs so I could do laundry.

November 14, 2006

The four of us took a taxi to Makro today. We'd been told that the store is similar to Costco at home, but we were disappointed with their stock and found little to buy.

November 15, 2006

We spent a lazy day on board enjoying the rain, thunder, and lightning that continued all day.

November 16, 2006

Marc and I went downtown for the afternoon. We purchased some sewing supplies and then went to ... you guessed it ... Crepes & Waffles. We ran into the couple from CALIENTE there and spent a pleasant hour chatting with them. In the evening, we joined the couple from PALDAMAR at a simple outdoor pizzeria close to the marina. Afterward, we strolled to Mimos for (more) ice cream.

November 17, 2006

When we got up this morning we noticed that all the navy ships across the bay were decorated with flags; some of the ships were new to the harbor, and one was a submarine. We spent the day sanding, filling, and painting and were surprised to hear a band playing late in the afternoon. It turned out to be a military band announcing the entrance of the large, three-masted sailing vessel GLORIA into the harbor. *(GLORIA is a Colombian Navy training ship.)* With our binoculars, we could see Colombian sailors lined up on the spreaders of the masts. Military personnel were also lined up and standing at attention on other ships in the harbor. It was quite a sight when all the vessels lit up at dusk.

November 21, 2006

I haven't been feeling well the last few days—probably the flu. Marc took the anchor windlass gypsy to a machine shop for repairs. The gypsy has been worn down from guiding anchor chain that's not the correct size. We'll look into getting new chain in Panama.

In the afternoon, Marc and Madeline grocery shopped for Thanksgiving dinner.

November 22, 2006

I'm back to a useful state. Marc sanded and I painted. I'm hoping this is the last layer of primer and we'll finish up with the top coat soon. The stainless steel stanchions haven't come back yet.

Marc and I walked to a butcher shop to buy a whole chicken for Thanksgiving tomorrow. While we were gone, Madeline made an apple pie.

Marc sold our old watermaker to Paul from PALDAMAR.

We're having generator problems.

The harbor is closed to outgoing boat traffic. I guess current offshore conditions (waves and swells) are dangerous and the coast guard is not letting boats leave. Aside from the rain, the inner harbor is unaffected.

November 23, 2006

HAPPY THANKSGIVING!

Madeline is making the dinner again, just like last year. She loves holidays.

Alex remains cheerful despite having no kids to hang out with here. Bruno lent him some computer games and he's been engrossed with SIMS 2 for the past week.

We are thankful for our family, friends, health, and MARAVIDA's dependability.

Love,
Sandy, Marc, Madeline, and Alex

P.S. The harbor was closed again today.

Staying for Christmas

From: sandy_n_marc
To: Davis News Group
Subject: Davis News
Date: Tue, 5 Dec 2006

We made the decision yesterday to stay here in Cartagena through Christmas. We are so far behind schedule that we actually have no schedule anymore. Madeline wants to be here for Christmas: She doesn't want to spend Christmas in "the middle of nowhere" (San Blas Islands), or in Colon Panama, which is "the unknown." From the reading I've done about Colon (where we will wait for our Panama Canal crossing), I get the impression that it isn't a very nice or safe place.

We feel safe here, especially with all the navy and coast guard ships docked just across the bay from our anchorage. There are always two small coast guard crafts patrolling the waters of this bay. On Saturday night (December 2nd), the three-masted sailboat GLORIA lit up like a Christmas tree, and then there were fireworks and a lighted boat parade.

It's hot here—hard to get used to, especially around the holidays. Because the grocery store is so pleasantly cool and convenient, we go there daily. We usually sit in the cafeteria and have a fruit smoothie before shopping.

Sometimes I have a coffee in the internet section. Half of the store was built into one of the stately buildings that line Calle Real. I love looking at these buildings and thinking about their history—they were probably once residences of the very rich. Many have been converted into businesses. Some are restored; others are run-down.

Sometimes I get a coffee on the street outside the marina. Tinto vendors are one of the most common street vendors in Cartagena and can be spotted easily on neighborhood streets carrying or pushing a wooden box filled with colorful thermoses. For 200 pesos, they will pour you a teeny cup of black coffee laden with sugar. If we are downtown, I sometimes get a coffee frappe at the Juan Valdez Cafe, which is similar to Starbucks and offers a better, though more expensive, alternative to street coffee.

Taxis rule the roadways in Cartagena. The yellow taxicabs are in good shape and have the license plate professionally painted on each side of the car (in addition to the real plates on the front and back). Motorcycle taxis are just as common. The driver wears a helmet and safety vest and carries another helmet for his passenger. Bicycle taxis are commonplace in the Manga neighborhood, and Old Town offers rides via horse and buggy, though the horses look skinny and sickly. Donkey carts often transport cargo. I'd say that owning a vehicle is not the norm here.

Marc is having a spear gun made at a local shop (as are the guys on DECIBELLE and CENTIME). Having heard from many cruisers about the success they've had fishing with spear guns, he has high hopes his fishing luck will improve with the device.

Marc has been taking a lot of taxi trips to the machine shop as he keeps coming up with things to be made or fixed for the boat.

Since we have finally finished the sanding and painting project (from the crash) and we've decided to stay longer, we are going to tackle putting the back bathroom together. It's a big messy project but will definitely be worth the time and effort when it's done.

Marc went to Club de Pesca today to pick up two free scuba BCs (buoyancy compensators) from PONCHE DE MAMA. The upscale Club de Pesca Marina is down the street from Club Nautico. They have a few spots for transient boats, but acceptance comes only with a recommendation from a club member. This is in contrast to Club Nautico's casual open invitation to all—with a special devotion to cruisers.

Madeline seems very content these days; she likes Cartagena. Alex has been taking the laptop to the marina (after finishing his schoolwork) to play internet games (we're too far away to get internet on the boat). This has helped him get to know the other kids. They are close to his age or younger and mostly girls.

Happy Holidays!

That's all for now—
Sandy

From: sandy_n_marc
To: Davis News Group
Subject: Davis News
Date: Sun, 24 Dec 2006

Greetings!

Alex has a new friend, eleven-year-old Henry. He and his parents joined us in the anchorage the day after my last e-mail. We've already spent a lot of time with them, and the boys have become fast friends. Jill, Andrew, and Henry are British but lived seven years in France before selling out and buying ESCAPADO in New York to go cruising.

Marc has volunteered to be the Wednesday morning net controller here in Cartagena. The net controller is like a disc jockey. He starts his show at a preset time and begins by asking his listeners to call in about any safety or security problems. Then he asks for new arrivals, departures, weather, social business, help wanted, and items for sale or trade. This service is incredibly useful for cruisers: We've listened to morning nets in St. Martin, St. Lucia, Grenada, Trinidad, and Curacao (and probably others I'm forgetting). Madeline, Alex, and I all groaned when we heard that our generous husband/father had committed himself again. Here's the story: Marc listens to the net every morning and is usually the first to help other people with offers of parts and things we have on the boat, or info on how to get somewhere, or he'll go to their boat and help with a computer, engine, plumbing, electrical, or other problem. I finally had to give him a little lecture a couple of days ago on how I love that he is such a generous person, but we're not getting much work done on our boat because he's always committing himself to others. I guess my talk made a bit of an impression on him this time: We got a lot more done on the bathroom project in the last couple of days.

After a long hot day of running errands or working on MARAVIDA, we often eat dinner at the Carulla grocery store cafeteria. It's a great alternative to cooking dinner on the boat. It's close, inexpensive, cool, and there's no wait. The other night, the four of us ate dinner for only 16,750 pesos (US$7.28). We also go there for refreshing *granizados*—slushies made with real fruit. The cafeteria has a granizado machine filled with a different flavor every day. The kids love them.

Marc had to give up net controlling because our VHF radio started to fail a few days ago and then finally quit. This was strange because it's only two years old. A guy at a local electronics shop took a look at it and found a fried component; he thinks the lightning storm *(on December 9th—more on that later)* might have caused the damage. The VHF part is unavailable here, so Marc ordered a new VHF, which will be sent with our port light from Florida. The window finally arrived in Florida, but we'll hold the shipment held until the radio gets there.

Bruno brought over the repaired stainless steel stanchions yesterday and they look better than before. (Very shiny!) Bruno's repairs to DOMANI are finished and DOMANI is now anchored beside us.

Marc is still going back and forth to the machine shop. Their current job is to make additional spears for Marc's new spear gun (and for spear guns for the guys on CENTIME, DECIBEL, and HEART OF TEXAS).

Friday night (the 22nd), we went on a Chiva bus trip to see Christmas lights. Chiva buses are colorful, open-air, wooden party buses with bench seats. We've seen them before, usually at night, and they're typically filled with enthusiastic drunken merrymakers. The Chiva bus riders greet the people on the streets with loud cheers. In all the neighborhoods we drove through (poor and rich), we saw people sitting or standing on the sidewalks, hanging out with their friends and neighbors. The adults, kids, and even teens were friendly, and it felt like a safe environment. In Trinidad, people hang around outside at night, but it feels very *un*safe.

A couple of days ago GLORIA moved to a dock next to our anchorage. This is probably why the coast guard asked us to move a couple of weeks ago. We tend to anchor MARAVIDA on the outskirts of anchorages because of her size and weight, but when the coast guard asked us to move closer to the marina, we didn't have a choice. The move was complicated, however, by MARAVIDA's unrecognizable anchor chain, crusted up with barnacles after five weeks in the filthy bay. As usual, though, Marc came up with a solution. He rigged up a saltwater pump so I could rinse while he wire brushed the barnacles off the chain. The process took a couple of hours, but we finally brought up the anchor and went in search of a new place to park. The only possible spot was a tight fit between other boats, but we made it work. The upside is we're now a closer dinghy ride to the marina. And, we know we are secure after staying on watch during that thunderstorm on the 9th and not budging.

It was a wild night. The weather became exciting after 10:00 p.m.; the wind howled, the water got choppy, the thunder boomed, and the lightning flashed. Lightning strikes hit in Manga and Bocagrande, and also in the water (our anchorage) between the two pieces of land. All the lights went out on the Bocagrande peninsula. We kept watch because we'd heard stories of boats dragging here in windstorms. Sure enough, a neighboring boat started to drag. We couldn't reach them by radio, so Marc valiantly jumped in our dinghy and drove over in the turbulent water to knock on their boat. The man came out to talk to Marc, but he didn't believe that his boat was dragging and went back to bed. Marc returned to MARAVIDA and we watched the boat drag, slowly at first, and then faster—headed for land and a concrete wall. The occupants finally came to their senses and emerged. The man started the engine while the woman went to the front of the boat to bring up their anchor. We stopped watching after lightning lit up their boat and we realized the woman was stark naked.

Our propeller must be covered with barnacles because we could barely get any speed up when we moved. Our newest worry is that barnacles will plug up the through-hulls at our water discharge points. We're okay so far, but we can tell it's getting worse because the toilet won't flush properly when the generator is running.

Tonight we will have a family Christmas Eve dinner on the boat. Bruno will join us and is quite excited about it. I think he's lonely since his girlfriend left for Spain.

The marina employees are off on Christmas day, so the cruisers have organized a 3:00 p.m. dinner. We pay US$5 per person to cover costs for the turkeys, dressing, gravy, ice, and table and chair rental. In addition, everyone brings a potluck dish, his or her own plates and silverware, and drinks. There are 150 people signed up!

MERRY CHRISTMAS!

Love,
Sandy, Marc, Madeline, and Alex Davis

Christmas and Beyond

From: sandy_n_marc
To: Davis News Group
Subject: Davis News
Date: Fri, 12 Jan 2007

December 25, 2006

We went to the cruiser Christmas dinner. The variety of food was great, and afterward there was a white elephant gift exchange featuring many humorous and bizarre gifts.

December 27, 2006

Marc and Madeline became sick with a fever and stomach problems. Since many cruisers have come down with the same illness, I'd guess the virus spread at the Christmas dinner.

December 28, 2006

We heard that a boat was boarded and robbed this morning near the entrance to this harbor. In response, the coast guard has offered to accompany boats as they enter or leave.

December 29, 2006

Our friends on ESCAPADO left Cartagena today. Alex was sad to see Henry go.

December 30, 2006

Marc installed the bathroom floor.

Madeline and I went to Castellana Mall.

Alex was throwing up in the evening (now he has the virus), so Marc and I postponed our dinner out to celebrate our 17th wedding anniversary. I'm not worried about getting sick because I think it's the same virus that I had a month ago.

January 1, 2007

Cartagena is a late night party town, especially at this time of year. We hear music most nights, sometimes well into the early morning hours (as late as 4:00). We also see and hear fireworks a few times a week, sometimes starting as late as 1:00 a.m.

Marc and I have a tradition on New Year's Eve of going to bed early and trying to sleep through midnight. That didn't work here. Along with the usual din of personal fireworks and celebrations, at midnight the Colombian Navy ships across the way and GLORIA (still docked near to us) started blasting their horns. To top it off, a couple of large fireworks displays started. And there we were, in the harbor, right in the middle of everything. Quite impressive.

January 4, 2007

We started out the day with two new problems. The generator overheated and the toilet stopped working.

The toilet through-hull became totally blocked with barnacles. Marc didn't tell me until after the entire episode was over, but he cleaned it out from inside the boat. He didn't tell me because he knew I'd freak out about the possibility of sinking if he couldn't get the through-hull closed back up promptly and properly. Anyway, he says he planned out his strategy ahead of time and then employed a "special technique" to execute it. He proudly asserts that we took on only about a gallon of seawater and were back in business the same day.

January 7, 2007

Bruno came over to teach us how to make homemade pasta, which we used to make a delicious lasagna dinner.

The rear head is almost finished. (I don't know if I'll ever get accustomed to calling the bathroom a "head.") Unfortunately, we can't finish the toilet installation because we can't get the PVC plumbing parts we need. We'll have to wait and get them in Panama.

We're attempting to identify and install all of the remaining interior pieces so we don't have to store them anymore. This process also identifies any leftover pieces for disposal, which includes the cumbersome Styrofoam insulation. Good riddance.

January 10, 2007

I heard on the radio net this morning that the single-hander on AFTER YOU (we met him here a few weeks ago) lost his boat on a reef yesterday in Panama's San Blas Islands. I didn't hear all of the details, but he's said to be okay.

Marc and Madeline went to a small foundry to have replacement pieces made to repair our fans. We purchased the plastic 12-volt fans several months ago. Installed at each berth, they've been instrumental in getting a good night's sleep in hot anchorages. Unfortunately, the plastic swivel piece has proven to be a weak point in the design, as it has already broken on a couple of the units, and it is only a matter of time until they all break. Rather than spend US$50 each for new fans that will just break again, Marc came up with the idea of having the swivel piece cast out of brass. The foundry will make a mold from the original piece, then melt metal and pour it into the form. Marc is having them make one for each fan and maybe an extra one or two for future fans. They will be very cheap compared to the price of the fans.

January 12, 2007

Today, we helped Bruno raise DOMANI's repaired mast into place. It broke on New Year's Day, when he took DOMANI to the clean water around the Rosario Islands (about four hours away). He wanted to charge DOMANI's batteries with the engine, since the generator still wasn't working. On the way, he ran into unusually rough conditions that put excessive stress on the mast (it had some rot near the base and loose rigging) and caused it to break during the passage.

Bruno rafted DOMANI up to MARAVIDA, and then THALIA came and rafted up on DOMANI's other side. Using winches on all three boats, the repaired mast was raised back into place. Madeline did the winching on MARAVIDA. She's stronger than I am, so we usually give her the winching job when Marc is occupied with another task.

I'm told it's now the dry season in Colombia. It hasn't rained here since the lightning storm in December, and any further precipitation is unlikely until around April. The air is cooler at night, too, which makes for easier sleeping.

We'll be leaving Colombia once we receive the window and radio shipments. We've enjoyed our stay here, but the barnacles are accumulating rapidly.

Take care—
Sandy

Another Week

From: sandy_n_marc
To: Davis News Group
Subject: Davis News
Date: Fri, 19 Jan 2007

January 13, 2007

Marc fixed the mainsail headboard attachment and brought a carpenter to MARAVIDA to look at some woodworking projects.

January 15, 2007

Yesterday, Marc installed the closet floor and toilet base in the aft head. This afternoon, the carpenter came aboard and worked for five hours.

January 16, 2007

Marc and Madeline went in search of screws and a filter for the generator.

We had three single-handers over for dinner.

January 17, 2007

We received both the port light and the radio today, and the carpenter put in a full day's work.

January 19, 2007

Over the past two days, Marc installed the new port light and the radio while the carpenter worked on his projects.

The kids and I went grocery shopping, and we all ate dinner at Danna's.

That's it for now—
Sandy

Shakedown Cruise

From: sandy_n_marc
To: Davis News Group
Subject: Davis News
Date: Tue, 23 Jan 2007

Bruno convinced us to do a shakedown cruise, so we followed DOMANI to the Rosarios Islands for a long weekend. The clear and turquoise water was a relief from the cloudy brown water in Cartagena Harbor. We swam, cleaned the barnacles off the bottom of the boat, and ran the watermaker.

> **Shakedown Cruise**
>
> A nautical term for making a voyage in order to test the performance of a ship and/or to familiarize the ship's crew with operation of the craft. In our case, a test run to make sure MARAVIDA would be ready for the impending passage to Panama.

Meanwhile, our carpenter has been staining and varnishing the pieces he made for us during the week: four shelves for two closets, a storage area under the refrigerator, woodwork around the washing machine, and a new curved door molding that we somehow lost along the way. We wouldn't have gotten around to doing those projects for a long time, so we jumped at the opportunity to hire a skilled carpenter for only US$4.50 an hour.

The shakedown trip shook out a new problem: the anchor windlass broke, but it turned out to be an easy fix. Yay!

We returned to Cartagena today. We now need to clean up, throw things away, and stock up on food while we wait for a weather window to leave for the San Blas Islands of Panama.

Talk to you later—
Sandy

Our Last Week in Cartagena

From: sandy_n_marc
To: Davis News Group
Subject: Davis News
Date: Tue, 6 Feb 2007

January 27, 2007

The carpenter came and installed the finished pieces of woodwork. They look great.

Marc met a refrigeration guy who could install tubing and charge the system for 60,000 pesos. The low price plus the promise of lower power consumption was enough incentive to go ahead and change the 110-volt refrigerator to 12-volt boat power.

January 28, 2007

The refrigerator work went according to plan yesterday, though additional parts cost 155,000 pesos. By this morning, though, Marc noticed it was weeping water and using too much power. So, he's decided the next step is to build additional foam around the refrigerator and cover it with gel coat.

January 31, 2007

The refrigerator guy came back today and installed larger tubing with insulation. Of course, he had to charge the system again, so we had to pay 60,000 pesos for that and 188,000 pesos for the new materials.

February 2, 2007

Marc still wasn't happy with the refrigerator, so he put a plastic vapor barrier around the foam and let a little gas out of the system. Because the refrigerator door needs a metal ring for magnetic closing, Marc is having a steel piece made and chromed at a local shop.

Meanwhile, the generator continues to run poorly and Marc is spending a lot of time working on it.

Since Bruno is also about ready to leave for the San Blas Islands, we're hoping to buddy boat with him. We officially checked out today because our 90 days are up and we don't want to pay for an extension. We're almost ready to go.

February 4, 2007

We can finally declare the refrigerator project a success. Now we have a 12-volt refrigerator that uses a lot less power and is just as cold as it was before the changeover.

February 5, 2007

We accompanied Bruno to the Megatienda grocery store and to the outdoor market so that we could provision for our trip. Mercado Bazurto is a huge and chaotic outdoor market, and I'm sure we would have gotten lost without Bruno as a guide. He hired a boy to follow us through the market with a cart, and we loaded it up with fruits, vegetables, eggs, and even shoes. Everything was cheap and fresh. The fresher the produce, the longer it'll last while we're in the remote San Blas Islands.

February 6, 2007

We've recently been venturing out to other neighborhoods to eat. After dark, the residents hang out on their neighborhood sidewalks or church plazas, and the children run about or ride around on donkeys. We are thankful to Bruno for introducing us to these places.

Last night, our restaurant meal cost US$1.50 each. It consisted of a lemon drink, soup, chicken, rice, and salad. We've dined with Bruno and Gerald (a forty-something German single-hander) a few times, and once with Andreas (a twenty-something German single-hander who transports backpackers back and forth between Colombia and Panama). The last two evenings, we were joined by Bruno's backpackers. He's decided to try taking two backpackers with him on the trip to Panama. His motivation is twofold: they'll provide both company and extra money (he's charging US$250 each).

I'll let you know when we leave Cartagena—
Sandy

Goodbye Cartagena

From: sandy_n_marc
To: Davis News Group
Subject: Davis News
Date: Wed, 7 Feb 2007

We left Cartagena at 6:30 this morning. Once anchored in the Rosarios Islands, we jumped into the refreshing clean water. Later, I sprayed off the decks and Marc scrubbed the barnacles off the bottom. We will rest tomorrow, and then leave early the following morning (Friday). We should arrive in the San Blas Saturday evening. (We think the passage will take about 36 hours.) I'll try to send out an e-mail within 24 hours of our arrival.

We will not miss the water and air pollution of Cartagena, or the dirt that accumulates on deck, or the barnacles that attach to everything under the boat. But we will miss the safe environment, the easy-going people, the cheap restaurants, charming Old Town, and panoramic city views from the anchorage.

Here's to calm seas!
Sandy

Cruising Guides

Elson, Constance. "Sailing the Caribbean Coast of Colombia, Part One: Islas Monjes to Cartagena." *Caribbean Compass,* Oct. 2011.
http://www.caribbeancompass.com/colombia_one.html

Elson, Constance. "Sailing the Caribbean Coast of Colombia, Part Two: Cartagena and the Southern Islands." *Caribbean Compass,* Nov. 2011.
http://www.caribbeancompass.com/colombia_two.html

Elson, Constance. "Sailing the Caribbean Coast of Colombia, Part Three: Sapzurro to Puerto Obaldia, plus Governmental Regulations for Cruising in Colombia." *Caribbean Compass,* Dec. 2011.
http://www.caribbeancompass.com/colombia_three.html

Nautical Publications. *Cruising Colombia.* Charleston, S.C.: CreateSpace, 2015. **I haven't read this cruising guide.**

CHAPTER 12

Three Months in Panama

> **Panama**
>
> Panama is a Central American country that borders Costa Rica, the Caribbean Sea, Colombia, and the Pacific Ocean. The country holds 3.5 million (2012) people on 29,000 square miles of land. Its highest peak is Volcan Baru at 11,401 feet. The jungle of the Darien Gap lies between Panama and Colombia and is the only break in the Pan-American Highway, which extends from Alaska to Patagonia.
>
> The wildlife of Panama is the most diverse in Central America, and the climate is tropical with a long rainy season.
>
> Panama's primary language is Spanish and primary religion is Roman Catholic.
>
> In 1903, the United States helped Panama secede from Colombia. From 1904 to 1914, the U.S. Army Corps of Engineers built the Panama Canal, and the ownership of the canal passed from the United States to Panama in 2000. Panama's currency has been fixed with the U.S. dollar since 1903. It uses the U.S. dollar for paper currency and its own balboa for coinage. Despite Panama's strong and growing economy in commerce, banking, trade, and tourism, it has a high rate of poverty and educational disparities.

San Blas, Kuna Yala, or Guna Yala

San Blas

What cruisers refer to as the San Blas Islands run along a 230-mile strip of the Caribbean coast of Panama. More than 350 small islands make up this archipelago. In 1938, the Panamanian government gave the indigenous Kunas control of the Comarca de San Blas, which covers both the islands and the strip of mainland along the coast for a total of about 900 square miles of land. The name was changed to Kuna Yala in 1998 and changed again in 2011 to Guna Yala, a more appropriate phonetic spelling. Approximately 31,000 Kunas (Gunas) reside there.

Guna Yala is divided into three districts, each headed by a high chief known as a cacique. Village elders called sahilas elect the three caciques, who in turn represent the whole Guna tribe in Panama's National Congress. The first sahila is in charge at the village level. The governmental positions under this chief include deputy sahilas, arkars (specialists in Guna traditions), police, minor chiefs in charge of specific places or things (cemeteries, airstrips, etc.), specialized healers, and secretaries to interpret Spanish to Guna. Probably because the Gunas follow this traditional governmental hierarchy—and because they're expected to abide by many strict rules—they are able to keep their culture and traditions alive.

Guna families are matrilineal. Though the men provide the food, the women distribute it; and though the men run the government, the women rule the house—with the eldest mother of a clan having the most power. A newly married couple moves in with the wife's family, and the groom takes on her family name and apprentices with her father.

Many of the men are fishermen who ply the waters in their dugout canoes, using paddles and sometimes sails. Others farm near the rivers on the mainland. I suspect they hunt as well, because we saw a Guna man carrying a rifle as he walked across a passenger bridge toward the mainland.

> The many uninhabited islands are watched over by coconut caretakers who maintain and harvest hundreds of palm trees. The Guna economy relies on coconuts, lobsters, and molas. Molas are fabric panels made up of three to five layers of fabric, hand stitched (applique and reverse applique) by the Guna women into abstract or animal designs.
>
> Because the Guna live at a subsistence level, the dense rainforests of their mainland territory remain undamaged. The road into Guna Yala is very rough, so most travelers come by boat or small airplane. The village islands are densely populated, but the other islands and the mainland are pristine.

From: sandy_n_marc
To: Davis News Group
Subject: Davis News
Date: Sat, 10 Feb 2007

Just a quick note to say we've arrived in the San Blas Islands of Panama.

We entered the island chain at Ratones Cays and will work our way west from here.

Marc

In the Islands

From: sandy_n_marc
To: Davis News Group
Subject: Davis News
Date: Thu, 15 Feb 2007

Our passage from Colombia's Rosarios Islands to Panama's San Blas Islands took less time than we thought it would. The 15- to 20-knot winds were ideal, but the waves were bigger than we like, at 6 feet and higher. We averaged 7 to 8 knots of speed until midnight. At that point, we took down the jib sail, which slowed our speed to 5 to 6 knots—a necessary action to avoid arriving before daylight.

We dropped anchor in Ratones Cays at 9:00 a.m. on Saturday the 10th. DOMANI arrived an hour later. Our total time at sea was 26.5 hours (only eight engine hours used).

We decided the anchorage at Ratones Cays was too rolly, so we moved to an area called Snug Harbor, which is located between the forested mainland and several palm tree-lined islands.

On Saturday afternoon, we visited the island of Playon Chico (also called Ukupseni) to pay our yacht fee. The Congreso charges $6 per month *(costs more now)* to anchor in their tribal district.

The drive to the densely populated island took about 10 minutes in Bruno's faster dinghy. We tied up next to a dilapidated Colombian trading boat and asked a Kuna sitting at the dock for directions to the Congreso. Rather than point the way, he jumped up and motioned us to follow him down the dirt road.

Our Panama cruising guidebook says the Kuna authorities can be found in the Congreso hut in the afternoon. Sure enough, a few men and women were sitting on beat-up chairs and benches in the large, sparsely furnished concrete building. The two tables in the room were empty, and there was no office paraphernalia except for the well-worn receipt book, which was used to document our payment. After we completed the transaction, we poked around the island a little. Although the Kunas didn't seem bothered by our presence, we felt like intruders. Just our own self-consciousness, I suppose. My impression is that the Kunas are patient, peaceful, contented people.

The island is packed with thatched huts made of palm fronds, canes, and reeds. Near the center is an open area with a large concrete basketball court. We saw at least 30 kids playing in this area.

Most of the women we saw wore traditional clothing: a red and yellow headscarf, a blouse with matching mola panels on the front and back, and a piece of patterned cloth that wrapped around the waist and hung down to the knees. In contrast, the men and children wore westernized clothing.

On Sunday, Bruno left Snug Harbor for Isla El Porvenir, where his wife, Veronika (amicably separated—not divorced), was due to arrive by plane the next day.

Marc and Madeline went fishing in the morning but saw few fish. In the afternoon, the four of us dinghied to the closest small island to play at the beach. Madeline decided to build a hut from dead palm fronds and got us all involved.

At night, it was pitch black except for one distant light. We felt truly isolated from the world. During the day, though, we saw a few fishermen in dugout canoes pass by on their way to and from their fishing spots. A few stopped by to see if we wanted to buy fish, crab, octopus, fruit, vegetables or molas. Unfortunately, we had to decline because we're short of U.S. cash (lots of 1's and 5's would be ideal to have here).

On Monday, the sailboat INFINITY joined us in the anchorage. We first met the couple in Curacao.

The following morning, we left on a four-hour passage to the outer islands of Coco Banderos Cays. We joined four other sailboats in this gorgeous anchorage that's surrounded by four small islands covered with white sand and palm trees. The water is crystal clear, and there are lots of reefs to snorkel.

On our first day here, a Kuna came by in a small boat with an outboard motor. He must have come all the way from one of the inhabited islands near the mainland because he had coke, beer, and Kuna bread to sell. We bought a bag full of rolls for $1.

The next day, Wednesday, Bruno came to the anchorage with Veronika. I think she's staying for a couple of weeks. Their relationship seems complicated. She usually visits him on the boat in the winter, and he visits their house in Italy for a few months in the summer.

We finally ran out of our stock of cat litter from Curacao. We could only find tiny bags of expensive, non-clumping litter in Cartagena. (We saw few cats there, though dogs were common.) Now that we're out, we've instituted operation sandbox. We moved the litter box on deck and added sand from the nearest island. Maria is thrilled with the substitution and is spending all her time on her own piece of paradise, though she's going to have to share it with Emily eventually.

Marc ordered a part for the generator and had it sent to Veronika in Italy so she could bring it here. Before he could install it, though, the generator's starting battery died ... permanently. Now we have to jury-rig the generator to the house batteries to get it started.

We held a family meeting to discuss our schedule. We haven't made any decisions yet, but we're concerned about the more than 2,000 miles we still have to travel before hurricane season starts on May 15th. We're below the hurricane belt now but have approximately 1,000 miles of hurricane territory from Costa Rica to northern Mexico ahead of us. One option would be to postpone our trip through the Panama Canal and have friends visit us here in the Western Caribbean. Another option would be to leave MARAVIDA somewhere cheap (perhaps Rio Dulce, Guatemala) and fly home for a visit, though only if the cost of airplane flights isn't prohibitive. Of course, the ultimate tropical paradise is right here in the San Blas, though rain and lightning storms are common in the summer months.

Our second concern (after hurricanes), is money. We probably have enough to last us two more years, barring any catastrophes. After that, I'm not sure what we'll do—since we can't see ourselves working 9-to-5 jobs.

Marc, Bruno, and Madeline just took their snorkeling gear to the large freighter wreck on the outer reef. It's a good time to do this because we've had unusually calm weather.

Talk to you later—
Sandy

Waiting for Vegetables in Nargana

From: sandy_n_marc
To: Davis News Group
Subject: Davis News
Date: Sun, 25 Feb 2007

We've decided to stay in Panama for a while. Our good friends, the Erreras, will visit us the last week of April. Lots of cruisers have friends and family visit them in the San Blas. It's an incredible opportunity to see these beautiful islands that can only be reached by boat. Bruno has asked us to look after his boat for about a month, starting at the end of March, and he says we can use DOMANI for extra berthing of guests if needed. So, let us know if you want to visit!

On February 17th, we took MARAVIDA and DOMANI to the island village of Nargana. It only took an hour to get there from Coco Banderos. There are no cars on the island, just soft sandy paths—perfect for walking barefoot. Despite the lack of cars and shoes, Nargana is one of the more modern villages in Kuna Yala because it has some infrastructure: a school, a clinic, a pharmacy, and a couple of small stores and restaurants. Simple technology is obvious from the rumble of the town generator and the sounds of television emanating from various thatched and concrete huts. Sanitation is still crude, however; the numerous outhouses that rim the island bear this out, each one perched over the water at the end of a crude dock.

We purchased potatoes at one tiny market and Kuna bread at another. Madeline paid 10 cents for a *dura*—a Styrofoam cup holding a frozen Kool-Aid type drink. Veronika bought meat, cheese, bread, and beer. The stores didn't have any produce other than potatoes, but the owners said they expected a vegetable delivery in a day or two, so we decided to stay in the anchorage and wait.

On the 18th, we took both dinghies down the Rio Diablo. We saw hawks, small blue herons, small white herons (I don't know much about birds), bamboo, coconut trees, banana trees, and many other trees I can't identify (nor do I know much about flora and fauna). Farther down the river, we spotted several small cemeteries. I'd guess that each one is owned and maintained by a family.

That night we ate dinner at a Nargana restaurant. We had to walk through a house to get to the eating area (most likely the owner's house). The restaurant itself was open-air with a thatched roof and sand floor—and two cats waiting for scraps. We had a tasty, simple, and inexpensive fish dinner.

The wind blew hard that night and three boats dragged. Not us, thanks to our mighty anchor.

On the 20th, Bruno, Veronika, Marc, and Madeline took a dinghy ride to check out the island of Tigres. They were gone a long time. When they returned they were soaked and too exhausted to give me a report. I did manage to find out that the island was much farther than they had anticipated, the voyage was rough, and it had rained hard.

Marc spent part of the next day working on MARAVIDA and part of the day working on another boat. He finally figured out why our generator has been turning off by itself for no reason—because of overspray paint on the grounding attachment. We're thrilled to have such an easy fix for the generator, though we still need to get a starting battery for it.

Marc and Bruno were each paid $100 to remove the broken transmission on a French boat in the anchorage. The $100 will go toward our entrance fee when we go to Porvenir to check into Panama. We've put off the trip to Porvenir because we heard the immigration people have been out of the office.

Tired of waiting for vegetables, we left on the 22nd. Bruno and Veronika gave up two days later. We discovered that our wait in Nargana had been foolish, because yesterday a dugout canoe selling vegetables visited us— way out here in the Holandes Cays. Lesson learned: They will come to you.

We're in the Eastern Holandes Cays, far from the mainland (a three-hour trip from Nargana—into the wind). We anchored in the "Hot Tub" anchorage next to DECIBEL, whom we'd originally met in Curacao and then saw again in Cartagena. They left the next day to take their guest to

MISSIVES FROM MARAVIDA

Nargana, where he will fly from San Blas to Panama City. DOMANI has joined us in the anchorage; all six of us dinghied over to nearby Sand Island yesterday, where we burned our accumulated garbage along with some garbage we found on the island. We swam and snorkeled around the tiny island, then went back to MARAVIDA for dinner.

Our French friends on LA COLOMBE—we originally sailed with them from Trinidad to Venezuela a year and a half ago—arrived today in the "Swimming Pool" anchorage. We'll go over to see them tomorrow.

Let us know if you want to come visit—
Sandy

Problems

From: sandy_n_marc
To: Davis News Group
Subject: Davis News
Date: Fri, 2 Mar 2007

The week started out well. On Monday morning, Marc speared his first fish; we visited our friends on LA COLOMBE in the afternoon; and in the evening, we went to the weekly appetizer potluck on BBQ Island, where our kids ran around with eight other kids. Life was good ... until the inverter and the generator stopped working. Darn.

On Tuesday morning, Marc got the generator running again, so he started up the watermaker. His mission for the day was to fill LA COLOMBE's water tanks because their watermaker was broken and they were almost out of water. Unfortunately, before we were able to fill our own water tanks, the generator stopped working again.

The kids spent the afternoon with a bunch of other cruising kids making a video, and later we had dinner on LA COLOMBE.

On Wednesday morning, LA COLOMBE left for Green Island and Marc started work on the generator. His final prognosis was "no hope" without removing it from the lazarette, disassembling it, and probably buying parts. Meanwhile, without the inverter, we couldn't use our 110-volt outlets that operate our computers, television (DVDs and GameCube), power tools, etc. Luckily, the fridge is now 12 volt, and of course the lights are all 12 volt, but without the generator we knew we'd soon drain the batteries down to nothing. And of course we couldn't use the power hungry watermaker. So, by the end of the day, we were down to 20 gallons of water and a sink full of dirty dishes.

On Thursday, Bruno came to our rescue by rafting DOMANI up to MARAVIDA. This enabled us to hook into DOMANI's generator so we could make water and charge MARAVIDA's batteries.

A new problem arose on Thursday, though: Our laptop died. Bruno lent us his extra laptop, but we needed the winlink software in order to send and receive e-mail. So, Marc took the hard drive out of our laptop, used our portable hard drive converter to transfer the info to our other computer, saved it to a memory card, and then transferred it to Bruno's extra laptop (all because his laptop wouldn't respond directly to the converter). I can now send and receive e-mail, but only while Bruno's generator is charging our batteries. So be warned: We may be slow in answering e-mail.

In a couple of hours, Bruno will leave to take DOMANI to Nargana so Veronika can fly out early the next morning. We will leave for Porvenir (to finally check in to Panama) and will meet up with Bruno Saturday afternoon. We plan to leave San Blas for Portobelo in a week or so. There's a bus that goes from Portobelo to Colon or Panama City, which will give us better access to civilization for making our repairs.

Sorry this e-mail is disjointed. I'm unaccustomed to typing on a European keyboard.

We'll check e-mail when we can—
Sandy

Checking In and Out

From: sandy_n_marc
To: Davis News Group
Subject: Davis News
Date: Sat, 10 Mar 2007

On March 2nd, we motored to Porvenir, a three-hour trip from Holandes Cays. Once anchored, we officially checked into the San Blas Islands. The $150 in charges included Panama entry, San Blas entry, overtime charges (it was 4:30 p.m. on a Friday), and a *zarpe* (exit clearance) to leave San Blas for Portobelo. *(Beware, prices have risen tremendously since we were there.)* Fortunately, Marc had made the $100 for his work on the French boat in Nargana. Even with that, we only had $142 in cash, but they had to accept it because there wasn't a way to get more. We didn't feel too guilty about it, though, since the overtime fees were excessive.

We left the next day for the Eastern Lemon Cays, only an hour away. Bruno motored into the anchorage soon after us. We combined a fish that Marc caught with two that Bruno purchased from the local Kunas for a fish dinner, and then we watched a movie on Bruno's boat.

Marc e-mailed the generator company with several questions.

The next day Marc, Madeline, and Mr. G (a Kuna who says he owns the three islands we are anchored near—though that doesn't jibe with our understanding of Kuna laws) went with Bruno on DOMANI to the Carti Islands. They soon discovered that Mr. G was loony. His problem surfaced after he drank a couple of beers. He started to get angry at Bruno for no reason other than Bruno was German. He talked about Germans being evil and made Hitler references. He continued to get agitated and threatened to kill Bruno, saying he could have the job done for very little money. Naturally, the whole incident upset Marc, and he began arguing with Mr. G. By this time (luckily), they were close to the shore of one of the Carti Islands. Bruno told Mr. G to jump off the boat and swim to shore. He finally calmed down then; perhaps he couldn't swim. Once on the island, they separated, but they later saw Mr. G drinking more beer. They had no intention of letting him back on the boat for the return trip. He had to find his own way back, hopefully after sleeping off the alcohol that had dramatically altered his personality.

On Wednesday morning, we left for the Chichime Cays, our last stop before leaving the San Blas. At first, the engine wouldn't start because its starting battery was dead, but Marc temporarily hooked it up to the house bank of batteries so we could get going. The delay didn't matter, though, since the passage took only 45 minutes. We stayed two nights next to the two Chichime islands. Unfortunately, the beauty of the anchorage is marred somewhat by the constant traffic of boats coming and going; it's a popular stopover for boats entering and leaving the San Blas.

We left the San Blas Islands on Friday the 9th, headed west. Rather than endure an overnight passage to Portobelo, we decided to stop at a couple of anchorages on the way. We spent the first night at Bahia Escribanos, after a three-hour voyage. The next day we traveled four hours to Isla Linton. We rafted up with DOMANI in order to make water again and dined on the fish we'd caught on the trip: an Atlantic mackerel and a king mackerel. The latter was more than 3 feet long, delicious, and plentiful (we're still eating it).

There are dozens of boats crowded into the anchorage at Isla Linton. We're not sure of the attraction, though. It feels eerie to me.

More later—
Sandy

Portobelo

> ### Portobelo
>
> Portobelo is located on the Caribbean coast of Panama about halfway between the Panama Canal and the entrance to the San Blas Archipelago. Portobelo has a deep, large bay that is flanked by four Spanish colonial forts. The ruins of these forts were added to the UNESCO World Heritage List in 1980. Unfortunately, in July 2012, it was deemed necessary for the UNESCO World Heritage Committee to place the site on the List of World Heritage in Danger. The reasons they cited were "environmental factors, lack of maintenance and uncontrollable urban developments."

> The town was named Puerto Bello (beautiful harbor) by Christopher Columbus in 1502. Beginning in 1597, Portobelo became an important trading and storage center for the Spanish treasure fleets. The customs house (Real Aduana de Portobelo) still stands in town. It was once known as the "counting house," where gold and silver was counted, registered, stored, and distributed. A sign in front of the customs house states: "The Customs House was used to store the extraordinary riches traded between Spain and the Americas. For one century, more than one-third of the world's gold passed through this building."
>
> Despite its fortifications, Portobelo was repeatedly attacked by pirates. Many battles were fought up until 1740, when Spain started to ship its gold around Cape Horn. After that, the once important town became insignificant. Portobelo is now a sleepy settlement of less than 5,000 people, but the town and bay are surrounded by beautiful, forested hills that provide a scenic anchorage for cruisers like us.

From: sandy_n_marc
To: Davis News Group
Subject: Davis News
Date: Sun, 11 Mar 2007

We're now anchored in the large Bay of Portobelo. We went ahead and rafted up with DOMANI, since we're still dependent on her for MARAVIDA's power needs.

I feel more comfortable here because there's plenty of elbow room compared to crowded Isla Linton.

Though we stayed in the Linton anchorage less than 24 hours, it was long enough for people to call on Marc for advice. We finally managed to tear away by mid-afternoon, though we had a mishap as we left the bay. Marc's magnetic feet zeroed in on a bag of tin cans that I had placed in the cockpit for disposal at sea. This caused a large cut, lots of angry words, and copious amounts of blood. Once we doctored the injury, cleaned up the mess, and made our apologies, the voyage to Portobelo only took an hour and 45 minutes.

Talk to you later—
Sandy

Taking the Bus

From: sandy_n_marc
To: Davis News Group
Subject: Davis News
Date: Tue, 13 Mar 2007

Soon after arriving in Portobelo, we heard about a recent disturbance in the anchorage. A crazy Frenchman on an Amel sailboat had been seen trying to set fire to boats and even rammed one or two. On the morning of the 8th, the man was finally taken away by the authorities after he succeeded in destroying a boat with fire. His boat was removed two days later. We just missed the excitement (thank goodness).

Even though there are two small Chinese grocery stores in Portobelo, we decided to take the bus to the large Rey Supermercado in Sabonitas for our first serious grocery shopping in over a month. The ride took 40 minutes in an old school bus and cost $1 per person. We each had a food priority: mine was peanut butter, Alex's was tortillas and refried beans, and

Madeline's was hot dogs. After locating these important items and much more, the kids and I lugged the groceries onto the bus and headed back to Portobelo.

Marc and Bruno separated from us in Sabonitas and hopped a bus to Panama City (another two hours away). They spent the night so they'd have plenty of time to get their errands done the next day. Marc will try to get the generator injector looked at, buy a compression tester, and check prices on outboard motors, batteries, laptops, cameras, etc. I expect them back late today.

Sandy

Misfortune and Misbehaving

From: sandy_n_marc
To: Davis News Group
Subject: Davis News
Date: Thu, 5 Apr 2007

About three weeks ago, Marc took the generator apart and found the problem. Yes, I know we keep coming up with new answers to our generator problems, but this time Marc felt he'd finally solved it. The place where the saltwater cooling mixes with the exhaust had corroded through, allowing salt water to run into the engine each time it was shut down. The salt water damaged the cylinder, piston, and both the intake and exhaust valves. No wonder we'd had so many problems with it. We're relieved that Marc was able to convince the generator company to replace the motor.

Because we have two heavy items to ship from the U.S. to Panama (new generator engine and new inverter), we decided to go ahead and set up a shipment through a container company in Florida. We've been visiting Portobelo daily to make purchases and shipping arrangements online (either at the town library or the pizza place).

Two and a half weeks ago, Bruno took off for Guatemala (by buses) to pick up the motorcycle he'd left there two years ago. Madeline and I went with him as far as Panama City for a two-night/three-day adventure. We stayed at a simple hotel, called Hotel 2 Mares, for only $22 per night. We were thrilled with the full-sized beds, shower, and cable TV (see http://www.hotel-dosmares.com).

Because Bruno's bus didn't leave until late that evening, he had time to accompany us to the hotel, show us the shopping area nearby, and eat dinner with us. About halfway through our meal at a simple Chinese restaurant on the shopping street, the owner of the restaurant came to our table to warn us that the street was dangerous after dark. His warning came a little too late, since it was already dark. Our adventure took a dangerous turn several minutes later, when an employee of the restaurant told us that robbers were waiting for us to leave the restaurant—but not to worry because the police had been called. So, we waited ... but the police didn't come. Eventually, another customer approached us and said he was an off-duty cop and could walk with us down the street. We decided this was our best option and left with him. The four of us kept close to each other as we walked. Even though there were few people on the street, I felt anything but confident. And sure enough, without warning, the small purse hanging around my neck was ripped from its straps as a robber ran past at high speed. Oh, how I wished I hadn't been wearing a dress without pockets or that I hadn't felt uncomfortable about leaving my valuables in the hotel room.

Apologetic, our escort left us on our hotel street. We immediately went to the internet café, a block from the hotel, where I canceled my credit and debit cards. My purse had also contained $45 in cash and my photo ID (my expired Oregon driver's license and a laminated copy of my passport). Luckily, I'd previously given Madeline $60 to put in her pocket, and Bruno was able to lend us more cash before he left for the 10:00 p.m. bus to Costa Rica.

I found out—after the incident—that this shopping street (Avenida Central, located two blocks up from our hotel) is known for thievery after dark but is fairly safe during the day (though not from pickpockets). I usually read travel guidebooks before I visit new countries—they almost always address common safety issues—but this time I only had a cruising guide for Panama. Lesson learned: Read ahead about unfamiliar destinations, and wear a money belt in big cities and questionable areas.

The next day, Madeline and I focused on the positive side of our adventure: shopping for bargains. We found cheap clothing—the cheapest we'd ever seen. (Madeline spent $2 on a pair of pants, 75 cents on a skirt, and splurged on a $4 blouse. I picked up a denim skirt for $5 but paid only a buck for a tank top and 75 cents for another skirt.) We ate lunch at a Chinese restaurant for $2.75—for both of us, and shared a 2-dollar pizza for dinner. Later, we snacked on 40-cent ice cream cones and used the internet for only 50 cents an hour. Panama City is without doubt the cheapest place we've ever visited.

Back in Portobelo, we pay $1.50 an hour for internet and 25 cents for a double scoop ice cream cone. Needless to say, we get a cone every time we dinghy into town.

Speaking of dinghying, we've been barred from using the dinghy dock. Yes, you heard it right. We broke the rules too many times and were finally banned on March 23rd. Now we have to use the town dock on the west side of Portobelo next to Fort Castillo Santiago de la Gloria.

Here's the story. The dinghy dock in the middle of town is private but available for use by cruisers if they follow a specific set of rules. We tried our best, but the rules contradict the common dinghy dock etiquette that we've become accustomed to. One posted rule at the dock in question states that outboard engines should be raised; this goes against the courtesy of leaving your engine down so that your raised propeller doesn't pierce another dinghy. Another posted rule is to pull your dinghy out, away from the dock, with an anchor; this becomes a problem as people come and go, making it hard to remove your dinghy from the dock without hanging up on other anchor lines. We weren't in the habit of doing these things and often forgot, plus Madeline and I frequently went to the dock by ourselves and couldn't get the engine raised (the latch mechanism was corroded and hard to work). Later, we would return to the dock and receive a stern lecture from the grumpy old man in the house. We aren't sure about his relation to the dock because the sign says it's owned by a corporation, but we are sure that he spends way too much time watching for rule offenders. And thus we were ousted.

We've spent some evenings with Andreas, whom we first met in Cartagena, and also some time with Estelle and Thierry from Canada. They live on an aluminum catamaran that they built with help from the designer. We're impressed by its unique and practical design.

Marc got the master cabin toilet installed and working. He's now working on the sink. It'll be nice to have both a backup toilet and a backup sink in case one fails.

Maria fell off the boat a couple of days ago. It's been about nine months since her last unintentional plunge. We had no trouble locating her because her cries were loud and emphatic. We found her wound up in the green grassy stuff hanging from the boat at the waterline, but before Marc could jump in to rescue her, she managed to get herself free. We took the net to the back of the boat and urged her to swim to us so we could scoop her up, but on her way she spotted the stern anchor line and frantically clawed her way up the thick rope. At first, she was shaken by the unpleasant experience, but once again she seemed to forget about it rather quickly.

Marc thinks the slimy green stuff growing on the boat bottom is a product of the freshwater rivers that empty into this bay combined with the salt water from the ocean. The growth is a nuisance, but I prefer it to the barnacle growth in Cartagena. Once the water clears up, I'll jump in and scrape it off the waterline. Right now the water is too muddy because the heavy rain from the last few days has caused excessive runoff from the rivers. I think the rainy season came early this year.

Take care—
Sandy

Back and Forth between Portobelo and Panama City

From: sandy_n_marc
To: Davis News Group
Subject: Davis News
Date: Wed, 2 May 2007

All four of us went to Panama City on April 9th. Our primary objective was to renew our passports at the U.S. Embassy, but we also had time to stroll, shop, and watch television in our hotel. Thanks to cheap restaurants and affordable hotels, we were able to thoroughly enjoy our mini vacation. Hotel 2 Mares was booked, so we stayed at Hotel Veracruz just around the corner. We paid $44 per night for a triple room and stayed two nights. (See http://www.hotelveracruz.com.pa.)

(Note: I cited the prices we paid for many items and services in Panama. Please keep in mind that all prices have gone up since then, though they still may be reasonable in comparison to other places.)

Later in the week, while exploring the fort in downtown Portobelo (Castillo San Gerónimo), we met an engaging young woman who asked us lots of questions about our cruising life. She turned out to be Megan McCormick—in Panama with her film crew to tape the Discovery Channel's *Globe Trekker* show. *Globe Trekker: Panama and Colombia* is now available on DVD (see http://www.globetrekkerstore.com/dvpaco.html).

Bruno returned on Saturday the 14th and kindly accompanied Marc to Panama City the next day to help arrange for the procurement of our shipment. (Bruno's Spanish is better than Marc's.) They rented a car Tuesday morning, picked up the shipment and a customs agent, and headed for the town of Colon. The shipment contained our new generator engine, a new inverter, a used laptop from eBay, books from Grandpa and Grandma Davis, two sink foot-pumps, and a water pressure pump.

Since the shipment couldn't be surrendered to Marc until the Yacht in Transit paperwork was done in Colon, the goods had to be transported in the company of a customs agent. Once they arrived in the bonded area, Marc gave the customs agent bus fare to get back to Panama City.

Before leaving the free zone, the guys decided to check out the duty-free liquor store. The rum prices were too good to pass up, so Bruno bought several cases and Marc bought two. They purchased pints because they were cheaper per ounce than large bottles. Bruno grilled the sales clerk about this because it didn't make sense. He finally obtained an explanation: Rich people can afford big bottles, so the larger bottles should cost more.

Their liquor purchase presented a problem when they tried to exit the free zone. They were told that they must have a customs agent accompany them to the boats to prove the destination of the goods. So once again they crammed a customs agent into the car along with the cargo. When they got to Portobelo and pointed out the boats from the dock, the agent said okay and left.

On Wednesday, the 18th, all five of us took the rental car back into Panama City to shop at PriceSmart. We loaded as many purchases as we could into the trunk, then filled the back seat from floor to ceiling. The kids and I planned to take a bus to Hotel 2 Mares while Marc and Bruno took the purchases back to the boats. The next morning, Marc picked me up at the hotel and we drove to the U.S. Embassy to get our new passports. After that, we picked up the kids at the hotel, dropped off the rental car, and rode the buses back to Portobelo.

On Friday morning, Bruno took DOMANI to Colon to get fuel, and Marc started to install the new generator. He got it running just before the Erreras arrived from Connecticut late Saturday afternoon.

That evening we ate at a modest restaurant in Portobelo, dickered for molas at the small Kuna marketplace, and peaked into the windows of the Church of San Felipe. On Sunday, we piled into the Erreras' rental van to visit the Miraflores locks on the Panama Canal. I took lots of pictures with my new camera. It was one of the goodies that we'd ordered online and the Erreras delivered to us: they also brought another laptop, an iPod, a clamp meter (the original items had conked out), books, outboard parts, our replacement VISA cards, electronic games for Alex, and U.S. flags (ours was pathetically faded and in tatters). On our way back to the boat, we stopped in Sabonitas for last-chance grocery shopping before our departure to the San Blas Islands.

The Church of San Felipe

Built by the Spaniards and inaugurated in 1814, the Iglesia de San Felipe houses the Black Christ, a carved statue of Jesus made from dark wood. Every year on October 21st, El Cristo Negro is carried through the streets of Portobelo, followed by a procession of pilgrims. There are differing stories about the Black Christ, but most agree that it came from Spain, was washed ashore at Portobelo in the 1600s, and was responsible for miraculous deeds.

Back to the San Blas Islands

On Monday, Marc and Claude returned the rental van in Colon and we got MARAVIDA ready for ocean transit. We left too late on Tuesday to get to the San Blas Islands in one day, so we anchored overnight at Bahia Escribanos. The next morning we caught three fish during our three-hour transit to Porvenir. Once in Porvenir, the Erreras arranged for a Saturday flight out of Nargana.

After a lunch break, we motored another three hours to the beautiful Holandes Cays and anchored in the "Swimming Pool." From our arrival Wednesday evening through our departure Friday afternoon, our guests managed to snorkel, fish, halyard jump, and surf behind the dinghy. There was also an opportunity to buy more molas when three Kunas came by in a dugout canoe. The two older women wore traditional dresses, short haircuts, bright makeup, and gold nose rings. The third, a young girl, had long dark hair and wore western clothing—a tee shirt and shorts. Becky purchased more molas and leg beads for Madeline. The Kuna woman unwrapped the long string of beads from her ankle and rewrapped it around Madeline's ankle. We wondered if the pattern would be lost if Madeline's ankle was a different size, but the design stayed the same—only slanted.

We left for Nargana on Friday afternoon so that we'd be anchored near the airport for the Erreras' 7:00 a.m. flight to Panama City. The Corazón de

Jesús airport is on a peninsula of the mainland, across from the island of Nargana.

We enjoyed having our friends visit, though seven days wasn't long enough and the weather wasn't ideal: lots of rain and little wind. There was one sunny day, but it was uncomfortably hot and also without wind. Since their departure, the trade winds have come back and we've had minimal rain. Go figure!

We're back in the "Swimming Pool" and have just met up with Bruno. He was recently in Porvenir to pick up a German backpacker named Sonja. She'll accompany Bruno on the trip back to Cartagena. He then plans to fly out of Cartagena on June 9th for his annual three months in Europe.

The generator has been giving us more trouble; this time, it's using too much water. Marc hasn't found the leak and thinks he'll have to pull it out ... again.

I'll send another e-mail when we've decided where we're headed from here. We keep changing the plan, which provides soap opera entertainment for our fellow cruisers but makes us more nervous about making the final decision.

Talk to you again soon—
Sandy

The Plan

From: sandy_n_marc
To: Davis News Group
Subject: Davis News
Date: Fri, 4 May 2007

I'll start with the definite plans and then move on to the uncertain ones.

We've decided to start a full-scale attack to finish MARAVIDA. She's worth little in her unfinished condition.

Cartagena is the closest place to work on boats and has the cheapest labor costs. We've arranged to have Bruno's former helper, Guillermo, work with Marc for a minimum of three months. He's reliable and works hard for US$20 a day. Bruno will leave DOMANI in Cartagena, under our care, while he's in Europe.

We'll keep MARAVIDA out in the anchorage so the metal chips and dust don't disturb other boats. We may, however, put Bruno's boat in the marina and split the cost with him. This will not only save us the daily fee of US$2.50 for showers, water, and docking the dinghy but also allow us to hook up DOMANI to shore power and use air conditioning and wireless internet on the boat during the day. In addition, the kids and I can sleep there when MARAVIDA is closed up for grinding and sanding.

Marc bought an air compressor and welder in Panama City. He says our generator will be able to handle the load. The air compressor will power the needle gun, which we'll use on the rusty parts of the deck. The welder will be used for welding the stanchions onto the steel toerails.

We plan to stay in Cartagena for about six months, or until the boat is finished. Then ... we're not sure.

Unless we get an unexpected financial windfall or employment opportunity, we will need to sell MARAVIDA. We may take her to St. Martin for this. Bottom line: We need the money. Between the lines: The sailing life is perhaps a tad too stressful for us and it's time to try something else. However, we're not ready to stop our adventure. One option could be barging the river canals in Europe. We've enjoyed our time in the Caribbean but are ready to explore a different part of the world. Madeline says she doesn't want the adventure to end and would like to go to Europe, I agree, and Marc is game (he came up with the river barge idea). Alex has always wanted to go back to Oregon and his friends there, but we think keeping him in adventure-mode is good for his conservative personality. Besides, he's made many friends along the way and is always cheerful.

We plan to leave for Cartagena in a couple of days. Marc wants to follow the coast, stopping to anchor at a few spots along the way. I'm a little nervous about this, but we'll try to get more information about the route from fellow cruisers. In any case, we don't want to return by the same route we took to get here because we'd have to beat against the wind and waves.

Sandy

Ham Radio to the Rescue

From: sandy_n_marc
To: Davis News Group
Subject: Davis News
Date: Thu, 10 May 2007

Marc has been fishing a lot so we've been eating fish often. Thank goodness our picky eater, Alex, has expanded his limited diet to include fish.

A few days ago, we turned on the SSB (single sideband) radio to listen to the daily Panama Connection Net (8.107 MHz at 8:30 a.m.). The net operator was describing a Mayday announcement made a few minutes earlier from a boat taking on water in the Pacific Ocean. At that time, the location of the boat hadn't been determined because the transmission wasn't clear enough to understand.

Phone calls and radio transmissions were made to report the incident to various authorities, and eventually the Ham Radio Emergency Net at 14.300 MHz took over management of the situation and maintained contact with everyone involved.

We listened all morning as the ham radio operators tried to communicate with the captain on SAILABOUT. At that point, he could be heard clearly by them (and us), but he wasn't receiving them well. SAILABOUT'S location was eventually determined to be 700 miles out from the Galapagos, headed to the Marquesas Islands.

SAILABOUT is a Norwegian boat, 35 feet long, and crewed by a husband and wife team. The captain said the boat was taking on water and the forestay had failed and then the bowsprit broke. They had life jackets, but not a lifeboat. He was told to deploy his EPIRB (emergency position-indicating radio beacon) so the coast guard could track their location. The closest boat to SAILABOUT was another sailboat, MOKISHA, 87 miles away. It diverted in their direction but was 15 to 20 hours from SAILABOUT.

At 4:30 that afternoon, we turned on the radio again and heard MOKISHA being excused from giving assistance. Another sailboat, DAMARRI, was closer—only five hours away. DAMARRI said they could not tow SAILABOUT, so the captain of SAILABOUT was asked if he was willing to abandon ship. He agreed. After much discussion, the parties involved agreed that once DAMARRI rendezvoused with SAILABOUT, they should not make the transfer of passengers because the conditions were treacherous (and they didn't have enough food and water to take the couple to civilization). However, a Norwegian merchant ship, m/v BELNOR, could get there by morning and take them aboard.

DAMARRI duly arrived on the scene and stood by all night (in 14-foot seas and 25-knot winds) until the merchant ship arrived in the morning. The couple on SAILABOUT then abandoned their boat and were taken on board m/v BELNOR, about 26 hours after their original mayday. (More details about this event are available at http://www.mmsn.org/news/events/sailabout.html.)

Everyone was pleased that the crisis was successfully resolved, but I couldn't help thinking about the consequences if SAILABOUT had sunk soon after their original Mayday.

Luckily, we don't have to worry about getting into a similar situation since we have no plans for long distance ocean crossings. Nevertheless, I now understand the importance of the 14.300 MHz radio net for international marine emergency communications.

Leaving Panama

On Monday, May 7th, we left the Holandes Cays and motored five hours to Snug Harbor. The next morning, we hauled anchor at 6:00 and motorsailed 12 hours to Puerto Obaldia. A few miles from the Panamanian border town, we were greeted by dolphins, which is always an awe-inspiring experience, but this time it was extraordinary because the water was so clear that we could see them underwater as they frolicked with MARAVIDA.

Our welcome in the bay was more sobering. The greeting came from armed Panamanian police officers standing on the jetty. Even though it was dusk, they motioned for us to come talk to them, or so we thought. After we anchored, Marc dinghied over to the dock, but that wasn't good enough: They wanted MARAVIDA at the dock. Marc refused because the swells were large and the depth at the dock was most likely too shallow. But they insisted on searching MARAVIDA. So, Marc had to bring the drug-sniffing German shepherd and his handler over to MARAVIDA in the dinghy. The large dog was obviously not used to boats because Marc had to lift him in and out of the dinghy and down and up through the companionway hatch. We put the cats away in Madeline's cabin while the dog was on board. (It was interesting that they didn't ask to see the room with the cats.)

Despite the late hour, we were asked to check in at the police station. This took a while. When we finished, an officer walked us to the immigration office, but the immigration officer said he was ready to go home and eat dinner. Since we were ravenous ourselves, we gratefully agreed to come back at 8:00 a.m. After eating dinner on the boat, we retired to our beds exhausted.

The next morning we were eager to get away from the small ramshackle town full of heavily armed national police. (Were they concerned with drug trafficking and Colombian guerillas?) First, though, we had to spend two hot hours checking out of the country with immigration, the port captain, and the police. Finally, we were free to leave; with relief, we pulled anchor at 11:00 a.m.

Next stop, Colombia!

Sandy

Cruising Guides

Bauhaus, Eric. *The Panama Cruising Guide*. 5th ed. Panama: Sailors Publications, 2014.

Rains, Patricia Miller. *Cruising Ports: The Central American Route*. 6.5 ed. San Diego, CA: Point Loma, 2011.

Zydler, Nancy Schwalbe, and Tom Zydler. *The Panama Guide: A Cruising Guide to the Isthmus of Panama*. 2nd ed. Port Washington, WI: Seaworthy Publications, 2001.

CHAPTER 13

Colombia Again

Back in Colombia

From: sandy_n_marc
To: Davis News Group
Subject: Davis News
Date: Thu, 10 May 2007

Our first stop in Colombia was Sapzurro, only an hour motor from Puerto Obaldia, Panama. We anchored next to DOMANI and a sandy beach, where we could see a few houses tucked back against the jungle. Marc and Madeline dinghied over to DOMANI to chat with Bruno and Sonja while I rested with a headache.

Later in the afternoon, we visited the colorful village that looks more like a tiny resort town than a border town, though we did see several armed police officers. Narrow concrete sidewalks crisscross the small residential area and run in front of the few commercial establishments facing the beach. The town can be accessed only from the water or via walking trails from Puerto Obaldia or La Miel in Panama, or from Capurgana in Colombia. There are no cars; consequently, there are no streets. "Lo que es muy tranquilo."

Last night we were assaulted by rain, lightning, and thunder. I sure hope we have better weather for our crossing tonight. We plan to leave at 6:00 p.m. and head to the San Bernardos Islands, which are about 20 hours away. Isla Fuerte is closer, but it's supposed to have an uncomfortably rolly anchorage.

Two backpackers swam over to the boats and asked for passage to Cartagena. We declined, having already discussed, and agreed on, a policy of not taking strangers on crossings. Bruno was easier to convince.

I'll e-mail again after we get to the S.B. Islands.

Sandy

San Bernardo Islands

> **San Bernardo**
>
> The San Bernardo Archipelago consists of 10 islands. One of the 10, Santa Cruz del Islote, is listed as the world's most densely populated island. In contrast, the other islands are sparsely populated. Some are private and some are parklands; others have a small resort, hotel, or cabins available for rent.

From: sandy_n_marc
To: Davis News Group
Subject: Davis News
Date: Fri, 11 May 2007

We left Sapzurro at 5:30 p.m. and arrived at the San Bernardo Islands 18 hours later. We had to motor the entire trip because there was no wind, but the bonus of calm seas provided an easy passage.

As we neared the San Bernardo Archipelago, we had to tiptoe through a minefield of reefs to get to the anchorage next to Tintipan Island. Once there, the anchor didn't set well, so Marc dove on it. He reported a rock bottom with a thin covering of sand—a challenge for good holding—but since the anchorage was well protected, we decided not to worry about it.

We plan to take our time getting to Cartagena. We'll stay here through tomorrow, maybe longer, and then stop at the Rosarios Islands, where we'll relax for a day or two.

Madeline turns 15 tomorrow. She plans to drink her hoarded club soda, suck on her recently purchased lollipop, and watch her new *Buffy* DVDs (brought by the Erreras). She says that will be a fine birthday as long as we go to Crepes & Waffles, for froufrou ice cream, once we arrive in Cartagena.

Cheers—
Sandy

Stormy Weather—and Cartagena

From: sandy_n_marc
To: Davis News Group
Subject: Davis News
Date: Thu, 17 May 2007

When we decided our anchor's holding would be okay, we didn't consider the possibility that a storm would hit us, as it did on the morning of the 13th.

We awoke at 5:00 a.m. to 40-knot winds blowing us toward shore. Immediately, we turned on the engine and prepared to leave, but raising the anchor became a problem. Marc struggled to operate the anchor windlass on the bow of the boat while the boat bucked on high waves. At the same time, the anchor was catching on coral. Madeline had been watching the depth gauge, but I sent her up on deck to relay communications between Marc and me because we couldn't hear each other over the howling of the wind. I then called Alex to come up and watch the depth gauge while I handled the throttle and wheel. (The commotion had woken Alex and he'd started to play video games down below—at 5:00 in the morning!) By the time we finally extracted the anchor off the ocean floor, we had only a foot of water beneath the keel. I used full throttle to motor against the wind and drove us away from the island. We then radioed Bruno, who had just dealt with the same crisis on DOMANI and was now standing-by offshore. We all agreed that we should proceed to the Rosarios Islands.

Our rattled nerves eased as the storm settled down, and we arrived at Isla Grande, in the Rosarios Islands, at 10:30 a.m. After two days of rest, we left for Cartagena, with a lunch stop at Playa Blanca on the Island of Baru.

We were surprised at how nostalgic we felt as we sailed into Cartagena Harbor (yes, finally sailing). Upon entering the anchorage at dusk, we immediately spotted LARA. The family on board recognized us and dinghied over as soon as we anchored. We had lots to catch up on since we'd last seen each other (a year and a half ago!) at Bahia Redonda Marina in Venezuela, where they were converting a Texas shrimper into a mega yacht. TARA was approximately 95 feet long, and they made a good profit when selling her thanks to low material and labor costs in Venezuela and their own diligent work schedule. LARA is also a Texas shrimper but larger (about 115 feet long). This time they've hired crew in Cartagena to work on LARA in the anchorage. Alex and Madeline are happy to have Patrick (almost 10) and Sean (almost 16) as their friends in this port. Marc and I enjoy talking with Sam and Virginia and have already received helpful advice from them for our own—much smaller—project.

The primary topic of conversation around the anchorage and marina is the recent storm. The same storm that hit us in the Bernardo Islands also hit Cartagena. Many boats dragged in the anchorage, and a few masts slammed against each other in the marinas.

We are trying to obtain a slip for DOMANI in Club Nautico Marina and hope a spot will become available before Bruno leaves for Italy. Meanwhile, he's decided to do a backpacker run, to Panama and back, for extra cash.

We have a few days to get organized before Guillermo starts working for us. We cleared in to the country with Manfred this time. He's German and grumpy. I prefer David; he's local and cheerful.

It certainly took a while, but we finally broke down and bought a cell phone for local calls. No doubt, it'll be useful for our extended stay here.

Our current impressions of Cartagena:

- Hottest and most humid place we've been besides Trinidad. The days are almost unbearable, but the nights are pleasant.

- Less rain and fewer bugs than in Panama.

- Prices are higher here than they are in Panama, and I think the dollar has lost more value since we were here last.

- Old Town is charming.

- It is a beautiful city at night.

- We have good friends here.

Talk to you later—
Sandy

Daily Routines and Big Developments

From: sandy_n_marc
To: Davis News Group
Subject: Davis News
Date: Wed, 6 Jun 2007

We now have a regular work routine, thanks to Guillermo. He works from 8:00 a.m. to 5:00 p.m., Monday through Friday, minus a one-hour lunch break. We pay him 50,000 pesos per day and an extra 3,500 for lunch. He also works on Saturdays from 8:00 a.m. to 1:00 p.m. for a full day's pay. The exchange rate now is 2,000 pesos to the U.S. dollar, so his wage works out to about US$25 per day. He has already removed the stanchions, lifelines, and the nonskid on the deck; now, he's attacking rust with the grinder and needle-gun. At the end of the day, I clean up and paint primer on any newly exposed metal. Marc alternates between working on deck with Guillermo and working on interior projects. His Spanish is improving.

Madeline spent a couple of days last week working on her Spanish but hasn't kept up with it. I'm hoping she'll get back to it since she was quite enthusiastic at the beginning of her studies. However, she may be too distracted now because ... she has a boyfriend. Yep, Sean from LARA is her first boyfriend. Unfortunately, he will be leaving mid-August to attend an arts magnet school in Colorado near where his aunt lives. (His passion is computer animation.) Madeline and Sean, along with Alex and Patrick, get together regularly on weekdays after 3:00 p.m. and spend all day together on the weekends.

Bruno docked DOMANI at Club Nautico Marina today. He leaves for Europe tomorrow.

Our plans have changed after learning that my mother put her condominium up for sale and is moving to Oregon City to care for her mother. Her move directly affects us because half of her condo's two-car garage is filled with our stuff. We agonized over what to do about this but finally decided that I should fly home to personally deal with our belongings. Because there will be considerable chaos here while I'm gone (Marc and Guillermo are extremely messy and disorganized), I've decided to take Alex with me. Madeline will stay behind for a few reasons: first, there's the money issue; second, she already went home last summer; third, Marc needs company; fourth, she can live easily with the mess and might even get motivated to do some cleaning; and finally, she has a boyfriend here (might as well let them be together until he leaves). So, Alex and I will be in Oregon from June 15th through July 21st.

And the changes keep coming: As you know, we're working hard to get MARAVIDA to a finished state so we can put her up for sale by the first of next year. Here's our new plan from that point on:

We're going back to Oregon to work with Marc's mother and stepfather in Mulino, Oregon, a hamlet not far from Portland. We will learn all about their business, which is building components for the fiber optics field. The goal is for us to take over the business when they retire sometime within the next couple of years. We will live in the original farmhouse on their farm. Coincidentally, the business/farm is located near Oregon City, where my mother will be living with my grandmother.

The adventure is not over. We remain committed to continuing with traveling adventures as we get closer to retirement age...

Sandy

Back from Oregon

From: sandy_n_marc
To: Davis News Group
Subject: Davis News
Date: Sun, 29 Jul 2007

Alex and I returned to Cartagena on July 21st, after five weeks in Oregon. Though we've been back for a little over a week, I can't seem to acclimate to this sweltering climate. The temperature got up to 100 degrees Fahrenheit when we were in Portland, but it didn't feel as bad in comparison to here. It's the humidity that makes it so uncomfortable. Nevertheless, I'm the only one that's miserable. Marc sweats a lot—but he doesn't complain—and Madeline and Alex are completely unfazed by it.

Alex and I visited family and friends while we were in Portland. I also shopped for necessities (like new underwear for everyone in the family). I enjoyed eating a variety of foods I haven't had in a long while, and I went to Starbucks more than I ever had before. Most important, though, I moved our sentimental belongings from my mom's garage in Beaverton to an upstairs bedroom at the farm in Mulino. Mission accomplished.

The seventh and final Harry Potter novel, *Harry Potter and the Deathly Hallows*, was released the day Alex and I headed back to Cartagena. When Powell's Books—at the Portland airport—opened at 5:00 a.m., we were the first customers in the door. Alex didn't mind the long day of travel because he had his new Harry Potter book and a new Game Boy game. (Not surprisingly, Alex, Madeline, and Marc have all finished reading the new Harry Potter book already.)

Our four check-on bags were full of books, DVDs, and equipment for the boat. Luckily, the bags weren't searched at customs. All the items are duty-free because they're for personal use—but I was relieved I didn't have to answer questions about the hundreds of sheets of sandpaper, etc.

To prepare for our arrival, Marc hired a girl to clean the interior of the boat. She worked two full days for US$15 per day. Marc also had the guys (yes, guy is plural, see next paragraph) clean up the decks and cockpit.

Madeline says I would've been horrified by the mess, so it must have been pretty bad.

Yes, we now have two guys working on MARAVIDA: Guillermo and Estephenson. We first met Estephenson when he charged our refrigerator last January. The guys have spent the last few weeks sanding and filling the deck. Marc has farmed out the big pieces of stainless for repairs and polishing.

Last Tuesday, we removed all of the floorboards in the boat and took them to Ferroalquimar shipyard to be repaired, refinished, and revarnished by a painting crew. We went to check on their progress on Saturday, and the pieces looked great. The workers said that they don't often see such high quality woodwork. (Recall that MARAVIDA was custom built in Brazil.)

Today, Guillermo and Estephenson worked on the stainless steel stanchions, polishing and prepping them to be welded onto the toerails.

Madeline has been living by herself on DOMANI in the marina. Of course it's only temporary, but being independent at age 15 has been a fun experience for her and takes her mind off Sean's absence. She buys her own groceries and cooks for herself. She also has a job working on LARA five days a week from nine to noon. She is sewing curtains, bed coverings, shower curtains, and pillow covers for the converted mega yacht.

Alex enjoys playing with Patrick from LARA, and Olive and Rueben from YAMANA. All four are taking a summer break from schoolwork.

We will take MARAVIDA to the boatyard soon. We'll have her hauled onto the hard and hire a crew to paint her bottom while Guillermo and Estephenson weld on top. Then, we'll have the topsides and deck painted, and she'll look better than ever.

Everyone dreads going to the boatyard. There's always less wind in a boatyard than on the water, which makes it feel much hotter. And it's so dirty—either dusty or muddy, depending on the amount of rain.

We want to complete two other large projects before we leave Colombia: getting new upholstery for the seating on MARAVIDA and building a fiberglass shower from scratch.

Marc would like to take MARAVIDA to California to sell, but I don't think we'll have time since we committed to arrive in Oregon by January 1st to start learning Marc´s mom and stepdad´s business. My guess is we'll take MARAVIDA to Curacao.

Talk to you later—
Sandy

Dailies

From: sandy_n_marc
To: Davis News Group
Subject: Davis News
Date: Thu, 23 Aug 2007

July 30, 2007

In the morning, Marc went with Andy (a taxi driver/interpreter named Andrés, who charges US$10 per hour for his services; he was recommended by LARA) to order more varnish for the floor refinishers.

In the afternoon, we had an upholsterer come to the boat to take measurements for a quote.

July 31, 2007

We experienced one of the frequent early morning windstorms that occur here in the rainy season. These storms are intense and usually cause a few boats to drag. Fortunately, we haven't dragged here, thanks again to MARAVIDA's heavy anchor.

Madeline babysat two South African children (ages two and five) from the boat TIGER, while we went out to dinner with their parents. The kids had a great time on DOMANI with Madeline, Alex, and Patrick.

August 1, 2007

All four of us went for dentist appointments at a dental office that's only a few blocks away from the marina. The prices weren't cheap, considering we're in Colombia, but they were less than at home (US$40 per checkup/cleaning). It's likely the prices are higher at this dental office because it caters to this wealthy neighborhood.

August 2, 2007

We returned to the dentist to have some cavities filled (US$20 per cavity), then went out to dinner at a Chinese restaurant with the family from TIGER and Sam and Patrick from LARA. While we were eating, a storm came through and knocked out the power. The employees weren't bothered in the least; they brought candles to the table so we could see our food. Virginia and Sean weren't with us because they're in the States getting their recently purchased 78-foot sailboat settled in Texas and then finalizing arrangements for Sean to start school in Colorado.

August 4, 2007

Estephenson and Guillermo got the refrigerator on DOMANI working.

August 10, 2007

Marc got up in the morning to find Maria sitting in the salon, soaking wet. She apparently fell in and then somehow managed to get back onto the boat by herself. She must have been jumping back and forth between MARAVIDA and the dinghy ... but missed that time. She's been amusing herself with this new activity when there's no wind and the dinghy floats close to the boat.

August 12, 2007

A repeat of two days ago—Maria has no fear and doesn't learn from her mistakes.

August 13, 2007

Madeline and I walked to Old Town while Marc went to do errands with Andy.

August 15, 2007

Marc went out with Andy again. Madeline and I walked downtown, this time with Alex.

August 17, 2007

The new windshield panels were installed today, following a failed first attempt. Marc had farmed out the job to experts because Plexiglas is difficult to bend. Unfortunately, the tradesmen weren't as proficient with the plastic as we had hoped; the first piece they brought back was not even close to the correct shape. They eventually got the curves right, but the corners are pitted due to excess heat exposure. Nevertheless, we were relieved to have something acceptable for our money. In Colombia, once you've paid for the materials on a job, it's almost impossible to get a refund; the cost of materials usually exceeds the cost of the labor itself, and the laborers are too poor to replace their mistakes.

August 18, 2007

The paint store repeatedly assured us that our order of semigloss varnish would come in any day, but we finally had to give up and buy the gloss that was in stock instead. We were tired of being badgered by the floor refinishers—they just want to finish the floorboards and get their money. Our sympathy turned to anger, though, when they threatened to charge us an additional 100,000 pesos to renew their rental space where our floorboards were stored. Marc guessed that they were lying about the rental charge, so he called the boatyard to confirm. Sure enough, the rental charge was fabricated.

Around 8:00 in the evening, Madeline was on DOMANI watching a movie when she heard a sizzling sound. After lifting up the floorboards to discover that the wiring underneath had caught fire, she ran to the nearest boat that looked occupied. Guy on RARE METTLE grabbed his fire extinguisher and rushed over to DOMANI. His first move was to turn off the shore power, but when that didn't stop the fire, he had to use the fire extinguisher. Madeline called us on the radio when the fire was out. Marc jumped in the dinghy and raced to the marina. Once there, he made sure the fire was completely out and all power connections were turned off, and then brought a shaking Madeline back to MARAVIDA. Thanks, Guy!

August 19, 2007

Marc vacuumed up the fire extinguisher mess on DOMANI and located the wire that was responsible for the incident. If Madeline hadn't been on board, the wooden boat would have been destroyed by fire. Nevertheless, Madeline will not stay on DOMANI again until MARAVIDA goes to the boatyard and she has roommates. The incident dampened her enthusiasm for independence—for now, anyway.

MARAVIDA's floors were delivered today. The final coat has fisheyes and looks terrible. Marc says the crater-like pockmarks were likely caused by surface contamination. The painters were probably in too much of a rush to finish the project and get their money. Nevertheless, we're relieved to have the pieces back and to be finished with the whole ordeal. Later, we'll have Guillermo and Estephenson sand the top coat down and reapply a nonglossy finish.

The windshield and floor fiascos have increased Marc's consternation about how things work in developing nations. He's so ready to be done. We are fortunate, though, to have Guillermo and Estephenson working on MARAVIDA six days a week. They are dependable and hard workers.

Today Marc finished plumbing the aft bathroom. Now the toilet and sink both work. I'm excited that I can brush my teeth in the bathroom instead of the kitchen sink.

August 21, 2007

We hired a marina worker to scrape MARAVIDA'S bottom and propeller. The cost was 50,000 pesos (US$25). He worked most of the day and did it without a scuba tank!

Marc simplified DOMANI's shore power wiring to bypass the existing mess of wiring.

August 23, 2007

The kids and I moved onto DOMANI yesterday, and today Marc, Guillermo, and Estephenson took MARAVIDA to the Ferroalquimar boatyard. They had to pull up the anchor without the windlass because the cracked chain gypsy is being recast at a machine shop. I heard that Marc did an excellent job backing the boat into the travel-slip, and the lifting and chocking of the boat went smoothly. Marc says MARAVIDA looks huge out of the water.

Marc was exhausted in the evening. Nevertheless, he went with us to YAMANA's going-away costume party (with a pirate theme). It took place downtown on the rooftop of a hostel. Our kids will miss Olive and Rueben, but Patrick is still here.

I didn't get a chance to appreciate the recently installed moldings (including all window moldings) before we moved off MARAVIDA.

DOMANI is cramped with our things on top of Bruno's things. The good news is that we've installed our window air conditioner in DOMANI (last used at Bahia Redonda Marina in Venezuela almost two years ago). The boat may be cluttered, but it feels comfortably cool.

Our tentative plan is to leave Cartagena at the end of October or beginning of November and sail to Curacao. We will put MARAVIDA on the hard at Curacao Marine in December, list her for sale, and then fly home to Oregon.

More later—
Sandy

Boatyard

From: sandy_n_marc
To: Davis News Group
Subject: Davis News
Date: Thu, 27 Sep 2007

August 24, 2007

First day of work at the yard. The guys are welding the stanchions to the toerail.

August 25, 2007

More welding today.

August 26, 2007

It has rained the entire day. Good. It's better to rain today (Sunday) than tomorrow so that Marc doesn't have to come up with indoor projects for the workers.

August 27, 2007

Three additional workers started today: Jaime, David, and Flavid. They will sand and paint the entire exterior of MARAVIDA while Guillermo and Estephenson work on other projects. Marc insists on paying by the hour, which isn't a standard practice here, but it gives us more control. Guillermo and Estephenson were hesitant at first but now realize that the wage is reasonable and consistent, and the work is long-term.

August 28, 2007

Guillermo and Estephenson finished the stanchions and then started on a new assignment: find the hole that's causing the keel fuel tank to leak into the bilge. They cut a large section of the keel open and inspected the interior thoroughly but found nothing obvious. So now, they'll re-weld the seams, grind the surfaces, and then paint with tank epoxy. Once the keel is welded closed, they'll start inspecting the inside surfaces of MARAVIDA—looking under the floorboards, beds, etc. for any new or previously missed rust since MARAVIDA was epoxy-painted in Trinidad three years ago.

August 29, 2007

We have to use Club Nautico's laundry service since we don't have access to our own washing machine on MARAVIDA and doing the laundry by hand isn't an option here because the marina forbids hanging it in public view (a common rule in marinas—for aesthetic reasons). I'm not complaining though; they wash, dry, and fold for US$5 per load, saving me lots of work.

Madeline and I went to Castellana Mall and found some new outfits for her. To Madeline's mind, there's only one thing better than going to the mall, and that's buying clothes at the mall.

August 31, 2007

After three trips to the Yamaha dealer, we finally got Bruno's 15-horsepower Yamaha outboard repaired and tuned. Marc can now drive our dinghy—with Bruno's outboard—directly to the boatyard (our 4-horsepower engine is too slow). This saves a lot of time and taxi money each day and is better for Bruno's engine than letting it sit for months without use.

September 1, 2007

I accompanied Marc to the boatyard today since it's a shorter work day (the quitting bell rings at 2:00 p.m. on Saturdays).

Chocked up next to MARAVIDA is a traditional Colombian fishing boat that's almost as long as MARAVIDA. Its old worn boards are being recaulked with cotton and some type of goo. One worker chops on a log with an ax (making replacement boards, I guess). Altogether, ten guys work on the boat while the Patron sits in a chair reigning over them. Marc said he saw the Patron call for one of the workers to come over and squash a bug. The whole operation is primitive, suggesting that time has stood still here.

We went to dinner on LARA for Virginia's birthday. Sam and Virginia also invited an American missionary couple who have been living in Cartagena for about four years: Dan and Berit Wick. They operate a foundation called "Friends for Colombia" (see http://www.friendsforcolombia.org).

September 2, 2007

It's Sunday, Marc's day off. Midmorning we took the dinghy across the bay to Boca Grande. There's no place to leave the dinghy, so Marc and Alex waited while Madeline and I walked the few blocks to McDonald's and brought back Egg McMuffins. It's a special treat that reminds us of home.

September 3, 2007

The boatyard has two restaurants that sit side by side. The yard workers are loyal to one or the other. Marc buys lunch for all five of our workers and himself every day but Saturday. For 4,000 pesos each (US$2) they get a hearty and filling meal of soup, meat, rice, salad, and a fruit drink. Guillermo was tired of the race for service at their usual restaurant and wanted to switch to the other one, which has smaller portions but provides table service to patrons in order of arrival. Marc approved, so Guillermo, Marc, and Estephenson have defected and are now considered "traitors," but Guillermo is much happier.

September 8, 2007

Alex went with Marc to the boatyard today (Saturday). They took the laptop so Alex can use the free wireless internet.

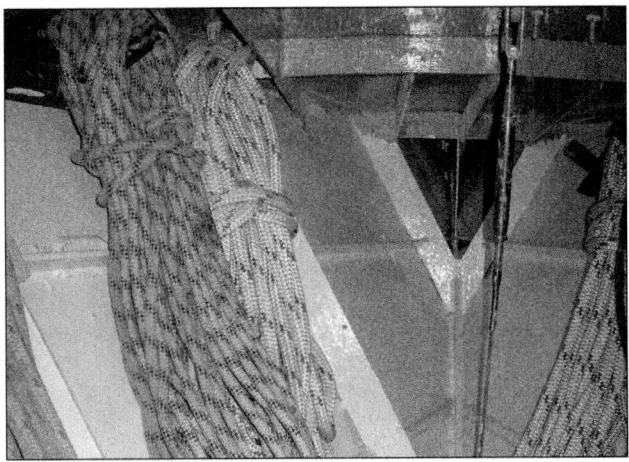

September 11, 2007

The upholsterer can finally start work on our cushions now that the foam has arrived (the leather order came in on time, but the foam was late). He will use the old cushions for patterns, which Marc will drop off as needed.

The upholstery shop is located next to the water, right on Marc's route to and from the boatyard.

September 12, 2007

Marc came back to the marina at noon to use the ATM to get money for paint. Madeline decided to accompany him back to the yard for the remainder of the workday.

Medical Tourism in U.S. Dollars

September 13, 2007

Marc and I went to Dr. Francisco Holguin, director of Medihelp Services Clinic, for general checkups (US$60 each). He was recommended to us by a friend who went to the private hospital to have a kidney removed back in May. The cost was only US$7,000, including a week's stay in a luxurious private hospital room. (See http://www.medihelpservices.com/en.html.)

Health care services aren't as cheap as in Venezuela, but they're certainly cheaper than in the U.S., so we're getting as much done as possible before we return to the States. Back home, we'll only be able to afford a major-medical insurance policy.

September 14, 2007

The next day we went back for lab tests. (My lab tests cost US$75, Marc's cost $64. My sonogram was $135, Marc's was $88.) When we met with the doctor to discuss the results, we learned that I have one fibroid in my uterus and Marc has two gallstones in his gallbladder. We don't feel as if we have to act on those particular problems immediately, but we were a little concerned about Marc's abnormal liver enzyme levels. The doctor asked Marc about his alcohol consumption. Marc said he drinks a few beers in the afternoon/evening (the cans are smaller than those at home). The doctor asked him not to drink alcohol for a few days and then come back for another liver test.

September 16, 2007

Sunday, Marc's day off. The four of us walked downtown in the afternoon and treated ourselves to ice cream at Crepes & Waffles.

September 18, 2007

Marc and Madeline went to renew their visas. Alex and I don't have to renew because our time was reset when we returned from the U.S.

September 19, 2007

Berit (the American missionary) met Marc and me in Boca Grande and then we all headed to my gynecologist appointment with Dr. Monica Guerrero. Berit translated for me. (Exam—$60, Pap smear—$15.)

After the appointment, we met Berit's husband, Dan, at their condo in a Boca Grande high-rise. The elevator opens right into the living room of their 3,000-square-foot home. Because the condo occupies the entire floor, every room has a stunning view. After a tour, the four of us went out to lunch at a deli that trains underprivileged young people in restaurant service.

The medical visits continued after lunch, with Berit translating again, this time at our appointments with a dermatologist. (Dr. Rodrigo Valez—$40 each). After that, it was back to the gynecologist for me for a follow-up sonogram. It was $92, but the doctor thought it might help determine why I'm having chronic bladder discomfort. (The results showed two fibroids, each about an inch in diameter.)

September 20, 2007

Marc and I returned to Boca Grande for additional tests: mammogram—$85; liver test for Marc—$15; and a more complex urine test for me—$30. Marc's liver test was normal this time. He really was drinking too many beers! Since carbonation quenches his thirst and sodas are too sweet, he's decided to switch to sparkling water for his primary beverage choice.

September 22, 2007

Madeline babysat four kids between the ages of three and five. They are from two boats: BLUEPRINT MATCH and RED THREAD. Madeline enjoyed the kids and was paid well.

September 25, 2007

The dermatologist removed seven spots from my body, five for testing. The doctor numbed each area with a shot or two (ouch and double ouch), and then cut the piece out and stitched it closed. This would be fine for one or two spots, but seven times left me feeling like a pincushion. (The procedure was $200, and the biopsy tests were another $100.)

September 26, 2007

The decks are finally done despite a small disaster at the start of the job. Marc went on an errand after explicitly telling the painters how to mix the two-part epoxy primer and specifying which hardener went with which paint. Here's what happened, in his words:

> When I returned to the boat, they had mixed and applied about a third of the paint to the deck. I was pleased with their work until I counted the number of cans left and found one extra can of hardener and one missing can of the enamel topcoat's hardener. When I confronted them and told them they had used the wrong hardener for the paint, they denied it. But then I showed them the cans of paint. They said, don't worry, it'll work fine even with the wrong hardener. I got angry because I knew it wouldn't work. I told them that all of the paint had to be removed quickly before it started to dry. I yelled at them for being careless and costing us a lot of money in paint. They asked if they were fired. I said no, but I was very unhappy because they hadn't been careful. They just sat and stared at me. Frustrated, I yelled 'MOVE' at the top of my lungs and they jumped into action.
>
> I had to leave the boat because I was so angry. When I got about 50 feet away from the boat, I let loose and screamed 'F**K' as loud as I could. All work in the yard stopped and everyone looked at me.
>
> They got the paint cleaned off, I bought more paint, and this time they mixed it correctly.

The last step to finish the decks was to spray on the nonskid compound after masking out Marc's design. Unfortunately, the masking had to be redone a few times before the painters could finally spray. The problem wasn't due to human error, but because of rain and faulty tape.

Right now, two of the painters are applying filler to the topsides and the third is refinishing the teak cockpit seats. Guillermo and Estephenson will be working on a different project for a couple of weeks—grinding and welding on ANDREA CLAIRE, another steel boat in the yard.

September 27, 2007

The anchorage and marina are starting to fill up after a quiet summer. Familiar boats and old friends are arriving daily, and the din of chatty cruisers has increased at Club Nautico's Wednesday Night Happy Hour.

Alex is going to be 13 on Sunday. How weird to think we'll now have two teenagers!

That's more than enough for now—
Sandy

Nearing the End...

From: sandy_n_marc
To: Davis News Group
Subject: Davis News
Date: Sun, 14 Oct 2007

September 28, 2007

Marc went with Andy (the taxi driver) to drop off the Mercedes fuel injectors—they need overhauling—and to purchase a new injector to replace one that broke in the cylinder head. The parts were ready for pickup in only a few hours. How gratifying to have success at both acquiring a new part and getting fast turnaround service.

We went to a barbecue dinner on LARA to celebrate their project completion.

September 29, 2007

When Marc isn't out purchasing supplies for the boat, he's laboring side by side with the workers. He had a funny mishap the other day when he was working on the top tier of some scaffolding, sanding near MARAVIDA's toerail, about 12 feet off the ground:

> Suddenly, part of the scaffolding collapsed. I fell down through several layers of scaffolding with boards crashing down around me. Fortunately, I was able to ride the boards as if I were surfing and landed on my feet. Because I'd finished working in that area anyway, the next section of scaffolding was undamaged, and I was still holding the sander, I climbed onto that scaffolding and started sanding again.
>
> Later the supervisor of the paint crew, Jaime, came over and said, 'Marc, I thought you'd be dead and we would lose our jobs because you were dead. You are the toughest man I've ever seen. I would never get in a fight with you.' He was uninterested in my explanation that it hadn't been a big deal.

September 30, 2007

Sunday, Alex's 13th birthday. After he opened his presents, which were books I had brought back with us from the States, we picked up Patrick and headed downtown to the naval museum and Crepes & Waffles. For dinner we went to our favorite Mexican restaurant (the only Mexican restaurant we know about here), and then headed for DOMANI, where we finished off the day with birthday cake from one of the many cake shops in Cartagena.

October 1, 2007

Berit accompanied me to the dermatologist to get my test results and have my stitches removed. A spot on my arm tested as melanoma, but it was small, and fortunately, all of it had been removed with the biopsy. A spot on my face, however, is basal cell carcinoma and much more has to be removed. The dermatologist has recommended a plastic surgeon to perform the procedure.

We went out to dinner with Fin and Susan from ANDREA CLAIRE. They told us they found Guillermo sleeping on the job today. But they knew what they were getting into—we had warned them that Mondays had become a problem for Guillermo. He calls in sick, or he comes in late and works listlessly. We figure he is partying too hard on the weekends. Estephenson is more diligent and responsible, but he has a family to support. Though Guillermo has a son, he isn't married, and his son doesn't live with him.

October 2, 2007

Marc accompanied me to my 4:00 p.m. consultation with the plastic surgeon. His office is located in a high-rise office building next to the hospital. It's an old building, nothing like the ultramodern Medihelp building down the street.

Madeline and Virginia shared our taxi to go to the English-Speaking Women's Group meeting being held at Berit's condo, just across the street from the plastic surgeon's office. Madeline has already volunteered at a shelter for teenage girls that the women's group helps support. The day shelter houses the girls every morning and feeds them lunch. The first time Madeline went there (with Berit and Virginia), she brought our sewing machine and iron and helped on each girl's sewing project. On her second visit, Madeline helped the girls with English.

October 3, 2007

We've hired a carpenter to work on MARAVIDA. His first, and most important, project is to install woodwork around the new refrigerator.

Several of the boat owners in the yard contributed to a fund to help Javier, a hearing-impaired boat worker. He had been working on a large powerboat project, but since the owner of the boat has been out of town, he's been working on ANDREA CLAIRE. He's well liked in the boatyard, and the workers are kind to him. Susan and Fin got the idea to collect money to get him a hearing aid, but first they arranged for a hearing test to see if a hearing aid would actually help. The results were positive, so a few boat owners pitched in money. The total was short of what they needed, but Susan and Fin decided to go to the audiologist anyway and explain the cause. It turns out that charitable giving is a strange concept to Colombians, but once the staff at the audiologist office understood that many people had contributed money, they offered to do the fitting of the aid for free and even worked with the supplier to get a discount. Javier was nervous about the whole process, but once he got the hearing aid he became amazed and excited about his new soniferous world.

October 4, 2007

Marc went with Andy to buy wood, varnish, and general tool supplies. Andy isn't an official taxi driver; he's a tour guide and often takes cruise ship passengers around the city. He's a good guide because he has a pleasant personality, speaks English well, and knows his way around town. He makes our life easier because he always knows exactly where to get the supplies we need, which saves us the time we'd otherwise spend searching out the right places for particular items. In addition, he translates communications between Marc and the merchants, which helps eliminate misunderstandings.

Andy taught Marc the expression "listo Calisto," which is similar to "ready Freddy" or "we are finished and ready to go." Marc now uses the phase frequently, much to our annoyance.

We went out to dinner with the couple from GECKO. We first met Anna and Ian in Venezuela. They're from Seattle and work in the television broadcast industry when they're not cruising on their catamaran.

October 5, 2007

Marc went out with Andy again, this time to get hydraulic work done on our backstay and buy a part for our paint gun.

We ate dinner on LARA with JEDI and Sam and Virginia's broker. The broker has come to visit and take pictures of LARA.

October 7, 2007

On Sunday, Susan and Fin treated us to a Rosarios Island tour as a thank you for giving Guillermo and Estephenson time off to work on ANDREA CLAIRE. We met them at 8:00 a.m. at the excursion dock downtown. We boarded a long, narrow boat that held about 50 people and had two 200-horsepower Yamaha outboard engines. The trip to the Rosarios Islands took only an hour and was surprisingly comfortable in the open ocean. We disembarked at a small beach resort (dilapidated by American standards, but normal for here), where we swam in crystal clear water that was a refreshing contrast to Cartagena's dirty harbor. We then boarded the same boat for a trip to the nearby aquarium. An hour later, we returned to the resort for a delicious fish lunch, more swimming, and lounging. The outing provided us a much-needed and appreciated break. Thanks, Susan and Fin!

October 9, 2007

I went in for my scheduled outpatient surgery at Medihelp Services Clinic. The doctor said the procedure took longer than normal because there was more cancer to remove than they had anticipated. The incision was an inch long and I will have a scar, but the plastic surgeon said he planned it to integrate with future facial wrinkles. (Total cost—US$800.)

October 10, 2007

Guillermo and Estephenson finished welding on ANDREA CLAIRE and are now working on the plumbing for two different items: the large electric bilge pump and the washing machine. The former had never been completed, and the latter had been temporarily diverted into the cockpit to exit through the cockpit drain.

Marc supervised seven workers today (counting the engine mechanic who worked at the boat for part of the day). Because Marc's presence was necessary to keep everyone on task, I went out with Andy to do boat errands. When we finished, he dropped me off at the boatyard with my purchases.

Marc asked me to look at the carpenter's woodwork. After thorough analysis and discussion, we decided his work is substandard. Marc will have to terminate him and some of the work will have to be redone.

October 12, 2007

I went out with Andy again to do more boat errands.

October 13, 2007

Today a big rainstorm came through town while Madeline and I were shopping at the Carulla grocery store. We decided to wait it out in the cafeteria. By the time the rain had stopped, the street had transformed into a 6-inch-deep river with a swift current. Luckily, we were just a block and a half from the marina and only had to ford the river once.

I'm afraid that all this rain will ruin the painters' plan to paint all day Saturday and Sunday in order to be finished by Tuesday.

> **Rain in Cartagena**
>
> Cartagena averages about 40 inches of rain a year. The rainiest months are May through November.

Other Stuff

When Alex and I came back from Oregon, I was astonished at how much Marc's Spanish had improved. Guillermo and Estephenson both understand Marc's unique brand of Spanish, and they speak back to him in simplified Spanish so that he can understand them. It amazes me that Marc speaks fast and with confidence; even his pronunciation is good. However, his vocabulary is limited and his grammar is poor. His key words are: mira, problema, eso, rápido, ahora, necesito, comprendo, acá, aqui, más tarde, cambio, pasado, mañana, futura, facil, trabajo, etc. (Translation: look, problem, that, quick, now, I need, understand, here, here—more specific and formal, later, change, past, morning, future, easy, work, etc.) His boatwork-specific words are: tornillo, soldadura, aceite, instala, repara, óxido, corriente, ferretería, agua con sal, manguera, tubo, calor, caliente, duro, fuerte, acero, inoxidable, pintura, papel de lija, máquina, aluminio, etc. (Translation: screw, weld, oil, install, repair, rust, current, hardware store, salt water, hose, pipe, heat, hot, hard, strong, steel, paint, sandpaper, machine, aluminum, etc.)

Marc and I walk the short distance to the marina's wharf each morning at 7:00 to get coffee (Club Nautico offers free coffee every morning). A few other early risers usually come by to chat. Eventually Marc leaves for the yard, and I return to DOMANI to work on chores. Later in the morning, Madeline and/or Alex walk with me to the grocery store to purchase meal items and internet time (the marina's internet isn't working well). We also stop at the ATM, where I use my debit card and Marc's debit card to withdraw the maximum cash allowed. I do this because we pay the workers daily and we also have to save up for the weekly cash-only marina bill and the future cash-only boatyard bill. In the afternoon, Patrick comes over to play with Alex, and Madeline usually convinces me to walk downtown with her.

Despite having air conditioning and the many other perks of being docked at a marina, we are not enjoying life on DOMANI:

- For one thing, we don't fit comfortably on the boat. Marc and I sleep on either side of the back cabin, which has the only functioning toilet. Madeline sleeps in the pilot house/salon on the settee. Alex sleeps on a mattress on the floor of the salon. He can't sleep where the mattress normally resides because the boat leaks directly over it.

- It literally rains inside the boat. And because it's been raining so much lately, we have to sidestep all the drip pans we've placed throughout the boat. (Remember, DOMANI is wooden and was built in the 1950s).

- There are cockroaches. Lots of them. I dread each night when the creatures come out from hiding and crawl up the walls, taking control of the boat and making us the minority. Unfortunately, MARAVIDA has also been invaded by cockroaches at the boatyard. We plan to mount a brutal attack against the beasts once MARAVIDA is back in the water.

- We've experienced so many problems with Bruno's electrical and toilet systems that we feel MARAVIDA's problems aren't so bad. (So, I guess this is actually a good thing.)

- It's been seven weeks, we're tired of DOMANI, and we're antsy to get back on MARAVIDA.

Sandy

Last Two Weeks

From: sandy_n_marc
To: Davis News Group
Subject: Davis News
Date: Sat, 27 Oct 2007

October 15, 2007

Green painted on starboard topside.

October 16, 2007

Green painted on port topside.

Got my stitches removed after a two-hour wait in a crowded doctor's office with too few chairs. I guess plastic surgery is a booming business here.

October 17, 2007

Bottom painted, ornamental lines taped on topsides, half of floors revarnished.

October 18, 2007

Lines painted, floors finished.

October 22, 2007

We took our lettering designs to a motorcycle decal shop last week. They used a computerized machine to cut the letters. The decals were made exactly as ordered—no screwups! And it gets better: An employee of the shop brought the decals to the boatyard today and applied them himself. We were surprised and grateful to have an expert do the job. I think he was thrilled to put decals on a yacht instead of a motorcycle.

October 23, 2007

When we picked up the last of the reupholstered cushions today, we were disappointed to discover that the navigation seat cushion was made upside down. Unfortunately, there's no time left to get it remade. *(It still sits, to this day, leather-side down.)*

MARAVIDA is almost ready to go. She was lowered into the water today, and then side-tied to the boatyard's dock.

October 24, 2007

We moved most of our personal gear back to MARAVIDA via one dinghy trip and two trips in Andy's car. We're excited to be able to sleep in our own beds.

This was the workers' last day. We gave out bonuses: US$100 to Guillermo; the welder as a gift to Estephenson; the compressor as a gift to Jaime; and US$50 each to Flavid and David.

October 25, 2007

It rained all day as we worked inside the boat, getting ready for departure.

At one point in the day, we heard a pop and smelled smoke. It was the new inverter/charger. Marc says it's only halfway broken because it can still charge the batteries when the generator is turned on or when the boat is plugged into shore power (the batteries run our 12-volt items). However, it won't produce 110-volt power anymore, which is a problem because we need the laptop to run the navigation software during our passage.

Susan and Fin came to MARAVIDA for dinner (ANDREA CLAIRE is still in the yard). They've been staying in one of the tiny rental rooms here at the yard. The accommodations include a bathroom, a bedroom, and a one-burner electric hot plate. They use the hot plate to cook dinner because the boatyard restaurants aren't open after lunch, and there aren't any grocery stores or restaurants in the vicinity (the boatyard is located in an industrial area).

Susan and Fin gave us a mini inverter. Thanks guys.

October 26, 2007

We spent the day cleaning Bruno's boat, shopping for groceries, and getting our *zarpe* (outbound clearance document for leaving the country). We left Club Nautico at night in our dinghy, which was overfilled with our remaining belongings. The trip to Ferroalquimar was long (because of our slow outboard motor) and a bit scary (it was very dark), but we eventually made it and had a good night's sleep. What a relief to be done.

October 27, 2007

The last week and a half in Cartagena has been an exhausting push to finish the boat projects. Today, we made last-minute preparations for the crossing.

In the evening, Susan and Fin came over for our "last supper" in Cartagena. They brought the raw ingredients for the meal, and we cooked them up.

We'll be on our way tomorrow—
Sandy

Leaving Cartagena

From: sandy_n_marc
To: Davis News Group
Subject: Davis News
Date: Sun, 28 Oct 2007

We said goodbye to Ferroalquimar, and Cartagena, at 9:00 a.m. Even though it's Sunday, some of the workers came to say farewell.

It's 6:30 p.m. right now. Conditions are calm so far, and we're motoring without sails.

Sandy

En Route

From: sandy_n_marc
To: Davis News Group
Subject: Davis News
Date: Tue, 30 Oct 2007

As we approached the Santa Marta area on Sunday night, we started to get into uncomfortable seas. After much debate, we decided to tuck into Five Bays for the rest of the night. We anchored at 1:30 a.m. next to our Canadian friends, Bill and Benita, on ALCHERINGA II. We also recognized the other boat in the bay, CAT COQUETTE, owned by a Danish couple we'd met in Trinidad about three years ago. Monday morning we all met on ALCHERINGA II for coffee, and that evening we had a potluck dinner on MARAVIDA. We plan to leave this morning (Tuesday) to continue our trip to Curacao.

P.S. Our friends were surprised and impressed by MARAVIDA's new and improved appearance. I hope to send pictures out once we get to civilization. We are proud of our beautiful boat.

Sandy

Los Monjes Islands

> **Monjes del Sur**
>
> Monjes del Sur is the site of a Venezuelan Coast Guard station. It consists of two small rocky islands that are linked by a solid rock dam/bridge. In front of the dam, boats can hook onto a rope that is stretched between the islands with individual finger lines attached.

From: sandy_n_marc
To: Davis News Group
Subject: Davis News
Date: Fri, 2 Nov 2007

On Tuesday, promptly at 9:00 a.m., we left Five Bays. The seas were calm and there was some wind, so we hoisted the main sail and let out the jib. At dusk, we rolled up the jib for better visibility in the dark. During Marc's turn on night watch, he saw a couple of squalls on the radar and changed course to avoid them. While I was on watch at dawn, the seas started to get higher; around 9:00 a.m., a squall hit us with a blast of rain and 35 knots of wind. Surprisingly, we didn't heel over much, even though the mainsail was raised. We were even more surprised when our speed got up to 10 knots, which must be a record for us. As the day progressed, the seas remained high and uncomfortable, making us all seasick (except Alex). Thus, our decision to make a stop was an easy one. We arrived at the Monjes Del Sur anchorage in Los Monjes Archipelago at 3:00 p.m. on Wednesday.

We managed to tie up without too much trouble by easing up and grabbing a line with the boat hook. Because boats are expected to line up along the rope facing the dam, the wind must typically come from the direction of the dam. Today, however, the winds are coming from the side and making us drift parallel to the rope. I'm glad there aren't any other boats here because we'd probably hit them at this angle.

Two coast guard personnel came down to the dock and indicated that they wanted us to bring MARAVIDA over to them. We didn't want to deal with the ordeal of docking, so Marc swam over to talk to them. Fortunately, Marc ascertained that the water depth at the dock was too shallow for MARAVIDA, so docking was out of the question anyway. Nevertheless, the coast guard officials asked to do their paperwork on our boat. Since we also didn't want to go through the trouble of launching the dinghy to pick them up, Marc came up with a plan. We unhooked from the tether, and Marc nosed MARAVIDA to the dock. Madeline and I motioned the men to climb aboard by grabbing and stepping over the pulpit. Marc then slowly backed over to the rope, and we hooked up to the line again. This took a long time, and then we had to repeat the time-consuming process in order to return the men to the dock.

The two young coast guard officials didn't speak English, but they managed to understand Marc's simplistic Spanish. Once the men finished filling out their forms, Marc sent them off with two mini rum bottles and said he'd go mañana to examine the island's broken watermaker, which they had disclosed was a big concern for the current residents of the island.

Since the weather looked more promising for Friday, we ended up staying another night, a much-appreciated reprieve. We also decided to break up the last 120 miles to Curacao with a stop in Aruba so that we won't have to endure any additional overnight crossings.

Marc cut short a swim around the boat when he discovered there were at least a hundred 4- to 6-foot-long barracuda circling in the small bay with MARAVIDA at the center of their circle. He says the fierce-looking predators aren't known to attack swimmers very often, but he didn't want to risk it with that many eyeing him.

In the afternoon, we blew up the spare dinghy and rowed to the dock. (Why oh why didn't we do this yesterday?) We hiked up to the lighthouse, greeting various coast guard personnel on the way. On our way back, Marc looked over the island's watermaker system with the commandante and proposed some ideas for fixing it. Meanwhile, we watched as men lugged buckets of water up the hill to a water tank. The water came from a small navy ship that had just arrived for the monthly delivery of personnel and provisions. Since everyone we talked to was worried about running out of water before the next delivery, Marc offered to make them more water with our watermaker. They eagerly accepted, so Marc ran the watermaker all afternoon and evening. Again and again he filled our water jugs with fresh water and delivered it to the dock; from there, a couple of guys hauled the jugs up the hill. They all worked until way past dark and the final tally was 85 gallons.

This morning at 5:15, we awoke to the sound of the anchor alarm. The wind had reversed direction and blown us over the main rope, close to the rocks. We bumped bottom once but didn't get stuck, thank goodness. Marc quickly pulled us away from the rocks using the tether rope. Then we used one short burst of power from the engine to get back to the correct side of the main rope. We immediately shut the engine back down to avoid getting the rope stuck in the prop as it passed under the boat. This worked out well, and we thought the worst was over. But then Madeline pointed out that our forward motion had stopped abruptly, and we had started to back up: The tether line had gotten stuck on the rudder. I fetched Marc's mask and fins, and he dove down to free the rudder. By this time, the wind had returned to its normal direction, and we prepared the boat for departure without any additional problems.

We left the anchorage at 6:40 a.m., bound for Aruba. So far, we've encountered gentle seas and enough wind to sail.

Sandy

Crime

A "pirate attack" happened while we were in Colombia that I didn't write about at the time, so I have to pull it from my memory banks. I did find reference to it online, though. It happened on sailing vessel PIPER III. I remember that Marc helped Donald and Kelley splash PIPER III soon after MARAVIDA's arrival at Ferroalquimar. I don't recall if the boarding occurred before or after their stay at the boatyard. Anyway, we heard about the incident on the morning net. PIPER III had been boarded when anchored next to the island of Baru. Donald had fought off the robbers successfully, but not before being slashed on the head with a machete. (He's okay.) Here's the full story as it appears online: http://yachtpals.com/pirates-sailboat-4061.

The locals in Cartagena do not stand by and ignore crime; they often get involved. One day as Marc was walking back to Club Nautico after running an errand, he saw a guy come clipping around the corner clutching a basket of raspberries. A second later, three men on foot, one man on a bicycle, and another on a motorcycle all chased him into a corner and surrounded him. One of them grabbed the raspberries, and then a couple of them started to beat on him. None were police officers.

The situation probably wouldn't have been much different if there had been police officers involved, as demonstrated by another skirmish that Marc got mixed up in.

> I was working on MARAVIDA in the anchorage when I heard a bunch of yelling and screaming. When I checked to see what the commotion was about, I saw a guy in a rowboat chasing after a swimmer. They were both about 100 feet from land, and the swimmer was swimming parallel to shore. A large crowd on land was yelling as the man in the rowboat would row to the swimmer and whack him on the head with one of his oars. As the swimmer got away, the guy in the rowboat would row toward him again and repeat the attack.
>
> I was afraid for the swimmer's life, so I jumped in my dinghy and rushed over to assist him. The hitter said he had caught the swimmer on his boat trying to rob him. I told the swimmer to swim to shore, but he refused. I assumed this was because he was afraid of the people on shore. I told him to get into my dinghy so I could take him to the police. He wouldn't do that either. So I went to the dock and picked up two policemen who were standing with the crowd. I drove them out to the swimmer and they hauled him into the dinghy. They proceeded to beat him up right there in my dinghy; kicking and hitting him. Then they got on their radio and called the coast guard and had me take them over to the small coast guard cutter that was nearby. The police officers shoved the guy up onto the cutter and then the coast guard started beating on him. The entire incident was very disturbing.

We believe the crime in Cartagena is related to extreme poverty. However, the more wealthy Cartagenians seem to have zero tolerance for any crime. They want their city to be safe. Because of that, and because armed police officers stand on many corners of the city, I felt safe when we were there.

One more incident, but this one is humorous. Three cruiser women, walking in Cartagena, were stopped by a young man with a knife who demanded their money. The women started laughing, which confused him, so he ran off in embarrassment.

Update on Javier

From: andreaclair
To: sandy_n_marc
Subject: Hello, hello
Date: Mon, 27 Apr 2009

Hello Davis Family,

We are back in Canada and have been meaning to e-mail you with a few news items from Colombia. We thought you would appreciate an update on Javier, the hearing-impaired young man whom we all chipped in a few bucks to help. He is doing amazingly well, still happily wearing the hearing aid. His speech has become a lot less like that of a deaf person, and his confidence is greatly increased. He was happy to see us and show us how he was doing. The bad news from Colombia is that the work sort of disappeared after we left, and many of the workers have had no work at all for the last 18 months or so. It seems that a lot of people in the region stored their boats in Panama since Shelter Bay got their operation going. We did store there last year, but this year they raised the rates considerably, so we didn't return. Also, it is fairly expensive to get work done there, and since we needed a bit of work (including a leaking speedo), we hauled earlier than usual, in March instead of waiting until the fall. Estephenson and Guillermo came and worked for about three weeks. Guillermo's work attitude left something to be desired, unfortunately, and even Bruno won't have him back. Estephenson was great as usual. They both say hello to all of you and asked many questions about what you are all doing now. Jaime seems to have vanished; we heard a number of tales about why this happened but chose to believe it was just the lack of work. He is rumored to be in Barranquilla but does not have the same cell phone number or answer his e-mail.

We are well, mostly recovered from our great motorcycle adventure, and our children are well and becoming more independent every year. (Yay!)

Let us know how you are doing—
Susan and Fin

CHAPTER 14

Aruba and Curacao

Aruba

> **Aruba**
>
> The 69-square-mile semi-arid island of Aruba has a population of just over 100,000. Approximately 80% of its inhabitants are mixed white/Caribbean Amerindian and 20% are other ethnicities.
>
> Aruba is the "A" in the ABC islands. We visited "B" and "C," Bonaire and Curacao, in July through October of 2006.
>
> Like Curacao, Aruba is a Kingdom of the Netherlands and the official languages are Dutch and Papiamento, though English and Spanish are widely spoken.
>
> Though the U.S. dollar is widely used in Aruba, the florin (AWG) is the official currency.

From: sandy_n_marc
To: Davis News Group
Subject: Davis News
Date: Sat, 3 Nov 2007

Since our inverter is broken, we decided it would be wise to spend a week or two in a marina so that we'd have power to complete our final boat projects. The question of whether to stop in Aruba before Curacao was settled when Marc remembered that Curacao has 50 Hz power and Aruba has 60 Hz power. MARAVIDA needs 60 Hz shore power to run the 110-volt system.

We arrived in Aruba at 3:30 p.m. and tied up at the cruise ship dock, where boats are required to wait for clearance from customs and immigration. At 6:00 p.m., we motored around the corner to Renaissance Marina, where marina employees waited to help us dock (see http://www.renaissancemarina.com).

As we maneuvered into the slip, the gearshift lever stuck—first in forward, and then in neutral. We managed to get into the slip, but we'll have to fix it before we can leave.

The next morning, we checked in at the marina office. After learning that you get two days free when you pay for five, we decided to stay an entire week. That should give us enough time to complete our projects and fit in in some downtime.

This is a perfect place for R & R. The marina is part of the Renaissance Resort Complex, and marina guests have access to all hotel facilities, including three swimming pools and a private beach within a short walking distance, a private island accessed by boat shuttles leaving every 20 minutes, and a couple of fitness centers and spas.

The marina is in the middle of Oranjested, within walking distance of all the town has to offer. This is the cleanest, friendliest, and most Disneylandesque Caribbean island we've been to—just what we need after months of hard work in a developing country.

We hope that LARA won't leave Curacao for St. Barts before we get there. Maybe they'll wait a little longer since it's still officially hurricane season, and storms are brewing out there.

That's all for now—
Sandy

The Last Couple of Weeks...

From: sandy_n_marc
To: Davis News Group
Subject: Davis News
Date: Sat, 17 Nov 2007

November 4, 2007

Yesterday, we walked to Dunkin Donuts for breakfast, checked in at the marina office, swam, and ate at Taco Bell for dinner. A day of leisure and American fast food—both a treat for us.

After dinner, as we were boarding MARAVIDA, we heard a distant meowing. We finally determined that the cry was coming from Maria, who was sitting on the excursion catamaran moored next door. Madeline had to climb onto the boat and carry her back, which seemed odd since Maria could have come back on her own ... but then we saw the German shepherd on the boat across from us. Maria must have decided to stay on the catamaran for her own safety. Maybe she'll stay on MARAVIDA now that she knows about the dog.

Madeline and I took a long walk and grocery shopped today while Marc hooked up MARAVIDA's shore power and started work on the transmission linkage. We all went swimming in the late afternoon. While at the pool, we were surprised to see the Colombian Navy sailing ship GLORIA departing from the island. We first saw GLORIA last Christmas in Cartagena.

Gloria

I learned a few more facts about GLORIA from the Aruban English-language newspaper. She's 249 feet long, was built in 1966, and is completing a round-the-world voyage with 10 officers, 70 students, 37 sub-officers, 3 marines, 10 civilians, and a music band. When she finishes up the voyage in Cartagena, the students will graduate with the rank of second lieutenant. This particular voyage is historic because it is the first class to graduate with female officers.

November 5, 2007

In the morning, Marc and I hauled a couple of bags of laundry over to the hotel. The cost of $1.25 per load is a good deal. You have to do it yourself, but it's easier to use the dryer than it is to hang out the laundry on the boat (outdoor drying is not allowed at the marina anyway).

At 1:00 p.m., XJ—an employee of the marina—generously gave us a ride to the large IGA supermarket. We had an hour to shop while she took her lunch break. We were thrilled with the choices, but tried to contain our buying to current-use items since stocking up isn't necessary anymore. *(XJ—Xiomara Jansen—is bubbly, friendly, helpful, and knowledgeable. In June 2009, after 12 years of service, she became a managing partner of the marina.)*

November 6, 2007

In the morning, we took the shuttle boat to Renaissance Island. We had a great time swimming in the ocean and lounging under the palm trees.

In the afternoon, Marc and Alex went to the swimming pool at the Renaissance Aruba Ocean Suites while Madeline and I went shopping.

November 7, 2007

Marc worked on MARAVIDA's electrical system this morning while I worked on a variety of tasks. The kids went to the pool by themselves. In the late afternoon, XJ's 12-year-old son came over to play video games with Alex (and brought a friend). A little later, his 15-year-old sister came over, too. XJ's kids have names that start with an X also: Xiovon and Xiavronique.

November 8, 2007

Marc's 45th birthday: pancakes for breakfast, beach midday, kids to Taco Bell for dinner, and Marc and I out for a simple dinner by ourselves. Madeline made apple pie for dessert.

November 9, 2007

Our week is up, but since we haven't accomplished all our tasks, we've decided to stay another week. Now we need to get serious about getting the work done on the boat.

November 10, 2007

Radio Shack, electrical work, swimming.

While Marc was chatting with a neighboring boat owner, he learned that our black cat had been seen roaming the decks of the mega yacht, LYS D'O, late at night. All week we'd thought Maria was afraid to get off MARAVIDA because of the dog, but she had us fooled.

November 11, 2007

The marina manager, Sanders, has loaned us his table saw. Marc got to work cutting floor pieces.

November 12–16, 2007

Alex has been hanging out with a boy, Chris, whom he met at the pool. Today, Alex came back from the pool with Chris and another boy, Jared, to play video games. Chris will leave tomorrow, but Jared just arrived. These aren't Alex's typical companions (boys living on boats); they're boys staying with their families at the resort.

Marc and I have been working on putting the new shower together.

Now that our second week in Aruba is up, we'll be looking for a weather window to cross to Curacao. Conditions are not so great at the moment.

I made reservations for MARAVIDA at Curacao Marine starting December 6th, and I booked our airline tickets to Oregon for December 11th.

Sandy

Thanksgiving in ... Curacao

From: sandy_n_marc
To: Davis News Group
Subject: Davis News
Date: Thu, 22 Nov 2007

Happy Thanksgiving!

The long-range weather forecast predicted worsening conditions, so we decided we'd better leave for Curacao as soon as possible. On Tuesday, November 20th, we got the boat ready and checked out of the marina.

When we took MARAVIDA to the cruise ship/customs dock to check out, we had a difficult time getting docked. Madeline and I were able to jump off with the lines when Marc first pulled up to the dock, but we couldn't hold and pull the boat in because the wind was pushing MARAVIDA away from the dock. For a while it looked like we were stuck on the dock, and Marc and Alex were stuck on the boat. But finally, a couple of dock workers and the immigration officer took pity on us and helped pull in the lines.

We left the dock at 4:00 p.m. and motored two hours to the southernmost anchorage of Aruba—San Nicolas Baai. Though you're supposed to leave Aruba immediately after checking out, we decided to ignore that rule because it would have been too hard to go through the check-out procedure and still make it to Curacao in the same day. The two-hour motor was in rough waters and the anchorage turned out to be quite rolly. Not what we expected for the lee side of the island.

We started our journey to Curacao on Wednesday morning at 8:30. Or so we thought. Early into the voyage, we ran into complications. First, the mainsail tore and the boom fell. Fortunately, it landed on the dinghy on deck, which kept it from falling onto the bimini top and us underneath. Next, the staysail partially unfurled itself (a knot held the top half closed) and started flapping about in the wind. At this point, Madeline was throwing up off the side and we were all miserable from the rough seas. So, at 10:00 a.m., we turned back.

Once we got back to the San Nicolas anchorage, Marc climbed up the staysail and cut the knot, then removed the entire sail. We then tried to relax while we waited for the next weather report by SSB radio fax. To our dismay, it showed—once again—that this was the best window we were going to get. So, despite still being seasick, we took off again at 5:00 p.m., this time without sails. We beat straight into 25 knots of steady wind with corkscrew seas. Our average speed was only 4 knots. Sadly, this final crossing was our most unpleasant passage ever.

We were relieved to finally arrive in Spanish Waters, Curacao, at 9:00 this morning. We've lots to do in the next couple of weeks but have accomplished the most important step just by getting here!

Sandy

Finishing Up in Curacao

From: sandy_n_marc
To: Davis News Group
Subject: Davis News
Date: Tue, 11 Dec 2007

November 23, 2007

We took the 10:00 a.m. shuttle to the grocery store and Budget Marine. It was nice to have a large variety of food choices at the grocery store and useful boat supplies at the chandlery.

In the afternoon, Marc and I took the public bus downtown to check in with customs and immigration. We came back to the boat to find five kids lined up on the back sugar scoop of the boat. It was great to see our kids swimming with their friends: Patrick from LARA and Alex's Dutch friends, Sieba and Jelle.

We finished up the day on LARA, dining on Virginia's delicious homemade pizza.

November 24–28, 2007

We continued to work on the shower, finished up the electrical wiring, and varnished the companionway stairs and the area around the refrigerator.

November 29, 2007

LARA left for St. Martin, and then St. Barts for Christmas.

November 30, 2007

We rented a car from Limestone Resort (nearby in Spanish Waters) to do a bunch of errands. This included visiting every pet store on the island in search of two cat carriers small enough to fit under airplane seats. The cats will not be allowed in the cargo hold because the flights are routed through Chicago, which gets too cold this time of year.

December 1, 2007

The generator broke. Darn it! Since leaving the marina (and shore power), we'd been managing without the (broken) invertor by running the generator whenever we needed 110-volt power. Now we're out of options. We can't run the watermaker, the washing machine, etc. We can run the main engine to charge the batteries, but that's hot and noisy. Nevertheless, we'll do it as needed to keep the batteries charged, and we'll have to be careful with our 12-volt power use. On the 3rd, Marc ordered the necessary parts to fix the generator. He asked them to be sent via FedEx international priority to Limestone Resort.

December 2–4, 2007

In addition to working on the boat, we have to sift through all of our belongings. We have to divide it between: throw away, give away, leave on boat, and bring on the airplane.

December 5, 2007

We checked into Limestone Resort (see http://www.limestoneholiday.com). The small group of holiday apartments is set on a rise and all the units look out onto a cove in Spanish Waters. There's a small pool and a small private beach. Our unit has two bedrooms, two baths, a sitting area (with cable television), a kitchen, and a balcony. We're both overwhelmed and delighted by its vast size. Maria immediately went into exploration mode; Emily went into hiding.

December 6, 2007

We drove MARAVIDA to Curacao Marine in Willemstad. She was pulled out of the water and placed on her stanchions by midafternoon.

December 7–9, 2007

A car is included with the apartment rental. We're using it every day to drive to the boatyard to work on MARAVIDA.

We took the cats to a veterinarian for new rabies shots and health certificates—a necessity for admittance into the States.

We lined up our eight suitcases and four backpacks in the apartment hallway. Over our six-day stay in the apartment, we packed and weighed, and repacked and reweighed the luggage, trying to get each bag to weigh in at just shy of 50 pounds (the airline's limit and probably the most our bags could handle anyway).

December 10, 2007

Our last full day in Curacao: We went to immigration to check out of the country, finished cleaning up the boat, and talked with the broker. (The generator parts did not show up.)

MARAVIDA is now officially put to bed.

December 11, 2007

We loaded the taxi-van and left for the airport at 5:30 a.m. What a familiar feeling—so much like our first trip to Trinidad, with eight suitcases and four backpacks. Only this time we're on our way to Oregon instead of leaving Oregon.

Our first flight, from Curacao to Miami, left on schedule. Maria meowed all three hours of the flight. She was not scared, she just wanted out of her kennel. Emily went into shut-down mode (paralyzed from fright) and was no trouble at all, thank goodness.

Our Miami-to-Chicago flight was scheduled to leave at 1:35 p.m. After many delays, the airline finally admitted that our airplane had to be grounded for repairs. We're staying overnight in Miami and will get to Portland via Dallas tomorrow.

We're now at the Airport Regency in Miami, courtesy of American Airlines. We didn't ask if the hotel allows animals. That way, we could avoid the awkward situation we'd be in if they said no. Marc had the brilliant idea of placing the toilet tank lid upside down on the floor to hold cat litter.

Our fingers are crossed for better luck with the flights tomorrow.

Almost to Oregon—
Sandy

Cruising Guides

Aruba Cruising Guide. Web. http://www.aruba-cruisingguide.com.

Epilogue

Back to Terra Firma

New Abode in Oregon

From: sandy_n_marc
To: Davis News Group
Subject: Davis News
Date: Wed, 19 Dec 2007

After our overnight stay in Miami, the flights to Dallas and Portland went smoothly—that is, as smoothly as plane rides with two cats can conceivably go.

We're busy setting up our new life on land. Unpacking the 12 bags we brought with us was easy, but going through the many boxes in storage is overwhelming. When we downsized three and a half years ago, we didn't downsize enough.

Madeline is delighted to have so much space in her room on the farm compared with her tiny room on the boat. Her only complaint is the cold.

We have to rearrange furniture before we can put Alex's room together. He doesn't mind, though, because we have internet. He's informed us that he loves the trees and doesn't mind the cold.

It's so beautiful here—despite the clouds, the cold, and the rain. The fir trees, the hills and mountains, and the wonderful smell in the air tell us we're home.

Our new abode is a charming remodeled farmhouse on Marc's mother and stepfather's 40-acre farm in Mulino, Oregon. They live in the main house.

The business office, shipping area, and testing area of the fiber optics components business are housed in their basement; the production area is in the converted garage; and the oven room and gas filling room are in one of the barns. We start work on January 1st.

Meanwhile, we'll unpack and organize our belongings, purchase necessities, and prepare for Christmas. Some friends have generously lent us their spare car until we find a car to buy.

Happy Holidays!
Sandy

Note: I've got to tell you the whole story about our experience flying to Oregon with the cats. We had asked the veterinarian in Curacao (the one who gave the cats their required shots and health certificates for entering into the U.S.) for a sedative that would allow the cats to stay calm and maybe even sleep through most of the long day of flights. The sedative seemed to work on Emily, or maybe she was just in shock. Maria, on the other hand, was angry about being confined to a cage. She meowed loudly during the entire three and a quarter hour trip to Miami.

While waiting in the Miami airport for our next flight, Madeline tried to get Maria to stop meowing by removing her from the cage and putting a small dog collar (purchased in Curacao) on her. Maria was excited to get out but became extremely frustrated; every time she tried to take a step or two, she fell. It appears that she was affected by the sedative after all.

We waited impatiently as our flight to Chicago (the initial connection to Portland) was pushed out several times. Finally, it was canceled and we were given hotel vouchers. But what about the cats? We were worried that the hotel wouldn't allow cats (and dared not ask). We came up with a plan: Marc and I would check in while the kids hung back with the cats. The carriers would be disguised as baggage, each draped with a sweater. Then, we would all make a beeline to the elevators. It worked. Marc's improvised litter box (upside down toilet lid) was a great idea, but the cats never used it. They didn't eat anything, either.

When we arrived at the security gate, the inspectors insisted the cats be taken out of their crates and carried through the pedestrian passageway. This was fine for Maria, but Emily was already scared out of her mind. The result? She let loose and peed all over Madeline as she was carrying her through. Once Madeline was able to return Emily to her cage, she ran to the bathroom to clean up. Unfortunately, she was not able to remove the urine smell completely.

Maria meowed loudly for the entire trip to Dallas. Immediately upon arriving at the airport, we took the cats into a family bathroom, got out their food and water bowl, and put some litter on a puppy-training pad we'd purchased at the pet store in Curacao. We took turns being on watch in the bathroom, waiting for them to eat, drink, or do their business, but they refused to partake of any of these amenities. We finally gave up, as the departure of our flight to Portland was imminent.

Maria, once again, complained during the entire flight, but Marc felt it was a little less stressful because there were two or three babies crying on the flight.

I have never seen a cat in an airplane and most of the people on our flights seemed surprised. The worst part was when a couple of people complained that they were allergic to cats. I was afraid that we might be kicked off the flight, but the flight attendant seemed to think that we were within our rights to stay and managed to move the people to seats farther away from us. The best part was the cat lovers, all of whom were very supportive. All in all, the whole idea of taking cats on airplanes is highly stressful—I wouldn't recommend it.

Merry Christmas

From: sandy_n_marc
To: Davis News Group
Subject: Davis News
Date: Tue, 25 Dec 2007

Merry Christmas to all!

Attached is a photo of our new house. We had a bit of snow today, which added to the holiday spirit.

Hope all is well with you.

MARAVIDA's crew on shore leave—
Marc, Sandy, Alex, and Madeline

P.S. Susan, can you show this to the guys in the yard?

(Susan and Fin of ANDREA CLAIRE were still on the hard in Cartagena.)

Reconnecting

From: sandy_n_marc
To: Davis News Group
Subject: Davis News
Date: Thu, 3 Jan 2008

We spent the first couple of weeks back in Oregon reconnecting with friends and family before starting work. Marc didn't wait until the 1st to start learning the ropes of the business because he was too excited.

The house is small but feels huge compared to the boat. We love having hot tap water and a full-sized refrigerator.

It's been raining a lot, but that doesn't bother me, maybe because I was born and raised in Oregon. However, I do hate getting up in the morning to a cold house.

Maria isn't fond of the cold either. Her solution is to spend the entire night with Marc and me under the blankets of our bed.

Well, that's it for now.

I'll keep in touch—
Sandy

Living in Mulino

From: sandy_n_marc
To: Davis News Group
Subject: Davis News
Date: Wed, 28 May 2008

We've been living and working here at the farm in Mulino for five months.

We finally have health insurance. The first company we applied to denied us because we didn't have any doctor history (in the States) for the last three years. The second one accepted us after a thorough inquiry. Our deductible is a whopping $6,000, but at least we're insured for any major medical health issue.

The kids took classes in Oregon City at a charter school for homeschoolers (the school year ended last week). They visit their friends in Beaverton when they can, though Beaverton is an hour away and gas is $4 a gallon. Madeline plans to fly to Colorado in July to stay two weeks with her boyfriend, Sean, and his family. She'll be attending Clackamas Community College in the fall, and Alex will take more classes at the charter school.

Our Canadian friends, Fin and Susan from the boat ANDREA CLAIRE, came and visited us last week. It was fun to see people from our cruising life, but it felt odd to talk about boats again.

MARAVIDA is on the hard at Curacao Marine. We pay $540 per month to keep her there. If she doesn't sell before November 23rd, we'll have to take her out of Curacao (temporarily or permanently) to avoid taxes.

We see my family often since they live nearby. My mother, her mother, and her sisters all live in the Oregon City area.

We do laundry next door and fight over our single bathroom. We are living with hand-me-down furniture and tablecloth-covered boxes that double as makeshift tables. Fortunately, we put a lot of kitchen gear (silverware, pots and pans, small appliances, etc.) in storage when we left on the trip, so we didn't have to purchase those items when we returned.

It's peaceful here. We like to take walks either on the property or along the country roads. To add to our goal of living healthier, a friend recommended a book called *Nourishing Traditions*. The book has inspired us to improve our diet and eat local products when possible. In addition to eating veggies from Marc's mother's large organic garden, we're purchasing eggs and raw milk from a local farm, honey from a neighbor, and meat from a nearby butcher.

E-mail us back and let us know how you're doing.

Sandy, Marc, Madeline, and Alex

Moving Back to Portland

From: sandy_n_marc
To: Davis News Group
Subject: Davis News
Date: Thu, 6 Nov 2008

Another five months have passed. Unfortunately, we discovered that the fiber optics business was not as committed to us as we were to it. After months of uncertainty, Marc's stepfather finally said, "No, I don't want to retire."

On October 27th, Marc started work at NVIDIA in Beaverton. We will move to the Beaverton area as soon as possible because Marc hates wasting three hours of his day in the car. Because we poured our remaining funds into finishing up work on MARAVIDA so we could come here, we are now short on cash and will have to rent (no money for a down payment on a house). If MARAVIDA would sell, we'd be in fine shape; I don't have high hopes, though, since she's in such a remote place and the world economy is distressed.

A couple of months ago, the boatyard owner assured us that we would be able to get another customs extension, but one week after Marc started his new job, we found out that an extension isn't possible. The boat has to be taken out of the country (for a minimum of two days) by November 23rd.

Marc has been granted a leave from NVIDIA to make the trip, but he needs crew to help him take the boat over to Aruba and back. If anyone is interested in a last-minute adventure and can pay for their own airfare, Marc would love the company. He plans to leave the week of November 17th and will return on Thanksgiving weekend. He'll spend the first few days getting MARAVIDA ready to launch and then make the overnight crossing to Aruba. After a couple of days docked at the Renaissance Marina in Aruba, he'll take MARAVIDA back to Curacao and put her back to bed on the hard.

Putting aside our recent troubles, here's what we're grateful for: Marc was able to get a job despite the ailing economy, he likes his job, and he was generously given leave to go to Curacao. Beaverton has a good school for homeschoolers where Alex can take classes (which will add to his home-based education), and he's thrilled to be moving to closer to his friends. Madeline is taking writing and golf at Clackamas Community College. She enjoys being a college student and looks forward to attending Portland Community College next term.

One more thing: We are offering an opportunity for adventure to a person, couple, or family. Must be trustworthy, mechanically minded, and ready for a challenge. MARAVIDA is a $600-per-month liability to us where she sits.

In Oregon, storage costs would be under $300. We don't have the time to move her or the money to pay to have her moved, but maybe someone else does. They could take their time (a year or more) to bring MARAVIDA to Oregon ... and have a free boat to cruise in. We have too much invested in MARAVIDA ($200,000 in cash and countless hours of labor) to cut our losses and give her away, but if we could get her to Oregon, we'd be able to use her and have an easier time selling her.

That's what's happening with us. Would love to hear from you!

Sandy

Thanksgiving in Oregon

From: sandy_n_marc
To: Davis News Group
Subject: Davis News
Date: Sun, 16 Nov 2008

We had an eventful weekend. On Saturday morning, Marc and I signed the paperwork for an apartment in the Beaverton area (northwest Portland). Madeline's 17-year-old boyfriend, Sean, flew up from San Diego (where his parents have just purchased a sailboat). He's going to hang out with us for a while. Today (Sunday), I took Marc to the airport. I'm happy to stay behind, because even though two weeks in Curacao and Aruba may sound like a dreamy tropical vacation, I know there won't be time for any R & R. There's a lot of hard work to do in sweltering temperatures, and most likely some seasickness to endure.

The kids and I will start moving boxes to the apartment next weekend and intend to finish up the following weekend when Marc returns on the 30th. This way, he'll have a short commute when he starts back to work.

I'm happy to spend Thanksgiving with my family this year, though we'll miss Marc....

I'll let you know how his trip went when he gets back.

Happy Thanksgiving!
Sandy

Marc's Trip to Curacao

From: sandy_n_marc
To: Davis News Group
Subject: Davis News
Date: Wed, 10 Dec 2008

I worried about Marc's boat-moving task because of the many potential complications that might arise—the possibility of mechanical problems, unexpected weather issues, etc. Though not without some problems, the mission was a success. Marc had a frustrating first day at the boatyard. Once he finally located a ladder to enter MARAVIDA, he found a couple of windows open (by the broker) and the bilge full of water—so much for leaving her high and dry. He also discovered that the electric cord had been unplugged, which caused the batteries to be dead.

The second day went better. His crew arrived and he was cheered by the company. One member is a family friend, the other an acquaintance. The former, Tim, is the youngest of the Errera family (recall that we stayed with them in Connecticut four years ago). He's 13 years old and enthusiastic for this adventure.

The guys did some maintenance work on the boat, cleaned up, then left for Aruba. Without warning, the acquaintance made a feeble excuse and simply left them in Aruba, forcing Marc and Tim to make the return crossing without him. If we had even suspected that might happen, we would have paid the airfare for Sean to go: if anything had happened to Marc on the crossing, Tim was too young and inexperienced to have taken charge. Sean, though only 17, has grown up on the ocean and could have taken control if necessary.

Tim was a good sport during the difficult return crossing. Marc said it was the worst crossing he'd ever experienced. It was moonless and raining, with waves 7 to 15 feet on the beam and winds 30 knots on the nose. They both stayed up all night, wet and sick. There was no danger for the boat, only a miserable time for the crew.

Meanwhile, back on the home front, the kids and I packed up a 17-foot U-Haul and moved most of the house on the weekend of November 22nd. The Opp family helped us unload. Sean was a tremendous help; he's much stronger than the rest of us and worked hard.

Sean may stay with us rather than sail from San Diego to Thailand with his folks. He and his mother haven't been getting along and need a break from each other. If he stays, he'll probably take classes at Portland Community College.

We're settled into the apartment, but Sean has to sleep on the couch. This isn't unusual for him because he's often slept on the salon couch in the various boats he's lived on over his lifetime. We would prefer, however, to give him his own room. Our ultimate goal is to purchase a four-bedroom house in this vicinity.

Happy Holidays!

Love,
Sandy, Marc, Madeline, Alex, and Sean

P.S. Teenagers are the majority in our household now.

A New House

From: sandy_n_marc
To: Davis News Group
Subject: Davis News
Date: Sun, 21 Dec 2008

Season's Greetings!

We're buying a house thanks to my mother, who's lending us money for the down payment. Two months of offers and counteroffers on a house we've been eyeing got the price down to our allowable budget. Patience and persistence paid off in this case.

The house is in Northwest Portland in the Cedar Mill neighborhood, only a few blocks from our last house. Built by the current owners in 1964, it is 2,000 square feet, with four bedrooms and two bathrooms. Half of the square footage is in the daylight basement, which is not fully finished. It's set on a half-acre lot with a 30- by 34-foot shop. The house needs new windows, a new roof, a new kitchen, and new flooring—but that's nothing we haven't faced before. The large lot size, the shop, and a prime location within the urban growth boundary of Portland make it a good investment—even if home prices continue their downward trend.

Meanwhile, we've been sticking close to home while Portland experiences unusual winter weather—lots of snow and ice.

Merry Christmas!
Sandy and family

Moving

From: sandy_n_marc
To: Davis News Group
Subject: Davis News
Date: Thu, 19 Feb 2009

We signed the closing papers yesterday and will make the move this weekend. Moving into our own house is exciting, despite the fact that this will be our second move in three months.

Short update:

- Marc enjoys working at NVIDIA.

- Madeline and Sean are taking math and drawing at Portland Community College. (Madeline is also taking driver's ed.)

- Alex is taking a robotics class at Village Homeschool.

- I've been busy with moving chores since we left Mulino at the end of November.

Gotta finish packing ... again.

Sandy

Lots Going On

From: sandy_n_marc
To: Davis News Group
Subject: Davis News
Date: Wed, 21 Oct 2009

Wow, it's been a while, hasn't it? News about MARAVIDA: No, she hasn't sold—but we've made a decision and are getting ready to implement it.

Marc and our friend Glenn (he worked with Marc at Intel and became a cruising sailor after that) will leave for Curacao on November 10th. Another year is up and MARAVIDA has to leave the country again, this time by November 25th. We've accepted Glenn's offer to bring MARAVIDA to Portland. Not only is he a seasoned cruiser, but he's recently unemployed and giving up his house. He will take his time and move along as weather conditions permit.

Marc will take three weeks off from work to help Glenn get acquainted with MARAVIDA, make some repairs, and do a shakedown cruise to Aruba. Glenn has been assembling a cast of crew for various parts of the long trip to Oregon.

The last newsletter I sent out was back in February when we were about to move into our new house. Here's a brief summary of what's been happening since then.

Marc:

- Still working at NVIDIA.
- He lost a dear friend and co-worker this year in a small airplane crash.
- Marc goes to "Thursday Lunch" with the same group of friends he's been lunching with for many years.
- He also still goes to "Hangar Night" at the Hillsboro Airport to meet up with his airplane buddies.
- He's been organizing his shop ever so slowly. It's outfitted with the woodworking and machine shop equipment he put in storage while we were gone.
- He has purchased a huge CNC milling machine (a bargain because the spindle speed control had failed). Last weekend, he finished the repairs and it's working.
- This summer he did a beautiful tiling job in the upstairs bathroom and installed six new windows downstairs. We'll have to wait until next spring and summer to purchase and install the rest.

Sandy:

I'm still working hard to personalize the house: I've acquired bits and pieces of furniture to make us comfortable, I've painted the rooms cheerful colors, and now I'm painting the peeling gray exterior green. In addition to working on the house, I chauffeur the kids to school, schedule their classes, and help with homework.

Madeline, Alex, and Sean:

Madeline and Sean are still attending Portland Community College (PCC). Alex also chose to go to PCC this fall (at age 14) instead of high school. The school makes admission difficult for kids under the age of 16; they must obtain college level scores on a series of placement tests. Students over 16, however, merely take the tests for placement, not admission. Fortunately, Alex tested well and was admitted.

Madeline drives now, but we don't have a third car, so I'm the chauffeur; unfortunately, Alex has classes at a different time of the day than Madeline and Sean.

Besides our three teenagers, we often have one or two other teens over for computer gaming. This means we don't have to worry about where they are or what they're doing. And we discovered that the layout of this house is perfect for teenagers—while they hang out downstairs, Marc and I have peace and quiet upstairs.

Emily & Maria:

The cats love the spacious accommodations. Their favorite pastime is sitting at the windows and watching birds and squirrels in the trees. Emily is still timid but has started to sit on Marc's lap when he sits in the recliner. Maria thinks she's in charge of the humans in the house. She looks right at you and meows when she wants something. One common demand is to be picked up when people are standing around talking—she wants to be up at our level so she feels she's in on the conversation.

That's all for now—
Sandy

Curacao: Communications from the Front

From: sandy_n_marc
To: Davis News Group
Subject: Davis News
Date: Mon, 30 Nov 2009

Marc and Glenn arrived in Curacao on November 11th, a third crew member arrived on the 14th, and MARAVIDA was splashed on the 23rd.

From Marc

November 12, 2009

Work is going good. Need some welding done. Sails will be ready on Friday. Glenn's a big help.

November 13, 2009

We found a small hole in the hull under the forward hall cabin, but it should be easy to fix. It took a day to get the basics running: lights, fans, etc. The charger died—the one we purchased just before leaving for Portland—so I went to Cost-U-Less and bought a regular car charger. We pulled out the old anchor chain, which was in bad shape. It was a good call to replace it. *(Marc purchased many boat parts before leaving for Curacao. He packed the lightweight items in his luggage and shipped the heavy items.)*

Today we worked on the stiff rudder. We removed the old packing, oiled the shaft, and then put in new packing. It's fine now. Tomorrow I'll get the engine running and Glenn will work on the generator.

We try to work early in the morning and then return after dark to do a bit more. We'll start cooking on the boat tomorrow. *(They stayed in a hotel for the first couple of days until they were sure that enough systems were operational to make the boat livable).*

November 14, 2009

Don't want to call at $2 a minute. I got the engine running. The stove works. The pumps work. Radio/e-mail seems to work. Now I'm working on the running lights. No major problems.

November 15, 2009

Removed windlass. Working on generator.

November 16, 2009

I prepped the boat for the welder while Glenn spent some time up the mast working on the lights. Other than that, we went to buy parts, tools, and food. The 95-degree temperatures make the work especially difficult.

(I didn't receive any more e-mail messages from Marc until the 25th, though I did get a couple of short phone calls. On November 18th, they picked up the new windlass, chain, and batteries from customs. The installation took a few days.)

November 25, 2009

We checked out of Curacao. We plan to motor up to the end of the island, then anchor until early morning, when we'll cross to Aruba. It's just Glenn and me on this crossing because the other crew member wasn't a good fit and we all agreed he should fly home. In Aruba, we'll pick up a new crew member, but I've decided I should stay with the boat for the four-day passage to Panama. The boat's in good shape and should make the trip fine.

November 26, 2009

We had a nice motor to Santa Cruz Bay and will leave here early tomorrow morning. The distance to Aruba is 58 miles, so the trip should take about nine hours. All systems are working. *(Santa Cruz is on the northern coast of Curacao. I believe stopping there shaves 20 miles off the trip to Aruba.)*

Aruba

November 27, 2009

Text from Marc: (2:00 p.m.) "At the dock in Aruba. Ok trip, no problems, just a bit rough."

From Sandy

I changed Marc's airplane ticket to fly out of Panama on December 5th. This means more unpaid vacation time, in addition to the $8,000 we spent to get MARAVIDA out of Curacao and on her way to Oregon. (That figure includes airfare and the cost of some much-needed new equipment.) The consolation is that once MARAVIDA gets to Oregon, if necessary, we could sell the house and live on her, though the kids would never forgive us. Better yet, we could sell MARAVIDA. Our San Diego broker says she will sell easier in the States.

We are thankful that Glenn is in a place in his life that allows him to take on this adventure. He knows the ins and outs and the ups and downs of the sometimes hard, sometimes glorious life of cruising. We will pay for boat diesel, maintenance expenses, the Panama Canal crossing fees, and Glenn's food.

Glenn has arranged for crew to join him at various stages of the trip but doesn't have crew lined up for the entire trip. If you might be interested in joining him, don't be afraid to ask us about it. But, don't expect a "margaritas on the beach" vacation jaunt. You'll be on a moving boat, helping Glenn when he needs it. You may get miserably hot at times—or cold and wet as MARAVIDA gets closer to Oregon; you may feel claustrophobic in your bunk; and you may get seasick. Single-handing MARAVIDA is not easy, and Glenn would appreciate the help if you're up to the adventure.

November 30, 2009

Text from Marc: "We checked out of Aruba and are heading out."

He's Back

From: sandy_n_marc
To: Davis News Group
Subject: Davis News
Date: Sun, 6 Dec 2009

Marc is home now but is too exhausted to write, so I'll give you the scoop on the rest of his journey.

They left Aruba on Monday morning and arrived in the San Blas Islands of Panama on Thursday evening. The trip went fine, despite high seas (the highest that Marc has ever experienced). Luckily, Glenn and Katie (she's the new crew member they picked up in Aruba) don't get seasick, and Marc only had to take seasickness meds a couple of times. Once they arrived in Panama, Marc had one full day to enjoy the beautiful islands before he took off in a puddle jumper airplane at 6:30 a.m. Saturday, bound for Panama City. He arrived in Portland today (Sunday) at 11:30 a.m. to freezing temperatures.

The good news is that the MARAVIDA is in great shape, everything worked perfectly, and Marc was happy for the chance to see the San Blas Islands again.

The bad news is that the expenditures added up to $12k for the last three weeks. We'll have to live even more frugally than before, but we're experienced penny pinchers who believe that practicing thriftiness is always a good lesson for the kids.

A new issue came up while I was writing this e-mail tonight. Marc received a phone call from Glenn and Katie in the San Blas. When they tried to leave the anchorage in Porvenir right after Marc's departure, they couldn't get MARAVIDA's engine to start. This was a surprise—we've never had problems with the engine before. Marc gave them some suggestions and we're standing by with our fingers crossed.

Sandy

(Glenn spent a lot of time messing with the engine, and in the end he discovered it was a small air leak in the fuel line.)

Brian's Panama Adventure

From: sandy_n_marc
To: Davis News Group
Subject: Davis News
Date: Wed, 6 Jan 2010

Here's an e-mail that Marc's father, Brian, sent from MARAVIDA.

Happy New Year!
Sandy

From Brian—Dear Family and Friends

A week ago, I flew out of Managua (Nicaragua) and landed in Panama City. I left my wife, Nancy, in the good company of her eldest son, Sam, and our caretaker, Cherry. *(This is at their house in Nicaragua; they divide their time between their two homes—one in Grenada and the other in Portland).* My plan was to meet Marc and Sandy's sailboat, MARAVIDA, at the Caribbean entrance to the Panama Canal and be part of the crew to take the boat through the canal. At the PC airport, I met up with Neon, a friend of Glenn's, who was also here to help out. The two of us crossed the isthmus by bus to the small harbor at Portobelo, near the Caribbean entrance to the canal, where we met MARAVIDA and her *capitán*, Glenn.

We headed to Colon the next morning. This went well except for the fact that I lost my cookies along the way and wasn't all that helpful.

The crew of three quasi-geezers seems to be compatible, which doesn't necessarily mean that we know what we are doing.

The Colon harbor is impressive and exotic. Huge freighters lined up to go through the canal and mountains of wacko paperwork waited for us. We were ready to pay our fees and schedule the transit through the canal, but the bank closed 15 minutes before we arrived to pay. To top it off, we bumped into the three-day New Year's holiday!

So, Neon and I headed into Panama City by bus for the three days. We took a ferry out to Isla Taboga (the Island of Flowers), a vacation spot off the coast where people escape from Panama City. This is a beautiful little island reminiscent of Greece.

Back in Panama City, we visited a great museum that traces the history of the canal's construction and evolution. The major force behind completing a railroad across the isthmus was to transport people and goods to California during and after the Gold Rush. We returned to Colon and the boat via that railroad along the canal itself.

We are now scheduled to start the two-day transit through the canal tomorrow.

Panama City or bust!
Brian

News from Glenn—Getting Ready for the Canal

From: sandy_n_marc
To: Davis News Group
Subject: Davis News
Date: Wed, 6 Jan 2010

And here's an e-mail sent out the same day from Glenn.

From Glenn—Hi Marc and Sandy

Today we're scheduled to have the advisor come to MARAVIDA, and then we'll proceed through the locks at 2:00 p.m. *(Vessels under 65 feet in length are required to transit the Canal with a transit advisor, while vessels over 65 feet will require a pilot. The "Canal Advisor," employed by the Panama Canal Authority, joins the crew onboard and oversees the passage through the Canal. His service is included with the cost of the transit.)*

We picked up a young couple, Karl and Cat, who will line handle for us. *(The vessel must have four designated line handlers to handle the four lines that are each a minimum of 125 feet in length. The lines go from the cruising vessel to the canal locks, two on the bow and two on the stern. When the vessel transits a lock, the vessel must be kept in the center of the lock by the line Handlers.)* Bill will also line handle while Benita stays behind to prepare Alcheringa II to go through the day after we finish. Along with Brian and Neon, that gives us one spare crew member, which is recommended to allow someone to do odd jobs like get food or drinks, etc. We'll spend the night in Lake Gatun and probably leave the last lock between 2:00 and 4:00 p.m. on Thursday. After that, we'll pass under the Bridge of the Americas, where there's a live video cam that broadcasts on the canal's website. We may have the jib up at that time.

Glenn

(You can see Panama Canal live webcams at http://www.pancanal.com/eng/photo/camera-java.html*.)*

News from Glenn—Made It through the Canal

From: sandy_n_marc
To: Davis News Group
Subject: Davis News
Date: Thu, 7 Jan 2010

From Glenn—Hey all

We're through the canal and anchored at Isla Flamenco. Kind of rolly here, but it's a relief to be done. Haven't decided what to do next, but will take a day or two to recuperate from the process.

We saw a crocodile sitting at the side of the entrance to the first lock. In the process of cutting a new set of locks for larger ships, they have drained a lake, and the crocs living in it have moved to Lake Gatun—where we were swimming!

Bill has gone back to Colon. Cat and Karl will spend one more night with us and leave tomorrow. Brian has a plane ticket for the 10th, which leaves little time for us to do anything more with him. Jorge—a new crew member—will arrive on the 14th, so we'll stay here until he arrives. Then we'll decide whether to head to Costa Rica (before our Panamanian cruising permit expires on the 29th) or to extend the cruising permit.

Well, I'm going to go relax. I hand steered 30 to 35 miles today, including through the locks, and then about four miles in the dinghy.

Cheers—
Glenn

MARAVIDA's Schedule

From: sandy_n_marc
To: Davis News Group
Subject: Davis News
Date: Wed, 27 Jan 2010

Glenn and MARAVIDA are still in Panama. Glenn is waiting for his renewed passport to arrive at the American Embassy. He's alone right now but is interviewing potential crew. He plans to hang out a bit in Costa Rica, then cross the Tehuantepec region in March, when the weather allows. Once in Mexico, he'll stay put until July, when he'll head up the California coast to Oregon.

Sandy

Close, But Not Quite...

From: sandy_n_marc
To: Davis News Group
Subject: Davis News
Date: Tue, 6 Jul 2010

MARAVIDA is almost home. Glenn has done a great job captaining her, often by himself.

He had a setback yesterday when the alternator failed. This happened just past San Francisco. He managed to sail toward Bodega Bay until he lost the wind, and then the coast guard towed him the rest of the way into the bay. He's working on the repairs now.

We rented a slip at St. Helens Marina (on the Columbia River, 50 minutes from our house). We're excited about seeing MARAVIDA again—it's been two and a half years since the kids and I last saw her. I'm sure she'll look a little rough after 4,000 miles. And I'm sure she'll need some repairs and sprucing up before we put her up for sale. We won't be able to work on her for a while, though, because we've torn out the second bathroom in our house and we need to re-roof this summer.

Take care—
Sandy

Weather Delays

From: sandy_n_marc
To: Davis News Group
Subject: Davis News
Date: Fri, 13 Aug 2010

On July 9th, Glenn took MARAVIDA into Brookings Harbor on the Oregon/California border. The weather was turning bad and the temporary alternator wasn't going to work in rough seas. While he was waiting in Brookings, he sent us the water pump for rebuilding. We sent back the rebuilt water pump and the correct alternator. He's been waiting for a good weather window since then.

The weather is finally going to cooperate. Marc was flown to Brookings yesterday afternoon by his friend Phil. Glenn and Marc left on MARAVIDA this morning at 10:30. They hope to arrive in Astoria on Sunday and leave early Monday morning for St. Helens. They are timing the early departure to correspond with the tides.

Sandy

Text from Marc

August 13, 2010

"We are off Cape Blanco now. The seas are big but long, so not bad. No wind. Love you."

Marc's Facebook Page

August 17, 2010

MARAVIDA is tucked safely into her slip at St. Helens Marina. We had a great trip up the Oregon Coast and Columbia River. It took me a day to get my sea legs back. My friend Phil joined us for the river trip. Coming up the river was great. Very pretty.

MARAVIDA shows the wear and tear of a 4,000-mile sea journey, but she looks great to us. It's nice to have her home. Glenn says he's ready to stay on land after nine months at sea.

Final Missive

From: sandy_n_marc
To: Davis News Group
Subject: Davis News
Date: Sat, 28 Aug 2010

We vacationed on MARAVIDA last week. How cool to be back on our boat again. I found that I feel more sentimental about MARAVIDA than I thought I would. We spent a lot of time working and living on her. Of course, we've done the same with houses, but our experience with MARAVIDA was different—perhaps because we didn't leave to go to work or school. And together as a family we experienced so much during those years with her.

MARAVIDA's interior looks as good as when we left her. Her green exterior paint has oxidized and she has a few scrapes. The white decks have a few rust spots. There are a couple of ports and hatches that need to be removed and resealed. All in all, not bad after sitting in Curacao for two years and then making a nine-month, 4,000-mile journey by sea.

So, now our house and our boat will take turns getting our attention...

Love to all—
The Davis Family

P.S. THANK YOU, GLENN, for devoting the last nine months to getting MARAVIDA from Curacao to Oregon.

Note: Every time Marc and I visit MARAVIDA (still docked at St. Helens Marina as of late 2012), we feel a pull. A pull to live on her again and go back to a life of cruising. We talk about cruising in Washington's Puget Sound at some point in the future. We have so much invested in MARAVIDA— money, time, and sympathies— that we are torn between keeping her, or trading her for a smaller powerboat, or ... we just don't know. As I finish writing this, we are still undecided. (As of April 2016, Maravida is still docked at St. Helens Marina but is for sale. I am hoping she will sell so that someone can once again give her their full attention. Otherwise, we will have to continue to visit her when we can and try to find time to do some repairs. Maybe we'll even take her out on short excursions.)

SANDY L. DAVIS

Helpful Wikis

Check online wikis to find detailed and (hopefully) up-to-date information on islands' general stats, anchorages, marinas, arrival/departure procedures, restaurants, etc.

Wiktionary.org defines Wikipedia as "an open-content online encyclopedia, collaboratively developed over the World Wide Web."

http://www.wiktionary.org

The wikis most handy to cruisers or potential cruisers are:

http://www.wikipedia.org/

http://www.cruiserswiki.org

http://wikitravel.org

http://wikimapia.org

Examples:

http://en.wikipedia.org/wiki/Vieques,_Puerto_Rico

http://www.cruiserswiki.org/wiki/Grenada

http://wikitravel.org/en/Cartagena_(Colombia)

Acknowledgments

I would like to thank my editor, Barbara Bigelow. She asked the right questions, pointed out inconsistencies, and improved the flow of my writing. I definitely learned a lot from her. http://bbigeloweditor.com/

Thanks to my mother, Janice Gunderson, for enduring our 3 1/2-year absence, and thanks to my husband, Marc, for creating my vision of the book cover and for his help and guidance in formatting the e-book. I now understand *html* a lot more than I ever thought was possible.

I'd also like to acknowledge two of my female heroes from our cruising days: Benita Richardson from ALCHERINGA II and Susan Leader from DAYDREAM. I was fortunate to encounter both of them in the Caribbean and sincerely appreciated their razor-sharp minds, their warm personalities, and their amazing ability to expertly maneuver their 40-something-foot-long sailboats. I'm sorry to report that Susan lost her battle with cancer in August of 2012. Keep strong Wayne!

About the Author

Oregon native Sandy L. Davis has spent most of her life living unconventionally. Her belief in out-of-the box thinking and do-it-yourself living is demonstrated in her books: *Missives from Maravida: A Family's Caribbean Sailboat Adventure* and *Two Months in Europe: Avec des Enfants*. In addition to writing, home remodeling, and traveling, she is mother, editor, and cheerleader to two college students, as well as nurturer to two well-traveled cats. She cherishes vistas, bright colors, libraries, and travel.

Comments or questions? E-mail her at:

sandy_l_davis@maravida.org

A Favor

Please take the time to review this book on Amazon. Here's how.

Instructions:

1.) Log in to your Amazon account.

2.) Locate *Two Months in Europe* either by keying the title in the search bar or by locating it in your order history. In the latter case, click on the box "Write a product review." Continue with number 5 below.

3.) Scroll down until you see the section on the page titled "Customer Reviews" and a gray box labeled "Write a customer review."

4.) Click on "Write a customer review."

5.) If you haven't done this before, it will ask you to "Set a customer pen name."

6.) Click on the number of stars. One is for unhappy and five for very happy.

7.) Type into the box labeled "Write your review here."

8.) Another box will show up asking for a "Headline for your review." Choose a title that best summarizes your review.

9.) When you've completed your write-up, click on "Submit."

Thanks!

Two Months in Europe Avec des Enfants

Two Months in Europe: Avec des Enfants documents the 57-day trip I took with my husband and our two young children. From Great Britain to France, then to Italy and back to France, the details of our trip are chronicled in journal form and supplemented with pictures, general information about the locations we visited, web links, and additional resource suggestions.

The goal? To travel to our ultimate destinations (with our kids!); to get out of the U.S. and our comfort zone; and to explore the history, culture, and landscapes of Western Europe.

Even the most careful traveler can't anticipate everything. The challenges of tired feet, hungry stomachs, and the occasional emergency (little ones who needed to "pee NOW") demand levelheadedness, patience, and improvisation. Yes, things didn't always work out as planned, but it was all part of the adventure and definitely worth it in the end. Read along and discover how we did it.

Locations visited:

- England: Winchcombe, Cheltenham, Warwick, Swindon, Longleat, Avebury, Bath, Cotswolds, Hidcote Gardens, Ludgershall Ruins, Minster Lovell Hall, Blenheim Palace, London

- Wales: Dan-yr-Ogof Caves and Carreg Cennen

- France: Paris, Versailles, Chambord, Cheverny, Chenonceaux, Saint-Malo, Le Mele-sur-Sarthe, Alençon, Le Mémorial de Caen, Pointe du Hoc, Arromanches, Chartres, Chamonix, Villefranche-sur-Mer, Èze, Bédoin, Mt. Ventoux, Vaison-la-Romaine, Les Baux, Seguret, Carpentras, Roussillon, Saint-Saturnin-les-Apt, Pont du Gard, Collioure, Peyrepertuse, Alet-les-Bains, Périgueux, Excideuil, Brive, Rocamadour, Les Grottes de Lacave, Hautefort, Sarlat, Beynac, Disneyland Paris

- Switzerland: Geneva

- Italy: Mont Blanc Tunnel, Portovenere, Castelfalfi, San Gimigiano, Chianti, Siena, Orvieto, Reggello, Cinque Terre (Vernazza, Monterosso, Riomagiore, Manorola, and Corniglia)

http://www.amazon.com/Two-Months-Europe-Avec-Enfants/dp/0988843218

Printed in Great Britain
by Amazon